KV-267-636

Solutions Manual to
MANAGEMENT ACCOUNTING

Norman Thornton
MA, MSc, FCMA, AMBIM

Principal Lecturer in Accountancy
Manchester Polytechnic

HEINEMANN : LONDON

William Heinemann Ltd
15 Queen Street, Mayfair, London, W1X 8BE

LONDON   MELBOURNE   TORONTO
JOHANNESBURG   AUCKLAND

First published 1978
© Norman Thornton 1978

434 91957 8

IMB typeset by Supreme Litho Typesetting, Romford, Essex
Printed and bound in Great Britain by Biddles Ltd, Guildford, Surrey

657·4

CARS 11381

THE HEINEMANN
ACCOUNTANCY AND ADMINISTRATION SERIES

General Editor:
J. BATTY, DCom(SA), MCom(Dunelm), ACMA, MInstAM, MIPM

Mr Wylie
FMA.

B 7027

3/8

ROCKET PROPULSION ESTABLISHMENT LIBRARY

Please return this publication, or request a renewal, by the date stamped below.

Name	Date
Miss Sandys	5.10.79
A.S Wilson	14/9/79
Mr Greenan	7.4.83
H. Stuchbury.	10.7.86.

(4/64) L23964 442077 Wt29280 D7061 10/64 10M T&Co **G871**.   R.P.E. Form 243

PREFACE

This manual gives suggested solutions to the questions in the main text. These assignments are designed to enable students to make contributions from their own experience or as given by the lecturer, in addition to their reading and understanding of the text. The solutions given outline the points that should be emphasised. In some cases, there may be more than one correct solution.

Norman Thornton

CONTENTS

INTRODUCTION

1 A Management Accounting Framework

1   Terms used in the quotation may be interpreted as follows:

'A system':
A collection of parts, each of which carries out an assigned function, but all of which are coupled together in such a way that a specified goal is achieved.

'Collecting information about an organisation':
(a)   Collecting financial information relevant to the purpose for which the information will be used
(b)   The recording and processing of data.

'Summarising information about the organisation':
(a)   In standard form for routine reporting
(b)   In appropriate form for special reporting.

'Analysing information about an organisation':
Using the characteristics for data division to produce information in a form of value to interested parties.

'Reporting in monetary terms information about an organisation':
Accounting primarily concerned with those facts that can be expressed in monetary terms.

The major purpose of accounting is to provide information to interested parties regarding the nature and significance of economic transactions. The interpretation of the accounting reports must be undertaken in order to emphasise significant features and explain the technical limitations inherent in the accounting process.

2   (a)   *The role of the management accountant*
To assist management to achieve their objectives by the provision of accurate, relevant and timely information, presented in such a way that it can form a basis on which decisions can be made.

2   (b)   *The function of management accountancy in a manufacturing company*

The function covers forecasting and planning so that policy can emerge; the co-ordination and control of the various parts of the organisation so that the policy is executed as planned; and the review and appreciation of results to measure the success of the policy and to discover those parts of the plan which have not been carried through effectively. Management accountancy also involves communication of what is possible from the lower levels of the organisation to the policy-makers; and the passage of financial information concerning policy and the plans from the top of the management structure to the bottom. It is also important that results should be communicated in understandable terms to the appropriate levels of the organisation.

Some of the techniques used by management accountants include budgetary control, standard costing, ratio analysis, funds analysis, marginal costing and cost-volume-profit analysis.

3   A logical presentation of the economic cycle affecting the business may emphasise the following factors;

(a)   *Capital acquisition*

The acquisition of the means of making investment. Money resources may be obtained from investors either in the form of shares or loans.

(b)   *Capital investment*

The investment of capital in the resources of the business. These may take the form of machines, buildings, utilities and materials.

(c)   *Resources use*

The measurement of the use made of the resources of the business. The resources of the business are stored in assets and in a given period a company may use these resources. As they are used they may be recombined into new products or services.

(d)   *Investment results*

The revenue/cost relationships arising from the use of the resources of the business. The resources are used to produce and distribute goods to customers. As a result of this distribution revenue is earned. The expenses chargeable to the revenue earned give a net result of profit or loss on business operations.

(e)   *Profit disposal*

The use made of the investment results. This usually involves a distribution of the financial results of the organisation's activities to proprietors, investors, lenders and the business.

4   There is little uniformity among companies regarding the duties and extent of influence of accounting staff and in particular, titles adopted for specific tasks. With this qualification, the duties of a management accountant in a typical medium-sized manufacturing company might include:

(a)   Assisting line managers in the formulation of the financial plans for the business

(b)   Establishing procedures to provide financial information to assist managers as in (a) and in the provision of information to permit a check to be made on how the actual situation is measuring up to the plans

(c)   Establishing procedures to provide costing information as a routine and assist with profit improvement opportunities

(d)   Providing, as necessary, financial information relevant to decision problems to assist management in arriving at a satisfactory solution to those problems

(e)   Interpreting the financial information provided to management

(f)   Providing financial information required by associated financial functions, e.g., stock valuations

(g)   Line authority over his own department.

5   To maintain the effective co-operation of managers whose work is assessed by the financial reports produced, the management accountant should:

(a)   Report the facts only

(b)   Use standards for assessment that have been independently compiled

(c)   To the extent that comments may be necessary, be as objective as possible

(d)   Release information to the supervisor later than to the subordinate to enable the latter to conduct inquiries he may think appropriate, providing the time-lag is not unreasonable

(e)   Where information appears to be unduly critical, check the detail to ensure that a mistake has not been made.

6   (a)   The management accountant should not have direct authority over functional departments other than his own. The role of the management accountant is advisory but it should be recognised that he is in a unique position relative to other line managers because he has access to interrelated information which may be vital to the valid solution of a works problem. The works manager may not have similar access. The relative status of line managers is a matter for company decision and the dominant personality of an individual is certain to affect personal relationships.

It is advisable to give sufficient seniority to the management accountant to ensure that his services are used to the best advantage and considerable care should be exercised in the choice of this official who should possess the following qualities:

(i) Tact, patience and diplomacy
(ii) An ability to impart confidence and generate a desire for co-operation on the part of line managers for the good of the company
(iii) An ability to present sound arguments that may be used persuasively, if necessary, to secure a desired result
(iv) A willingness to listen to the other person's point of view and profit from the experience gained.

Where views clash, it is top management's responsibility to resolve the issue with diplomacy and tact avoiding, wherever possible, the suggestion that one senior official is undermining the authority of another official whose views are necessary to secure a balanced opinion.

If staff relationships are established on a reasonable basis, the extreme action of resignation can be avoided. The advice to be given to top management would be to aim to secure the benefits of the management accounting service in the context of the above behavioural considerations.

6   (b)   With decentralisation of accounting work it is possible that:
(i) Records may be duplicated
(ii) Labour saving equipment may not be economical
(iii) A smaller staff may reduce the flexibility of dealing with absences such as sickness and holidays.

With centralisation of accounting work it is possible that:

(i) a loss of direct contact between the accountant and production staff could occur
(ii) There may be a loss in direct control of costs
(iii) It may be more difficult for the accountant to understand what the figures in his reports represent.

In effect, the issue is again a matter of the calibre of the management accountant and the way the accounting work is organised relative to the operating management. The management accountant should maintain personal contacts and his understanding of the significance of the financial information produced. It is not common practice for the management accountant to report direct to the works manager and if this is the case, the chief accountant should have functional authority over the work of the management accountant.

7   The factors affecting the structure of the reporting system for financial information for the internal management of a manufacturing company are as follows:

(a) The information required by management
(b) The concentration on significant information
(c) The need to provide information in time for it to be of use to management
(d) The need to integrate reports with each other by (i) providing schedules which explain in greater detail sections of an overall report for management; and (ii) providing reports for different levels of management which progressively break down the overall report for management
(e) The recognition of the levels and functions of management and management relationships particular to the company
(f) The provision of a communication link enabling the information to be interpreted to the user of the information
(g) Feedback on the follow-up action taken as a result of the information supplied
(h) Flexibility of the system and the systematic review of report provision and coverage.

8   The preliminary questions to consider when preparing a special report are as follows:

(a) Why has a request been made for a report or the accountant taken the initiative to produce a special report?
(b) If the report is the result of the accountant's initiative, what is the objective of providing the report?
(c) What type of information is required by management from the report: factual information only or the inclusion of conclusions and recommendations?
(d) How will the necessary information be obtained?
(e) How much time is available to obtain the information and is it possible to get the data required in the time available?

A special report should be presented as follows:

(a) In a form that presents the relevant information as a balanced picture of the subject
(b) Arranged logically so that the main topics of the argument emerge progressively
(c) The use of the standard format for the company, if applicable, e.g., introduction; main sections of the report, including reference to appendices (if applicable); conclusions and recommendations

(d)   The use of supporting techniques of presentation to assist interpretation, e.g., graphs and statistical methods

(e)   In a concise and as easy to read form as the accountant can present the report

(f)   Where opinions and recommendations are given, the assumptions on which they are based should be stated.

9   In preparing a special report the following steps should be taken at the investigation stage:

(a)   Define the matter to be investigated as clearly as possible

(b)   Define the use to be made of the information to be provided

(c)   Obtain past information available that may be useful in the investigation

(d)   Break down the investigation to identify the basic objectives to be covered

(e)   Identify any limiting factors to the investigation; time and the cost of the investigation are usually important considerations

(f)   Consider possible solutions to the problem to be investigated as a basis for creating a logical series of questions to aid inquiries

(g)   Within the limitations set, plan how each basic objective will be achieved; the planned use of the resources available is very important

(h)   Make the investigation ensuring that the plan is followed and the objectives are kept in mind.

In reaching the conclusions and making the recommendations from the result of the investigation the notes taken should be checked for inconsistency, incompleteness, and inaccuracy. Where these faults are found they should be rectified by further inquiries. Facts and opinions must be distinguished and if the information is insufficient to form a conclusion it may be necessary to carry out additional investigation into the ubject of the report.

In reaching conclusions the following should be avoided:

(a)   Selecting facts to fit a conclusion that one wishes to reach on the subject of the investigation

(b)   Judging the information by the wrong standard

(c)   Assuming that the present situation will continue without adequately confirming that this will be the case as far as can be reasonably assessed

(d)   Applying the results of studying a few cases to all cases without ascertaining the validity of this assessment

(e)   Assuming that a point for verification is proved true because the opposite cannot be proved

(f)   Comparing non-comparable information.

Recommendations should be based on the conclusions reached. The conclusions should be the result of objective reporting whereas the recommendations represent personal opinion. A reader of the report may accept the conclusions without question but may prefer his own solution to the problem.

10 A financial report should:
(a) Be as simple and concise as is consistent with the needs of the recipient
(b) Be prompt enough to enable action resulting from the statement to be taken in time
(c) Relate to the division of responsibility within the organisation as part of an integrated reporting structure to cover all management levels
(d) Generate from the accounting activity without involving excessive time and expense in compilation and presentation
(e) Be presented logically, with explanations where necessary and clear descriptions of data contained
(f) Include a basis for comparison
(g) Use, where appropriate, the principle of 'management by exception'
(h) Facilitate identification of trends and unusual occurrences
(i) Incorporate, where practicable, professional techniques in report presentation which will improve their quality.

11 Factors affecting the frequency with which reports are produced are as follows:
(a) The period should be sufficiently short to reveal significant variations in costs as early as possible so that remedial action can be taken
(b) The period should be long enough to allow a reasonable degree of averaging and yet avoid an undue volume of clerical work
(c) The periods adopted should contain, as nearly as practicable, the same amount of working time
(d) Custom in the trade
(e) Consolidation requirements where the company is part of a larger group.

Three common accounting periods adopted are as follows:
(a) The week – this period reveals information early for management but reports of this frequency can be expensive to produce and reasonable averaging of costs may not apply.
(b) The calendar month – this period is a convenient analysis of the financial year to link with other consolidated periods used in the reporting system, e.g., three calendar monthly reports to produce

quarterly information. The big disadvantage is the unequal length of many of the accounting periods rendering comparisons difficult.

(c) The four-week period — this period overcomes the difficulty of unequal working day duration in the months but involves additional clerical work.

12   Information regarding the company, not given in the case, would be necessary to give a detailed answer to the questions but a reasonable answer can be supplied on the basis of the information given.

(a) A medium-sized manufacturing company would require additional financial information for the control of the business for the following reasons:

 (i)   Information on company profitability, the financial status of the business and company liquidity and the ability to pay debts, is required more frequently than once a year
 (ii) The information supplied appears to be historical and information on the anticipated future progress of the business should be given
 (iii) Decision-making information is not mentioned
 (iv) No mention of the integration of the information other than the annual detailed schedules of operating expenses with the annual financial report
 (v)   No mention of comparative data and the identification of key information for control.

(b) The reporting system might include the following:

Description of reports	Frequency	Reason for the frequency given
(i) Balance sheet and profit and loss statement	Quarterly	The overall data not required more frequently and the four quarterly returns may be reconciled with the annual financial accounts
(ii) Product profit data and cost control information applicable to responsibility centres	Monthly	A reasonable period for control and may be consolidated and reconciled with the quarterly statement

(Table continued on facing page)

Description of reports	Frequency	Reason for the frequency given
(iii) Sales and production statistics	Weekly	The need for a shorter control period check. Some data may be given daily
(iv) Funds availability and projected use of funds	Weekly	The need for a shorter control period check. The general situation might be controlled monthly and cash balances daily.

(All the above reports should show significant variations from planned performance.)

In addition to the above routine reports, special reports should be provided giving relevant data for specific decision problems.

FINANCIAL STATEMENT CLASSIFICATION

2 Financial Data Classification and Terminology

1   Explanation of the terms used in the statement:

'Expenses':
The decrease in owners equity resulting from the operation of the business is called 'expense'. Expenses are expired costs in the accounting period.

'Losses':
Expenditure with no commensurate benefit to the business and irrecoverable. Expenses in excess of revenue.

'Function performed':
Functions are concerned with the manufacturing, marketing and administration of the business.

'Person responsible':
The person connected with a responsibility centre whether this person's authority is limited to expenses or extended to include revenue and assets.

'Form in which the services were contained':
Examples: rent, electricity, insurance and postage.

Other satisfactory classification systems:
(a)   Product classification
(b)   Time classification, e.g., projects of limited duration
(c)   Controllability classification
(d)   Technique classification: (i) budgetary control; (ii) standard costing; (iii) marginal costing; (iv) absorption costing
(e)   Cash flow classification: source and use of funds
(f)   Comparative classification: uniform costing.

2   Departmental division does not necessarily identify controllable costs. Where departmental costs include controllable and uncontrollable items, the analysis is not a duplication (see the example below).

Answers to the second part of the question will vary according to the student's practical experience. One example is given below:

In the case of footwear manufacturers, expenses of productive and service departments are classified as follows:

(a) *Productive departments*
(i) Expenses under direct departmental control:
Indirect labour
Supervision
National insurance
Holiday pay
Maintenance of plant and machinery

(ii) Expenses not under direct departmental control:
Machine rentals
Insurance
Depreciation
Redistribution of service departments' costs

(b) *Service departments*
(i) Expenses under direct departmental control:
Indirect labour
Supervision
Office staff
National insurance
Carriage inwards
Machine rentals
Lasts, knives and patterns
Maintenance of plant
Coal, gas and electricity
Maintenance of buildings
Travelling and car expenses
Stationery, postage and telephones
Sundry expenses

(ii) Expenses not under direct departmental control:
Rent, rates and insurance
Depreciation.

3   (a)   Where the main object of the company is manufacturing, the following income or expenditure may be considered outside the main activities of the business:
 (i) Rents from land and property

(ii) Trade investment income

(iii) Other investment income.

3   (b) Exceptional costs that require separate classification are items that are material and expected not to recur frequently or regularly:
  (i) Amounts arising out of a radical changeover of work or methods in factory or office
  (ii) Damages payable at law
  (iii) Penalties for late completion of contracts
  (iv) Losses from obsolescence.

3   (c) Costs that are normal are constantly recurring and abnormal when they are unusual or non-recurring. In the case of lost plant and machinery time, the classification of costs between normal and abnormal items depends on the reasons for the plant not being in productive operation:
  (i) Normal reasons for the stoppage of plant include:
    Cleaning
    Plant maintenance
    Inspection of plant
    Minor repairs
    Temporary mechanical breakdown
    Temporary power failure
    Delayed arrival of materials
    Occasional shutting down for short periods to balance production with that of allied products

  (ii) Abnormal reasons for the stoppage of plant include:
    Major repairs or overhauls of plant
    Seasonal cessation of production
    Planned shutting down to avoid over-production
    Raw materials not being obtainable
    Exceptional causes, e.g., fire, flood, strikes and fuel shortage.

4   Answers will vary according to the student's practical experience. Two examples are given below.

A Printer's Example

Term	Description	Examples
Non-manufacturing departments	Separate businesses apart from the printing or manufacturing divisions	Retail businesses (stationery shop)

(Table continued overleaf)

13

Term	Description	Examples
Productive departments	Departments engaged in direct production – a department in which preparatory, machining or finishing operations on jobs are carried out	Letterpress Lithography Carton making Die stamping Binding
Direct services	Departments which provide facilities directly for jobs – their costs are recovered by means of direct service rates recovered direct to jobs	Printed stock expenses. Block or plate store expenses. Paper maturing expenses. Selling expenses
Sundry service departments	Departments which are ancillary to production or to other departments (their costs are absorbed by the above departments, i.e., these departments give service to the other departments)	Canteen service Time-keeping service

A Footwear Manufacturer's Example

(a) Productive departments:
  Clicking
  Closing
  Bottom cutting
  Bottom preparation
  Heel building
  Heel covering
  Lasting
  Making
  Heel attaching
  Finishing
  Shoe room

(b) Service departments:
  Purchasing and stores
  Power
  Light and heat
  Planning, costing and wages
  Welfare and canteen
  Building expense
  Designing and pattern making
  General factory expenses

(c) General departments:
Administration
Selling and distribution.

5   Answers will vary according to the student's practical experience. Six examples of service departments from the iron and steel industry are given below.

Service Department	Description	Limits of classification	
		Cost from	Cost to
Water supply	Obtaining and distributing water from a river, well, reservoir or other source, including purchased water	The intake sluice or valve	The delivery of water to the consuming units or to the storage points in consuming departments
Water treatment	The process of softening, or otherwise treating water and delivering such water	The intake of water at the treatment plant	The delivery of treated water to the consuming units
Steam raising	The raising of steam for consuming departments	(1) For water: at the tank supplying the boiler feed pump (2) For fuel: (a) Solid fuel: (i) if arising outside the works at the boiler siding; (ii) if arising in the works at the boiler plant	The point where the steam is delivered to the mains which convey it to the consuming departments

(Table continued overleaf)

Service Department	Description	Limits of classification	
		Cost from	Cost to
		(b) Liquid fuel: at the storage tanks (c) Blast furnace and choke oven gas: at the boiler gas isolating valves (d) Waste heat: at the boiler plant	
Steam distribution	The distribution of the steam raised to the consuming departments	The point where the steam enters the main steam transmission lines	The point where it enters the steam ranges supplying the consuming departments
Electricity generation	The generation of electric power	(1) For steam driven generators: the receipt of steam at the turbine stop valve (2) For internal combustion engines and gas turbines: the receipt of oil at storage tanks or gas at the gas isolating valve	The generator bus bars

(Table continued on facing page)

Service Department	Description	Limits of classification	
		Cost from	Cost to
Electricity distribution	The transforming, transmitting, distributing and converting or rectifying of electric power	The receipt of electricity at: (1) the generator bus bars; or (2) the bus bars receiving purchased electricity	The switch supplying the bus bars of the consuming departments or an equivalent alternative exchange point

6   Costs that may extend beyond any one control period are:

(a)   *Fixed asset costs*
The amount capitalised is the acquisition cost which normally includes installation costs and expenditure involved in making the asset ready for use. The amount carried forward into a subsequent trading period is the book value of the fixed assets at the end of the current control period. (The book value is normally the acquisition cost of the asset less the accumulated depreciation charged to the end of the current control period.)

(b)   *Significant asset improvement expenditure*
Where expenditure is incurred which improves an existing asset beyond its condition as originally purchased and is significant enough to be considered capital expenditure, the accounting treatment is to treat the betterment in the same way as the fixed asset to which it relates.

(c)   *Prepayments and deferred expenditure*
This is expenditure incurred which is unexpired in the current control period. Insurance cover, for example, does not necessarily expire at the end of the trading period and the unexpired cost which is expected to expire in the future is carried forward to the accounting periods expected to benefit from such expenditure.

(d)   *Stocks held for further use, work-in progress and finished goods held for future sale*
In this case the costs associated with manufacturing the products for sale remain an asset of the business until the products are sold.

(e) *Intangible assets not currently written off*
Patent costs, for example, may be carried forward to subsequent trading periods because of their extended life beyond the current control period.

The reason for carrying forward expenditure into a subsequent trading period is the expectation that such expenditure will benefit the future period and is sufficiently significant to justify the carry forward procedure.

7   Answers will vary according to the student's practical experience. One example is given below:

(a) *Factory expenses*
(i)   Variable factory expenses:
     Machine royalities
     Consumable stores

(ii) Fixed factory expenses:
     (1) Productive departments
          Indirect labour
          Supervision
          National insurance
          Holiday pay
          Maintenance of plant and machinery
          Machine rentals
          Insurance
          Depreciation
          Redistribution of service department costs
     (2) Service departments
          Indirect labour
          Supervision
          Office staff
          National insurance
          Carriage inwards
          Machine rentals
          Lasts, knives and patterns
          Maintenance of plant
          Coal, gas and electricity
          Maintenance of buildings
          Travelling and car expenses
          Stationery, postage and telephones
          Sundry expenses
          Rent, rates and insurance
          Depreciation.

(b) *Selling and distribution expenses*

(i) Variable selling and distribution expenses (i.e., costed specially to products):
Travellers commission
Agents' commission
Discounts allowed

(ii) Fixed selling and distribution expenses (i.e., recovered over all production):
Indirect labour (cleaning)
Warehouse staff
Travellers' salaries
National insurance
Travelling and car expenses
Stationery, postage and telephones
Carriage and packing
Advertising
Showroom expenses
Redistribution of service department costs

(c) *Administration fixed expenses*
Office staff salaries
Management salaries
National insurance
Holiday pay
Exployers' liability insurance
Rent and rates
Depreciation
Travelling and car expenses
Stationery, postage and telephones
Legal and professional charges
Sundry expenses.

8 Costs may vary (a) with each vehicle; and (b) with mileage. A classification of typical transport costs of the company may be as follows:

Costs not varying with mileage	*Reason for the classification given*
Fixed costs:	
Garage rent and rates	These costs not varying with either
Transport administration	mileage or vehicle

(Table continued overleaf)

19

Costs not varying with mileage	Reason for the classification given
Variable costs per vehicle: Drivers wages and National Insurance	Drivers usually allocated to vehicles
Vehicle depreciation	Vehicle depreciation will certainly increase with increased mileage but the charge for depreciation is usually calculated as a rate per vehicle ignoring the mileage variation between vehicles
Vehicle licence	A cost identified with the specified vehicle
Semi-variable costs per vehicle: Vehicle insurance	A blanket cover insurance charge may be made plus an insurance premium per vehicle

Costs varying with mileage	Reason for the classification given
Petrol or diesel oil	A miles per gallon direct relationship is evident
Tyres	An anticipated mileage for tyre use is usually used to assign tyre costs to vehicles
Maintenance costs	Actual costs are usually averaged to vehicles on the basis of a rate per mile

Note
The following classification is sometimes used:
Fixed costs:
Wages and National Insurance
Insurance
Licence
Garage overheads
Transport administration.

Variable costs:
Petrol
Oil
Vehicle depreciation
Tyres
Maintenance costs.

9   Four examples of activity measures that may be used are:
(a)   Units sold
(b)   Sales value of units sold
(c)   Units produced
(d)   Sales value of production.

The choice of the activity base depends upon a consideration of:
(i)   The factor that reasonably reflects the variability of the cost
(ii)   The need to provide a base to represent a number of costs combined
(iii)   The wish to link the presentation with associated data.

With regard to (i), some costs may vary more closely with sales than production, e.g., selling costs. Similarly, some costs may vary more closely with production than sales, e.g., factory costs. With isolated costs, the factor preferred is the one that expresses the variability of the item more accurately.

With regard to (ii), the difficulty of using sales is the possible variation in stock levels, particularly in a company where the business is seasonal. In this situation, the factor preferred is the sales value of production.

With regard to (iii), the associated data used with the costs may be sales value to indicate cost-volume-profit relationships. In this situation, the factor preferred is sales because by convention revenue is not recognised in the accounts until the sale is made.

10   (a)   The assumptions on which the graph is based are as follows:
(i)   That variable costs are a constant cost per unit of volume
(ii)   That fixed costs are at the same amount for the range of volume indicated in the graph
(iii)   That the efficiency of operations is unchanged over the range of volume illustrated
(iv)   That mixed costs can be separated into their fixed and variable elements.

10   (b)   The machine shop manager's views are correct. Regarding the apparent absence of other costs not behaving as simply as the graph, suggests the explanation may be as follows:
(i)   Mixed costs may have been divided into their fixed and variable elements: the variable costs included in area (a) and the fixed costs included in area (b).
(ii)   Costs varying not in direct proportion to changes in the level of activity but predominently variable or fixed may have been regarded as such. This view may be taken if the error introduced is considered to be insignificant and unlikely to mislead management.

(iii) Stepped costs may be regarded as fixed for the range of output anticipated.

In the estimating area, the division of costs into their fixed and variable elements is important in so far as the changing relationships can be examined as a basis for decision-making. The study of behaviour patterns as outlined avoids the danger of over-simplification. In the interpretation of cost reports, the understanding of cost behaviour patterns is vital and the form of presentation used should recognise this. The accountant should always ensure that the basis on which information is supplied is understood by the users of that information and relevant for the purpose intended.

11 The following characteristics signify a managed cost in the context of management's financial control responsibility:
(a) The levels of cost are incurred at the discretion of management according to the policies laid down by top management. They can usually be easily changed by a variation of these policies and often are in a change of management, e.g., when an organisation is taken over by another business.
(b) There is difficulty in deciding what the level of expenditure should be. Typical managed costs that present problems are advertising and research and development costs.
(c) The control of these items tends to be a check on expenditure to a permitted level in the accounting period. There is no relationship to the common basis of the variation of cost levels, i.e., the level of business activity. Managed costs are, therefore, found in the fixed cost category of business expenses.
(d) If cost reductions are wanted, e.g., in a business crisis, it may be relatively easy to reduce managed costs but this may not be in the interests of the business. Improvement in performance may be secured by increasing rather than reducing the managed cost.

12   (a)

The requirements of the classification system	How met in this case
(i) To locate accounts quickly	Accounts identified in groups recognisable as standard divisions of an accounting system
(ii) To express a comprehensive accounting plan	Coverage of the manufacturing, trading, profit and loss and financial status accounts of the business

(Table continued on facing page)

The requirements of the classification system	How met in this case
(iii) To give flexibility where changes in the accounting system may be made	Extension possible within (i) main sections (ii) main groups, and (iii) sub groups
(iv) To assist in the preparation of control information	The group detail is in similar form to that required for financial reports
(v) To facilitate control	Control account classification provided
(vi) To facilitate data processing	Logical classification to serve as the basis of a coding system

12 (b) Further sub-classification may be expected in the classification system to meet the needs of management:
  (i) To recognise the nature of the responsibility of members of the business, e.g., responsibility centre classification
  (ii) To recognise the degree of influence exercised by a member of the business on specific financial items: e.g., controllable costs classification
  (iii) To recognise the magnitude and significance of the activities of the business, e.g., classification by major, minor and ancillary activities of the business
  (iv) To recognise similarities produced as a result of normal or ordinary conditions being attained
  (v) To recognise the relative effect of fluctuations in activity level, e.g., the classification of fixed and variable costs
  (vi) To recognise the principal classifications of types of material, e.g., plastics, timber, metal, etc.
  (vii) To facilitate control, e.g., sub-classification of personal accounts: trade debtors classified between sections A to L and M to Z
  (viii) To recognise product cost requirements.

3 Financial Data Division

1   Further analysis of the department's costs may be:

(a)   By locations sub-divided as to functions:

    (i)   Locations: the territorial divisions

    (ii) Functions: Selling:

                 sales salaries and commissions

                 travelling and car expenses

            Sales promotion:

                 advertising

            Sales administration:

                 sales office expenses.

This analysis sub-divides costs to those primarily responsible for expenses. By relating this detail to the appropriate analysis of sales turnover, the margin of profit by locations can be determined.

(b)   By single products or product groups:

With the analysis and the appropriate analysis of sales and other costs the margin of profit or loss can be determined for single products or groups of products.

2   (a)   The analysis of the profit potential of existing products will assist the executives in deciding on future product strategy. This classification may be as follows:

  (i)   The strong and established items of the line. These products provide the main sales volume and the company depends on these products for its main source of profits in relation to capital employed.

  (ii) Products that are new and as yet unproved. These are the products that are expected to provide good future profits and management is prepared to subsidise them during their development period.

 (iii) Products that have passed their peak in growth and profitability. Since these products can offer little in the way of future profits it may be expected that management effort may be diverted to other categories.

In addition the following questions should be answered:

(i) To what extent can growth come from increasing the company share and penetration of the existing market possible from existing products?

(ii) To what extent can growth come from creating new markets for existing products?

(b) The emphasis that management should place on the key areas of the categories defined above is as follows:

(i) Category (i) products are entitled to priority in day-to-day managerial attention to assure that they remain strong and flourish in accordance with their possibilities for as many years into the future as possible.

(ii) Category (ii) products require specialised attention and frequent review and reappraisal as experience and knowledge are acquired. To ensure an adequate flow of such promising new products, there should be an effective research and development programme.

(iii) Category (iii) products should be eliminated as their contribution drops to a level where management attention is no longer justified.

(c) The following information may be demanded if executives decide to divert their attention to new products:

(i) The extent to which research and development activity is aimed at identifiable market requirements

(ii) The length of the lead time between development work and the actual launching of new products

(iii) The timing of new product introduction

(iv) The effect of likely new products on the existing range of products in particular, an analysis of their profit impact and product line strategy, product elimination, competitor's reaction and stock levels.

3 (a) The anticipated value of the classification of distribution costs by form of transport may be:

(i) To ascertain the costs and establish cost rates for each transport group. Each group may consist of similar types of vehicles — make and carrying capacity.

(ii) To compare with other modes of transport, e.g., own vehicle use compared with private hauliers, British Road Services, rail or parcel post.

(b) The anticipated value of the classification of distribution costs by delivery routes may be:

(i) To ascertain the costs relating to delivery routes

(ii) To establish route standard costs

(iii) To assess the value of alternative routes to those used for deliveries.

(c)   The anticipated value of the classification of distribution costs by product may be to contribute to the evaluation of a product or product line.

Related information may consist of sales turnover, performance standards, and other comparable data such as comparable period costs and trend data.

4   The analyses chosen for principal departments would be as follows:

		Reason for choice
(a)	*Sales*	
(i)	Merchandise classification (units and value)	(1) Variable mark-ups on merchandise require groupings of goods by similar gross margins of profit (2) Buying and selling requirements (3) Stock control (4) Relationship to planned sales levels
(ii)	Type of sales (credit sales and cash sales)	(1) Nature of business (2) Cash control (3) Debtors control
(iii)	Sales in sale periods	Check on the effectiveness of sales promotional programmes
(b)	*Purchases*	
(i)	Merchandise classification (units and value)	(1) Buying control (purchasing commitments (2) Stock control
(ii)	Number and value of orders placed	Check on outstanding purchases
(c)	*Overheads*	
(i)	Variable and fixed cost classification	(1) To assist in the interpretation of cost movements (2) Relationship to planned cost levels
(ii)	Controllable and uncontrollable cost classification	To ensure costs specifically identified with individual managers
(iii)	Merchandising (buying and selling) expenses; publicity expenses; occupancy expenses; dispatch expenses; and administration expenses	To identify costs with departmental store functions

5   The basis of the statement in the question is the belief that certain costs of a responsibility centre may not be influenced by the action of the manager of that centre. To give this information, therefore, is irrelevant to the work of such an executive of the company.

The statement assumes that costs for a specific responsibility centre can be classified into their controllable and uncontrollable elements. A recognition of the duties of each manager indicating their influence exercised over costs should enable the classification to be made.

It is important that a manager should know the cost of the resources he uses and in some responsibility centres, if only controllable costs are recorded, a very distorted picture may emerge. There is the possibility that the manager may be able to influence indirectly the costs that are considered uncontrollable by himself.

6   The type of classified information regarding factory operations that may be provided to the managing director, works manager and departmental supervisor is as follows:

(a)   *Managing director*
Total costs analysed into their principal cost elements: labour, material and factory overhead.

Comparisons made between actual and planned or standard performance to isolate departures from the performance expected.

(b)   *Works manager*
As (a) above with the analysis of the costs to individual departments to the extent that these costs are controllable or uncontrollable by each department.

(c)   *Departmental supervisor*
The controllable costs in detail for the supervisor's own department.

Comparisons made between actual and planned or standard performance to isolate departures from the performance expected.

The integration of the three reports is accomplished by the progression in the detailed analysis supplied. The works manager has the departmental analysis not given to the managing director, and the departmental supervisor has the detailed costs of the department not given to the works manager. If the works manager or managing director want the detailed information, the link is provided by control totals in each report, e.g.

Managing director's report: his total costs will agree with the total departmental costs in the works manager's report

Works manager's report: his individual departmental controllable costs will agree with the total of detailed cost items in the departmental supervisor's report.

The breadth of reporting covered by each report is increased as the responsibilities of managers increase.

7   Answers will vary according to the student's practical experience. One example is given below:

Production Meeting Agenda
(a)   Production costs — a review of product and departmental statistics
(b)   The order book — a review of the movements in production
(c)   Stocks — levels of raw material, work-in-progress, finished goods, and a consideration of overdue supplies
(d)   Quality
(e)   Plant and accommodation — capacity review
(f)   Labour and manning — a review of works manning and labour requirements; week-end working
(g)   Production problems
(h)   Policy and development — this heading includes the consideration of work study investigations.

8   The details that may be required from managers requiring funds to be released for a capital expenditure project already approved are as follows:
(a)   Responsibility centre
(b)   Manager's reference
(c)   Authorisation office reference — if different from (b)
(d)   Project description
(e)   Reason for the expenditure — in particular, the specification of any changes since the approval of the capital expenditure
(f)   Type of asset classification
(g)   Purchase or lease?
(h)   Alternatives and/or quotations considered and rejected
(i)   Expenditure requirements (related to the date of asset acquisition) — year, month and amount
(j)   Effect of the authorisation:
    (i)   Amount of the capital expenditure authorisation
    (ii)   Amount of funds previously released (if any)
    (iii) This request
    (iv)   Total requested (ii) plus (iii)
    (v)   Balance available (if any)
(k)   Signature of the manager applying for the release of funds (also date signed)

(l)   Signature of the executive recommending and approving the application (also date signed).

9   The details that may be required from R and D personnel when completing a proposal form requesting funds for a R and D project are as follows:
(a)   Brief tital
(b)   Sponsoring department
(c)   Project reference number
(d)   Scope of the research project:
   (i)   To what questions is the research to provide the answers? The priorities?
   (ii)   What is the value of the information to be obtained and how is it to be applied?
(e)   Details of relevant literature
(f)   Brief details of any exploratory work that has been done which may indicate lines along which the research and development may take place
(g)   What facilities will be required
(h)   Supplementary notes and background information:
   (i)   Any ideas on how the work might be tackled
   (ii)   Any customers who would co-operate in experimental work
(i)   Anticipated cost of the research and development project (related to the date of required expenditure commitment) − year, month and amount.

10   Current assets are cash and other assets, both monetary and non-monetary, normally held for a short term, generally less than one year. They may be converted into cash or consumed in that period. Examples are as follows:

(a)   Monetary current assets:
   (i)   Cash at bank and in hand
   (ii)   Debtors − amounts owed by customers (trade debtors) and amounts owned by others, e.g., employees
   (iii) Short-term investments
(b)   Non-monetary current assets:
   (i)   Stocks − raw material; work-in-progress; finished goods; other stocks, e.g., maintenance spares and stationery
   (ii)   Prepayments, e.g., insurances

   Current liabilities are short-term monetary and non-monetary obligations to company creditors. Examples are as follows:

(a) Monetary current liabilities:
- (i) Creditors — amounts owing to suppliers (trade creditors) and amounts owing to others, e.g., for current taxation
- (ii) Accrued expenditure

(b) Non-monetary current liabilities: deferred revenue, e.g., advance payments by customers.

11 (a) Stock is normally classified according to the nature of the item and its ultimate use. For example, the natural classification may be:
- (i) Raw materials
- (ii) Factory supplies
- (iii) Work-in-progress
- (iv) Finished parts
- (v) Finished goods
- (vi) Tools.

Ultimate use classification is made possible by an application of production analysis where groups of materials which are allied in nature, and distinctive enough to be set apart from other items, are assembled into a class. The class will be judged in relation to end use. For example, in car manufacture the classes of materials and parts may be:
- (i) Engine
- (ii) Ignition and electrical
- (iii) Fuel system
- (iv) Wheels and tyres
- (v) Transmission
- (vi) Body
- (vii) Controls and instruments
- (viii) Cooling system.

(b) By grouping materials and components, etc., according to similarity in shape, size and material as suggested in (a) above by means of the classification system, a sound basis is obtained for the introduction of a standardisation programme. Each group can be examined for duplication or possible standardisation. In the case, standardised descriptions should be adopted and an age of stock analysis provided to identify the slow-moving items for review pending their possible disposal.

In addition to the above, the grouped components can also be examined for similarity of production process in order that the group may be produced using the same machines and tooling.

After elimination of obsolete stock, duplicate stock and standardisation, a review of stock levels appropriate to revised production requirements should lead to the lower investment of funds in stock.

12   Answers will vary according to the student's practical experience. Four examples are given below:

Example 1
Nature of business: Manufacturer of firelighters, polishes and similar household products
Number of employees: 250
Reports supplies:
(a)   Profit and loss variance statement – the details are analysed:
    (i)   the main product, and
    (ii)   other products
(b)   Standard works cost of sales, actual sales and gross profit – details per product
(c)   Service department variances – actual and budget comparisons for each cost centre
(d)   Production department variances – similar detail as (c) for each production department
(e)   Production and sales report – quantity information.

Example 2
Nature of business: Engineers and toolmakers
Number of employees: 550
Reports supplies:
(a)   Product statistics – orders, deliveries, output and stocks (a report for each product)
(b)   Targets – order and output projection
(c)   Inquiries – received, dealt with, outstanding and declined
(d)   Standard schedule of tools stocked – additions to the stock register
(e)   Steel supplies overdue and delivered late
(f)   Works manning – includes details of week-end and overtime working
(g)   Payroll analysis – employee cost information
(h)   Profit statement – analysed by main products
(i)   Operating costs – service department costs and quantity information on the service supplied
(j)   Balance sheet
(k)   Commentary on the monthly results.

Example 3
Nature of business: Engineers and contractors
Number of employees: 2,500

Reports supplied:

(a) Company operating statement – variances by product divisions
(b) Works operating statement – expenditure summary and variances on works expenses
(c) Central services summary – detailed costs and variances of central services
(d) Cost centre utilisation summary – analysis of utilisation variances
(e) Divisional operating statement – standard marginal costing data
(f) Sales control report – product group sales analysis
(g) Overhead expenditure – analysis of expenses included in the works operating statement.

Example 4

Nature of business: Cardboard box manufacturers
Number of employees: 4,000
Reports supplied:

(a) Divisional trading account – standard profit and loss account analysed by box-making divisions
(b) Direct labour control statement – cost comparisons for each cost centre
(c) Expense summary – analysis of expenses for each production unit
(d) Plant statistics – quantity information for each plant
(e) Utilisation report – analysis of utilisation statistics
(f) Sales report – product analysis
(g) Capital expenditure progress statement
(h) Transport costs – expense analysis

FINANCIAL STATEMENT INTERPRETATION

4 Accounting Information Relationships

1   If costs can be directly identified with the manufacture of a product and allotted to that product they are known as direct costs. These costs include the costs of raw material and labour incurred in the production of the specific product. All other factory costs are defined as the indirect costs of production.

The following problems may arise in respect of the distinction given above:

(a)   The significance of a cost item – although the costs may be directly identified with the manufacture of a product they may not be allotted to that product if, for example, the cost is insignificant or the cost of accumulation is not warranted.

(b)   The joint cost situation – raw materials used jointly in the production of more than one product may be difficult to identify specifically with any one product in any meaningful way.

(c)   Assignment of indirect costs – indirect costs are often allotted to product costs on an agreed basis although they are not directly identified with the manufacture of the product.

(d)   Disagreement on product costs – variable costs only may be allotted to products by some accountants.

2

Trading Statement
Three months ended 31st March 19....

		£	£	£	£
Net sales					25,000
Less cost of sales					
	Opening stock — raw materials	1,500			
	Add materials purchased	6,000			
		7,500			
	Less closing stock — raw materials	1,700			
	Raw materials cost		5,800		
	Direct labour cost		3,000		
	Direct expense		200		
(a)	Prime cost		9,000		
	Indirect labour		1,000		
	Maintenance materials		100		
	Electricity, gas and water		700		
	Rent and rates		1,100		
	Plant and machinery depreciation		800		
	Sundry factory expenses		1,200		
(b)	Total factory cost			13,900	
	Add opening work-in-progress			9,000	
				22,900	
	Less closing work-in-progress			8,000	
(c)	Factory cost of goods completed			14,900	
	Add opening stock — finished goods			12,000	
				26,900	
	Less closing stock — finished goods			14,000	
(d)	Cost of sales				12,900
(e)	Gross profit				12,100

34

3

Profit Statement
Three months ended 31st March 19....

		£	£	£
Net sales				35,000
Less cost of sales				17,000
Gross profit				18,000
Less operating expenses				
(d)	Administration expenses:			
	Office staff salaries	3,000		
	Office rent and rates	1,000		
	Printing and stationery	500		
	Telephone and postage	600		
	Audit fee	200		
	Sundry office expenses	1,000	6,300	
(e)	Selling and distribution expenses:			
	Salesmen's salaries and commission	3,000		
	Salesmen's entertaining expenses	100		
	Salesmen's car expenses	700		
	Carriage outwards	1,000	4,800	11,100
(a)	Operating profit			6,900
	Add investment income			2,000
(b)	Net profit before tax			8,900
	Taxation			2,000
(c)	Net profit after tax			6,900

4   (a)
Trading Statement
Three months ended 31st March 19....

		£	£	£	£
Net sales					40,000
(iv)	Less cost of sales				
	Direct material cost	5,000			
	Direct labour cost	4,000			
(i)	Prime cost		9,000		

(Table continued overleaf)

35

(a)   *Trading Statement (continued)*

	£	£	£	£
Brought forward		9,000		40,000
Factory overhead:				
Variable factory overhead	3,600			
Fixed factory overhead	6,400	10,000		

(ii) Total factory cost ... 19,000

			£	
Work-in-progress stock at the beginning of the period		3,000		
Work-in-progress stock at the close of the period		2,900		
Add work-in-progress stock variation			100	

(iii) Factory cost of goods completed ... 19,100

Finished goods stock at the beginning of the period		5,000		
Finished goods stock at the close of the period		4,800		
Add finished goods stock variation			200	19,300

(v) Gross profit ... 20,700

*Schedule of **Variable** Factory Overhead*
Three months ended 31st March 19....

	£
Lubricants	500
Labour cost incurred on defective work	1,000
Inspection labour cost	700
Plant and machinery repairs	500
Factory power	900
	3,600

Schedule of Fixed Factory Overhead
Three months ended 31st March 19....

	£
Factory supervision salaries	3,000
Factory insurance	500
Factory clerk's wages	1,100
Factory rent	1,000
Plant and machinery depreciation	800
	6,400

4   (b)   *Profit Statement*
                        Three months ended 31st March 19....

		£	£	£
Gross profit				20,700
Less operating expenses				
(i)	Administration expenses:			
	General office rent	1,000		
	Administration salaries	2,000		
	Telephone and telegrams	500		
	Postage and stationery	700		
	Audit fee	1,000	5,200	
(ii)	Selling expenses:			
	Sales salaries	2,000		
	Salesmen's commissions	900		
	Sales office rent	900		
	Travelling and entertaining – salesmen	600		
	Advertising	2,000	6,400	
(iii)	Distribution expenses:			
	Van expenses	1,000		
	Carriage outwards	1,500	2,500	14,100
(iv)	Operating profit			6,600

5   In calculating profit for a period, the sales figure is reduced by costs
and losses and while some of these items may be historical fact, e.g., sales
made or bad debts experienced, other items may be estimates as, for
example, the depreciation charge.

The trading and profit statements are not statements of objective
verifiable fact. They are a subjective estimate of profit, and the accuracy of
this figure is conditioned by the estimates and conservative provisions for
expected losses which have been made.

The depreciation charge, mentioned above, is usually an estimate of the
proportion of cost of the asset, e.g., plant and machinery, expired in the
period on an agreed basis such as use or time. The bad debts experienced
may be supplemented by the expected amount which will be lost to the
business through a customer's failure to pay for goods sold to them.

The estimating process involves an expression of opinion and there can
be differences of opinion. The trading and profit statements may have been

prepared by accountants competent in their work but the mixture of facts and opinion and the possible differences of opinion, possibly equally justifiable, means that calculated profits may vary given the same facts and transactions involving estimates.

6	*Balance Sheet as at 31st March 19....*			£
Capital acquisition				
Issued share capital				10,000
Revenue reserves				
Profit and loss account balance — at end of period				9,000
				19,000
Capital investment		£	£	£
(c)	Fixed assets			
	Freehold land and buildings		6,000	
	Plant and machinery		4,000	
	Office furniture and fixtures		1,000	11,000
(d)	Working capital			
(b)	Current assets:			
	Stocks	7,000		
	Trade debtors	6,000		
	Cash at bank and in hand	2,000	15,000	
(a)	Current liabilities:			
	Trade creditors	5,000		
	Current taxation	2,000	7,000	8,000
(e)	Capital employed			19,000

7   The controversy regarding intangible assets is concerned not only with their valuation but whether they should be shown in the accounts of the business.

(a)   Intangible assets are assets that have no physical existence but their possession confers a right to the business, e.g., goodwill. They are assets difficult to value because each intangible asset is unique and any comparison with similar items may be impossible.

(b)   Intangible assets are often shown separately in the balance sheet at cost or unwritten-off value. Patents, for example, may be written off over their legal life but other intangible assets, such as goodwill, may be eliminated from the balance sheet as soon as possible. The conservative approach may result in the intangible assets not being shown in the balance sheet at all rather than risk their over-valuation. If intangible assets are shown in the balance sheet, they are often shown as the first item on the assets side of the balance sheet.

8   (a)   Idle factory plant capacity is equipment not being used. An estimate may be made by taking an average over a long enough period to eliminate seasonal or other variations. If this view is taken, the idle facilities may be termed: normal idle factory plant capacity.

(b)   The possible causes of idle plant capacity may be:
 (i)   Insufficient sales orders
 (ii)   Shortage of labour in the industry
(iii)   Plant built in anticipation of future growth of the business
(iv)   Lack of material
 (v)   Changes in demand in the industry, e.g., movement from cotton to man-made fibres
(vi)   Breakdown.

(c)   Idle factory plant capacity costs are mainly the fixed costs of maintaining the plant not used and the depreciation charge if not computed on a usage basis.

9   Working capital is the net current investment required by the company and this short-term criterion is met by reducing the amount of current assets by the amount of current liabilities. The assumptions made in the provision of this figure are:
(a)   That the working capital components are continuously changing by frequent transactions in the ordinary course of business
(b)   That short-term liabilities are not generally regarded as providing permanent capital and, therefore, related to short-term changing assets (non-permanent assets)
(c)   That the settlement of current debts may be met by current assets
(d)   That there is a valid relationship between the classification 'current assets' and the classification 'current liabilities'.

10 (a)
 (i) *Operating assets*   £
      Fixed assets – at cost less depreciation   250,000
      Current assets   195,000

                                                            445,000

(ii) *Value of output*   £
      Sales   400,000
      Add closing work-in-progress   25,000

                                                            425,000
      Less opening work-in-progress   20,000

                                                            405,000

(iii) *Operating profit*   £   £
      Value of output   405,000
      Less cost of output
          Factory cost   304,000
          Administrative cost   33,000
          Selling cost   25,000
          Distribution cost   15,000   377,000

                                                             28,000

(iv) *Value added*   £
      Value of output   405,000
      Less materials consumed   141,000

                                                            264,000

(v)   *Factory cost*   £   £
      Materials
          Opening stock-materials and goods   310,000
          Add purchases   140,000

                                              150,000
          Less closing stock-materials and goods 9,000   141,000

(Table continued on facing page)

		£
	Brought forward	141,000
Factory wages — production employees		144,000
Factory salaries — works manager		4,000
Factory expenses		15,000
		304,000

(vi) *Administration cost*

	£
Salaries — management and clerical employees	11,000
Rates	7,000
Miscellaneous expenses	5,000
Other administration expenses	10,000
	33,000

(vii) *Selling cost*

	£
Sales manager's salary	5,000
Other selling expenses	20,000
	25,000

(viii) *Distribution cost*

	£
Van drivers' wages	6,000
Other distribution expenses	9,000
	15,000

(b)   The other adjustments that may be necessary to ensure that the information is comparable between member organisations in the Trade Federation Scheme may include:

(i)   Operating assets converted to current values

(ii)   Expenses converted to current cost levels, e.g., depreciation adjusted to amounts based on current values of assets

(iii) An adjustment of administration costs to include an economic rent estimate for property owned.

11   The main purpose of an accounts chart is to aid the processing of financial data by:

(a)   The grouping of financial items according to their common characteristics.

(b)   Encouraging the orderly presentation of financial data.

(c)   Allowing for the flexibility required where recording systems must be expanded to meet changing needs, yet preserve existing classification relationships.

(d)   Assisting analysis and synthesis in the most convenient form, usually related to the provision of financial statements for management.

(e)   To assist staff in the processing of data, usually through the use of symbols linked to the classification adopted. Coding incorporated in the accounts chart is essential to enable modern data-processing equipment to operate efficiently.

The accounts chart may also be used to relate costs to specific individuals in the organisation to assist the control process and accountability.

The accounts chart may be constructed as follows:

(i)   Decide on the objectives to be met by the accounts system and, in particular, users' needs in terms of information to be supplied

(ii) Design the classification of the data to satisfy (i) by the grouping of items according to their common characteristics

(iii) Identify the terms to be used and define each term adequately

(iv) Code the classification adopted by the use of alphabetical, numerical or a combination of these symbols, preserving the identity of not only individual items but also the groups of items detailed in (ii) above, e.g., Fixed assets:

101 Freehold property
102 Leasehold property
103 Plant and machinery
104 Fixtures and fittings
105 Motor vehicles

(Group identity given by the first digit '1' in the three-figure code.)

12   On the basis of a four-digit numerical code, the coded classification in question 12 (Chapter 2) is as follows:

Part 1 – Balance Sheet

Main classification Code	Sub-classification Code
01 Fixed assets	01 Leasehold land and buiding 02 Plant and machinery 03 Fixtures and fittings *(Table continued on facing page)*

| Main classification | | Sub-classification | |
Code		Code	
		04	Commercial vehicles
		05	Motor cars
		06	Other assets
02	Depreciation provisions	01	As for fixed assets
05	Current assets	01	Stock — raw materials
		02	Stock — work-in-progress
		03	Stock — finished goods
		04	Stock — other stocks
		10	Trade debtors control
		14	Prepaid expenses
		17	Other debtors
		20	Cash at bank
		25	Cash in hand
10	Current liabilities	01	Trade creditors control
		04	Accrued expenses
		07	Other creditors
14	Share capital	01	Ordinary shares
		04	Preference shares
16	Capital reserves	01	Capital reserve
18	Revenue reserves	01	Profit and loss account
19	Deferred liabilities	01	Future tax

Part 2 — Profit and Loss Account

| Main classification | | Sub-classification | |
Code		Code	
30	Sales	01 etc.	Sales by product groups
35	Factory cost of sales	01 etc.	Factory cost of sales by product groups
38	Material purchases	01	Raw materials
		05	Components
40	Expenses	01	Direct wages
		04	Indirect wages

(Table continued overleaf)

| Main classification | | Sub-classification | |
Code		Code	
40	Expenses (continued)	07	Salaries
		10	National Insurance
		12	Pension Fund
		14	Rent
		16	Rates
		18	Light, heat and power
		20	Carriage inwards
		22	Carriage outwards
		24	Car expenses
		26	Insurance
		30	Printing and stationery
		32	Postage and telephones
		35	Travelling and entertaining
		38	Bad debts
		40	Discounts allowed
		42	Bank charges
		44	Legal and professional fees
		50	Depreciation
		55	Directors remuneration
		60	Other expenses
50	Other income	01	Discounts received
		05	Rent receivable
55	Other expenditure	01	Loss on sale of fixed assets
60	Taxation	01	Corporation tax
		05	Income tax
65	Appropriations	01	Dividends – ordinary shares
		04	Dividends – preference shares

Further sub-analysis may extend the four-digit numerical code, e.g., extended analysis of materials, wages and salaries.

5 Ratio Analysis and Interfirm Comparison

1   As indicators, ratios indicate trends and areas of possible weakness in the business. As pointers, ratios may identify the possible causes of a poor business result, e.g., a low return on capital employed may be indicated and an analysis of this primary ratio into ints constituent elements may identify sections of the business that require further investigation.

Ratio information should not be taken in isolation from supporting data because incorrect conclusions may be drawn for the following reasons:

(a)   A ratio may indicate a satisfactory overall result but hide situations that should receive management attention, e.g., a good sales to debtors ratio may not disclose individual customer accounts where extended credit is being taken.

(b)   A ratio may indicate a poor result but a satisfactory explanation may be evident, e.g., a low stock turnover rate may show that stocks are greater than normal but this may be the direct result of the buyer purchasing additional raw materials because of an impending shortage. This action may be in the interests of the business yet give a poor ratio.

(c)   In a vertical combine, the organisation of the group may limit the possible performance in certain areas identified by ratio analysis.

(d)   Some of the factors that affect performance disclosed by a ratio may be non-controllable.

Having recognised the above limitations, ratios can emphasise relationships and generate further investigation which may be in the interests of the company.

2   Advantages of using capital employed as a ratio base for profit assessment, as compared with sales or cost of goods sold, are as follows:

(a) It emphasises to management that profit assessment is not limited to the profit margin but includes the turnover of capital

(b) It relates various aspects of business operation in one overall measure of performance

(c) It enables the business to detect sectors of activity requiring managerial attention

(d) It can serve as the basis for interfirm comparison through ratio analysis

(e) It gives management an emphasis to secure a reasonable rate of return on the capital employed in the business.

Disadvantages of using capital employed as a ratio base for profit assessment, as compared with sales or cost of goods sold, are as follows:

(i) It is difficult to reach agreement on the basis of calculating the figures to use in the return on capital employed ratio

(ii) Where segments of the business are to be assessed, the analysis of capital employed to responsibility centres is usually difficult

(iii) Management may be motivated to take action to improve the return on capital employed which may not be in the long-term interests of the business, e.g., leasing rather than ownership of assets.

3   Problems likely to arise in determining the figure of capital employed are:

(a) Deciding the items to include in capital employed
(b) Deciding on the interpretation of the terms used
(c) Deciding on the value of the items chosen.

Statement of Capital Employed as at 31st December 19....

	£000	Workings and reason for the figure given
Fixed assets		
Freehold land/buildings	408	$\frac{102}{100}$ x £400,000 = Current values
Plant and machinery	120	Replacement value 200,000
		Less depreciation to date
		$\frac{£200,000}{£150,000}$ x £60,000 = 80,000
		120,000

	£000		Workings and reason for the figure given
Brought forward	528		
Fixtures and fittings	65		Assumed current values
Motor vehicles	45	638	
Research and development		225	Best estimate of value
Loose tools		20	At valuation
Investments			
Trade	160		Assumed current values
Quoted	30	190	

Working capital

Assumed current values

Current assets:			
Stocks	1,090		
Sundry debtors and prepayments	750		
Cash and bank balances	70	1,910	
Current liabilities:			
Sundry creditors and accruals	550		
Current taxation	85		
Proposed dividends	38	673	1,237
Capital employed			2,310

Omitted items:
Goodwill omitted as an intangible asset
Bank overdraft because this is regarded as part of capital employed.

4   Responsibilities centres in this case may be linked to managers and products as follows (Figure 5.1):

(Figure 5.1 overleaf)

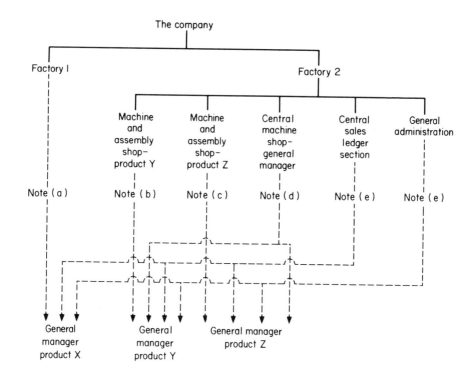

Figure 5.1

Capital employed	Basis for the analysis of capital employed to products
Fixed assets	(a) Factory 1 assets to Product X
	(b) Factory 2 assets in Product Y machine and assembly shop to Product Y
	(c) Factory 2 assets in Product Z machine and assembly shop to Product Z
	(d) Factory 2 assets in the central machine shop apportioned to Products Y, Z and sub-contract products on the basis of machine shop use (possible use of machine hours)
	(e) Factory 2 assets in the central sales ledger section and general administration apportioned to Products X, Y and Z and sub-contract products on the basis of product sales

(Table continued on facing page)

Capital employed	Basis for the analysis of capital employed to products
Working assets	To the extent that these current assets and current liabilities can be identified with specific products, the analysis will be a direct allocation. Otherwise, the amounts are usually apportioned on the basis of product sales.

Note regarding fixed assets:
Where factories are to be placed on a comparable basis it is normal to make an adjustment for owner-occupied property, as compared with the rented property. It is usual to include a notional rent in the former factory's costs (in this case: Factory 2). If this is done, the value of the property in the capital employed of Factory 2 should be eliminated from the above analysis.

5   Date ....
To: Managing Director
From: Accountant
Return on Capital Employed
Referring to the conference you recently attended, this memo explains features mentioned on the subject of return oncapital employed as a means of assessing business performance.

The return on capital employed as the product of the profit margin and asset turnover
Figures used in the following ratios as an illustration:

Profit:	£10,000
Sales:	£80,000
Capital employed:	£40,000

The profit margin: $\dfrac{\text{Profit}}{\text{Sales}} \times 100 = \dfrac{£10,000}{£80,000} \times 100 = 12\frac{1}{2}\%$

Asset turnover: $\dfrac{\text{Sales}}{\text{Capital employed}} = \dfrac{£80,000}{£40,000} = \text{Twice}$

Return on capital employed: $\dfrac{\text{Profit}}{\text{Capital employed}} \times 100 = \dfrac{£10,000}{£40,000} \times 100 =$

$= 25\% \text{ (i.e. } 2 \times 12\frac{1}{2}\%)$

The direction of management attention

It is agreed that attention should be directed to both areas of managerial performance to secure a reasonable rate of return on the capital employed in the business. Undue emphasis on, for example, the profit margin, may hide the fact that over-investment is taking place in the assets used to earn that profit.

Through the medium of the overall ratio of profit to capital employed it is possible to keep a check on business control activities — for example, a poor stock turnover rate, the stock control system or a poor credit period result, the credit control procedure. The principal control activities normally reviewed by ratios developed from the primary ratio (return on capital employed) are:

(a)   Material control
(b)   Labour control
(c)   Expense control
(d)   Capital expenditure control
(e)   Credit control
(f)   Funds control.

The ratios mentioned by the speaker emphasise significant financial relationships and generate further investigation that may be needed. They are no substitute for good management and a recognition is needed that other factors may be significant for the business, e.g., personnel management, research and development and customer relations.

Signed . . . .

6   The following criticisms may be made of the director's assertion:

(a)   The managing director claims this ratio is the only information required to measure the progress of the company. No one type of information can give management that measure of performance.

(b)   The ratio described is the added value for the week divided by the number employed and is not affected by any increase in cost apart from direct materials or represented by the number of employees. In this area, labour use could present a problem as, for example, a variation in the proportion of the labour force employed: part-time/full-time.

(c)   If the ratio does change, interpreting the movements in the ratio would prove difficult without a lot of supporting detail.

(d)   Important factors are ignored by the ratio such as the capital employed by the business and variations in stock levels.

(e)   The managing director refers to a predetermined standard to measure the progress of the company but does not define the basis of this standard. Given a satisfactory basis for the standard, the ratio is one measure that the managing director could use.

7

Ratio calculated	Objective of the ratio calculated	Additional detail
(a) Return on capital employed ratio: $$= \frac{£1,750}{£5,343} \times 100 = 32.8\%$$	A measure of the efficiency of operating management in achieving a desired profit on the funds invested in the business	Current values on assets employed with the appropriate adjustments to profit
(b) Net profit ratio: $$= \frac{£1,750}{£7,000} \times 100 = 25\%$$	An indication of the net profit margin	Product detail
(c) Capital turnover ratio: $$= \frac{£7,000}{£5,343} = 1.3 \text{ times}$$	The rate at which assets are turned over in earning the profit achieved	Current values of assets
(d) Liquid ratio: $= £1,318:£546 = 2.4:1$	To indicate the availability of liquid assets to meet short-term liabilities	Types of debtors
(e) Current ratio: $= £3,565:£546 = 6.5:1$	To indicate the company's liquidity expressing the working	

(Table continued overleaf)

51

Ratio calculated	Objective of the ratio calculated	Additional detail
(e) Current ratio (continued)	capital relationship in terms of short-term assets to short-term liabilities	
(f) Sales to debtors ratio: = £7,000:£1,277 = 5.5:1	To indicate the extent of the average credit being allowed to customers	Customer accounts analysis

The standards of comparison adopted for each of the above ratios could be:
(i)   Planned performance ratios
(ii)   The ratios for previous comparable periods
(iii) Interfirm comparison ratios.

8   Relevant ratios from the data:

Return on capital employed ratio $= \dfrac{£2,850}{£95,000} \times 100 = 3\%$

Net profit ratio $= \dfrac{£2,850}{£142,500} \times 100 = 2\%$

Capital turnover ratio $= \dfrac{£142,500}{£95,000} = 1.5$ times

Gross profit ratio $= \dfrac{£28,500}{£142,500} \times 100 = 20\%$

Selling expenses ratio $= \dfrac{£4,900}{£142,500} \times 100 = 3.4\%$

Per order $= \dfrac{£4,900}{7,770} = £0.60$

Warehouse expenses ratio: $= \dfrac{£6,750}{£142,500} \times 100 = 4.7\%$

$$\text{Per order} = \frac{£6,750}{7,770} = £0.90$$

Handling and clerical expenses $= \dfrac{£10,250}{£142,500} \times 100 = 7.2\%$

$$\text{Per order} = \frac{£10,250}{7,770} = £1.30$$

Administration expenses $= \dfrac{£3,750}{£25,650} \times 100 = 14.6\%$

$$\text{Per order} = \frac{£3,750}{7,770} = £0.50$$

Other relevant information from the data:

Order size	Number of orders	%	Sales income £	%	Average selling value per order £	Average gross profit per order £
Under £5	4,000	51	8,000	6	2	0.4
£5 to £29.9	1,750	23	17,500	12	10	2.0
£30 to £54.9	1,200	15	48,000	34	40	8.0
£55 to £79.9	400	5	24,000	17	60	12.0
£80 to £104.9	300	4	27,000	19	90	18.0
£105+	120	2	18,000	12	150	30.0
	7,770	100	142,500	100		

Comment

There is no information regarding the turnover of capital aspects of the business so comments are necessarily restricted to the following:

(a)   Most of the orders give little sales value and it should be in the interests of the company to attempt to reverse this pattern by, for example, changes in discount policy.

(b)   The cost levels need to be reduced wherever possible. No comparable information is given in the question but if profit has been as high as 5% of sales, cost levels in relation to sales have been better. It may be that there is a minimum cost level for the minimum service necessary and only increased sales could remedy this, but costs should be divided between their fixed and variable elements to give this information. If it is possible to reduce expenses every effort should be made to do so.

(c)   The volume factor mentioned above should be given attention and an attempt made to increase sales.

(d)   The profitability of individual orders should be examined and the results of such an investigation used to vary policy. The average costs per order in relation to the average gross profits show small orders as making a loss and as so many small orders are received the point made in (a) above is important.

(e)   It seems possible to achieve the target return on capital employed if the profit ratio can be increased to former levels.

(f)   Planned changes in policy should be judged against possible improved performance and the business controlled to achieve the expected results.

(g)   A check on asset turnover factors should also be made.

9   *Tabulation of Key Ratios*

	Ratio	Measure-ment	Actual		Plan
			Year 1	Year 2	Year 3
(a)	Profit before tax / Capital employed	%	8	8.9	9.1
(b)	Profit / Sales	%	5	7.3	6.4
(c)	Sales / Capital employed	Times	1.6	1.2	1.4
(d)	Materials cost / Sales	%	40	37	36

(Table continued on facing page)

	Ratio	Measure-ment	Actual		Plan
			Year 1	Year 2	Year 3
(e)	Labour cost / Sales	%	15	14	13
(f)	Administration cost / Sales	%	10.5	11.8	16.8
(g)	Selling and distribution cost / Sales	%	3.5	4.5	4.3
(h)	Liquid assets / Current liabilities	Times	2:1	2.5:1	2.4:1
(i)	Current assets / Current liabilities	Times	5:1	7.5:1	7.1:1
(j)	Cost of sales / Stock	Times	3	2.8	2.9
(k)	Debtors / Sales per day	Days	58	45	40

Interpretation of the ratios

The primary ratio of profit to capital employed increased significantly in Year 2 over Year 1 but only a small increase is planned for Year 3 and this return for the industry appears low. The increase in capital employed is being planned despite a reduction in expected profit margins owing to an increased turnover of capital.

Production costs have fallen in Years 1 and 2 and this reduction is planned to continue in Year 3. Administration costs are rising rapidly and need investigation. Planned selling and distribution costs are lower in relation to Year 2 but still higher as a per cent on sales on Year 1. They would merit further investigation.

Sales are continuing to increase in value and it would be useful to know the change in units.

The company appears to be financially sound and stock turnover is consistent. The improvement in debt collection shows increased attention to credit control.

Workings

Ratio	Actual		Plan
	Year 1	Year 2	Year 3
(a)	$\dfrac{10}{125} \times 100 = 8\%$	$\dfrac{16}{180} \times 100 = 8.9\%$	$\dfrac{18}{198} \times 100 = 9.1\%$
(b)	$\dfrac{10}{200} \times 100 = 5\%$	$\dfrac{16}{220} \times 100 = 7.3\%$	$\dfrac{18}{280} \times 100 = 6.4\%(c)$
(c)	$\dfrac{200}{125} = 1.6$ times	$\dfrac{220}{180} = 1.2$ times	$\dfrac{280}{198} = 1.4$ times
(d)	$\dfrac{80}{200} \times 100 = 40\%$	$\dfrac{81}{220} \times 100 = 37\%$	$\dfrac{101}{280} \times 100 = 36\%$
(e)	$\dfrac{30}{200} \times 100 = 15\%$	$\dfrac{31}{220} \times 100 = 14\%$	$\dfrac{36}{280} \times 100 = 13\%$
(f)	$\dfrac{21}{200} \times 100 = 10.5\%$	$\dfrac{26}{220} \times 100 = 11.8\%$	$\dfrac{47}{280} \times 100 = 16.8\%$
(g)	$\dfrac{7}{200} \times 100 = 3.5\%$	$\dfrac{10}{220} \times 100 = 4.5\%$	$\dfrac{12}{280} \times 100 = 4.3\%$
(h)	$\dfrac{36}{18} = 2{:}1$	$\dfrac{30}{12} = 2.5{:}1$	$\dfrac{36}{15} = 2.4{:}1$
(i)	$\dfrac{90}{18} = 5{:}1$	$\dfrac{90}{12} = 7.5{:}1$	$\dfrac{106}{15} = 7.1{:}1$
(j)	$\dfrac{162}{54} = 3$ times	$\dfrac{168}{60} = 2.8$ times	$\dfrac{203}{70} = 2.9$ times

(Table continued on facing page)

Ratio	Actual		Plan
	Year 1	Year 2	Year 3
(k)	$\dfrac{32}{200 \div 365}$ = 58 days	$\dfrac{27}{220 \div 365}$ = 45 days	$\dfrac{31}{280 \div 365}$ = 40 days

10   The CIFC attempts to make their studies comparable by:

(a)   Basing comparisons on a uniform accounting system regarding the data used in the ratios supplied

(b)   Providing participants with sets of instructions and definitions of terms used

(c)   Using field investigators

(d)   Not comparing firms as such but to reveal what effect certain differences in their features and practices have on their performance

(e)   Ensuring that data is sufficiently comparable for the object of the comparison to be met.

The choice of the key ratios would begin with the principal ratio:

$$\frac{\text{Profit}}{\text{Capital employed}}$$

as the main indication of commercial success. This primary ratio would be broken down to indicate:

(i)   Profitability: $\dfrac{\text{Profit}}{\text{Sales}}$

(ii)   Turnover of capital: $\dfrac{\text{Sales}}{\text{Capital employed}}$

These main factors would then be broken down to identify key areas of performance, e.g.

Breakdown of the profitability ratio:

$$\frac{\text{Factory cost}}{\text{Sales}}$$

$$\frac{\text{Selling and distribution cost}}{\text{Sales}}$$

$$\frac{\text{Administration cost}}{\text{Sales}}$$

Breakdown of the turnover of capital ratio:

$$\frac{\text{Fixed assets}}{\text{Capital employed}}$$

$$\frac{\text{Sales}}{\text{Average stocks}}$$

$$\frac{\text{Average trade debts}}{\text{Average sales per day}}$$

11 (a)   Date ....

To: Member firms in the Trade Association
From: Secretary, Trade Association

Interfirm Comparisons

I have examined the possibility of introducing an interfirm comparison scheme and report on the matters mentioned by members as worthy of investigation:

Advantages of interfirm comparisons

(a) Extends the comparative data available to the business to assess its performance
(b) Provides companies with information regarding profitability and productivity relevant to the specific industry and for companies of similar type and size
(c) Identifies specific areas in the business which may need managerial attention
(d) The production of information for management on a uniform basis.

Limitations of interfirm comparisons

(a) Companies not co-operating to the extent necessary in modifying their own methods to provide comparative data
(b) Lack of support by firms on a continuing basis
(c) Reluctance on the part of some firms to part with information notwithstanding assurances on confidentiality.

Type of information which could be produced

Interfirm comparisons are usually based on ratio comparisons, the primary ratio:

$$\frac{\text{Profit}}{\text{Capital employed}}$$

supplied with its two constituent elements:

$$\frac{\text{Profit}}{\text{Sales}} \quad \text{and} \quad \frac{\text{Sales}}{\text{Capital employed}}$$

Detailed analysis of the first ratio (the profit margin) and the second ratio (turnover of capital) can follow by further ratio analysis to give important information to participating companies, e.g.

The profit margin:

$$\frac{\text{Factory cost}}{\text{Total cost}}$$

$$\frac{\text{Administration cost}}{\text{Total cost}}$$

$$\frac{\text{Selling and distribution cost}}{\text{Sales}}$$

Turnover of capital:

$$\frac{\text{Sales}}{\text{Fixed assets}}$$

$$\frac{\text{Cost of sales}}{\text{Average stock}}$$

$$\frac{\text{Debtors}}{\text{Average sales per day}}$$

Further details of how a scheme of interfirm comparison could be introduced in this Association will be supplied on request.

Signed . . . .

(b) Possible explanations of the differences disclosed are as follows:

Possible explanations		Possible investigation
(i) Direct labour	Lower wage costs Different production methods	An examination of comparable wage rates An analysis of business methods — in particular, the extent of mechanisation relative to other firms in the scheme

(Table continued overleaf)

Possible explanations		Possible investigation
(ii) Direct material	Lower material costs	
	Different production methods	An analysis of business methods – in particular, the efficiency in the usage of material
(iii) Overhead	Excessive overhead cost	An examination of cost levels
	A different cost structure	An analysis of cost elements and cost behaviour related to business methods

12 (a) On the subject of confidentiality it would be pointed out that the Centre for Interform Comparison is an independent organisation and figures are only distributed to firms taking part, unless permission is given by companies for a wider use of their information. Each company is identified by code number only.

On the subject of comparability, information provided would be compiled on a uniform basis as outlined in detailed instructions given to member companies. The instructions are carefully prepared to ensure that data will be sufficiently comparable to meet the objectives of the study.

(b) The following meanings may be given to the terms used in the ratios:
  (i) Operating profit: profit before tax on the main activities of the business after meeting all expenses on the basis of current values (depreciation) and charging interest on all capital
  (ii) Capital employed: fixed assets and working capital at current values for the main activities of the business
  (iii) Sales: gross sales less trade rebates and sales allowances
  (iv) Cost of production: direct material, direct labour and production overheads
  (v) Cost of administration: expenses of non-manufacturing functions excluding marketing and research and development
  (vi) Cost of selling and distribution: expenses of obtaining sales, preparing goods for despatch after manufacturing and their disposal to customers
  (vii) Fixed assets: long-term assets at current values employed for the main activities of the business
  (viii) Materials consumed: raw materials consumed at cost
  (ix) Stock: average stock of raw materials for the period at cost

(x) Average trade debts: average of outstanding debts for the period

(xi) Average sales per day: average for the period.

(c)   The operating results for Electric Parts Ltd give cause for concern. Their return on capital employed is not only less than the results of the average company but is below that of 75% of the companies taking part. The possible cause of this poor performance may be judged by examining ratios 2 and 6 in both cases these are low.

The reason why the operating profit to sales ratio is poor may be judged by examining ratios 3, 4 and 5 and ratio 3 is above average. The reason why the sales to capital employed is poor may be judged by examining ratios 7, 8 and 9 and ratios 8 and 9 merit further investigation.

The ratios are merely indicators of possible poor performance but in the case, production costs, stock and credit control should be checked for inefficient operation.

In the case quoted, membership is worth while because information to assist the company in assessing its performance is provided which could not be obtained in any other way.

6 Cost-Volume-Profit Analysis

1   The factors that could invalidate the findings disclosed by break-even analysis are as follows:

(a)   Variable costs not remaining a constant per unit
(b)   Fixed costs not remaining fixed for the period under review
(c)   A change in efficiency possible over the activity range under consideration
(d)   Difficulty in the segregation of fixed and variable costs
(e)   Sales prices not remaining at a constant per unit
(f)   In the case of a multi-product business, the sales mix may vary for products with differing profits per unit of sale
(g)   Capital investment considerations including significant variations in stock levels.

These factors may be allowed for as follows:

(i)   A study of cost behaviour to assist in the division of costs into their fixed and variable elements. Statistical techniques such as least squares may assist with this problem.
(ii)   Adopting the planned range of output to minimise the effect of significant variations of costs and revenue.
(iii) The separate production of break-even charts for (1) each product group; and (2) possible changes in sales mix.
(iv)   The profit planning considerations of management not restricted to break-even analysis.

2   (a)   The break-even chart will show the following:
(i)   The break-even point — when total sales equal total costs, i.e., no profit or loss made by the company.
(ii)   Margin of safety — the extent to which a planned activity level can fall before a loss is experienced. The difference between planned sales and the break-even point.

(iii)   Profitability at different activity levels based on different planning assumptions regarding revenue and costs.
(iv)   Contribution at different activity levels based on different planning assumptions regarding revenue and costs (providing the presentation is in the form of Figure 6.8 per the text).

(b)   Providing the limitations of cost-volume-profit analysis (see the answer to question 12a) are borne in mind, the technique is useful as a profit planning tool assisting management to understand the significance of their plans. The detailed study of break-even chart relationships, prompted by the application of the technique, is particularly valuable because this analysis can go beyond the simple relationships that are the basis of the assumptions depicted on the break-even chart.

(c)   Since the break-even chart represents a static relationship, in a multi-product company the chart assumes a planned sales mix which can alter. If the mix favours products with high contribution per unit, the effect will show on the break-even chart by lowering the break-even point. If the sales mix varies in the opposite direction, the break-even point will be raised. The break-even chart can demonstrate these changes but the static assumption is a significant limitation on the chart's usefulness.

3   (a)   The cost-volume-profit relationships implied in the statements made by John Smith and Bill Green are as follows:

Statements made by John Smith
'greater volume in terms of sales was the answer to the company problem'. The high volume would aim at lowering the total unit cost per product. A low contribution per unit with high fixed costs would require high volume to obtain a reasonable profit. A low volume with high fixed costs could be serious for company profitability.

'the sales value was the same as the year before with no major volume change yet the profit had dropped . . . product 123 had not sold in the current year as well as in the previous year'.
This result appears to be due to a change in the mix of sales with a greater volume of less profitable products than product 123 making up the total volume of sales in units.

Statement made by Bill Green
'delivery of a costly new piece of plant and machinery and this should mean an increased production rate'.
This machinery will increase fixed costs. Although the increased production

rate will reduce unit cost, the profit implied in the increased contribution per unit is dependent on the increased volume. Higher fixed costs will have reduced the margin of safety.

(b)   A possible explanation of the chart supplied by Jim Grey is as follows:
Plan A gives the highest fixed costs and this gives the highest break-even point of the three plans and, therefore, results in the lowest margin of safety. Variable costs and revenue are indicated as a constant per unit. Fixed costs are indicated as a constant amount for the range of activity shown.
Plan B gives a lower level of fixed costs than Plan A which lowers the break-even point and increases the margin of safety.
Plan C gives increased profit for the same level of fixed cost as Plan B, thus lowering the break-even point further and giving the maximum margin of safety of the three plans.

    The increased profit may be explained by a reduction of variable costs; or a possibly improved mix of sales; or possibly both.

4   The break-even chart required (Figure 6.1):

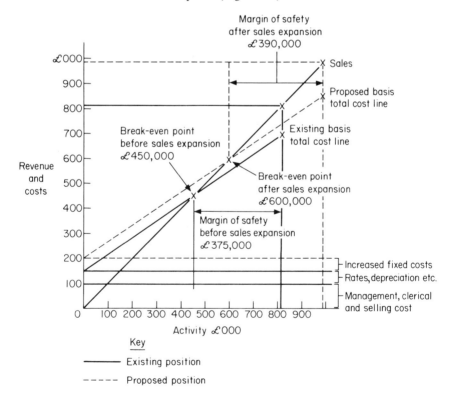

Existing basis sales: £825,000
Proposed sales: £825,000 + 20% (£165,000) = £990,000
Total costs before sales expansion:

		Litres		per litre		£
Product	A	30,000	x	£2	=	60,000
	B	20,000	x	£3	=	60,000
	C	40,000	x	£10	=	400,000
		90,000				520,000

Add distribution and bottling costs $\dfrac{90,000}{12}$ x £4 = 30,000

Variable costs	550,000
Fixed costs	150,000
	700,000

Total costs after sales expansion:

Variable costs: £550,000 + 20%	660,000
Fixed costs	200,000
	860,000

Answers to the question from the graph:

		Before sales expansion £	After sales expansion £
(a)	Break-even point	450,000	600,000
(b)	Margin of safety	375,000	390,000

5   The comparative profit graph required (Figure 6.2):

	Product A	Product B	Product C
Profits			
Contribution = Sales x P/V ratio	£60,000	£60,000	£60,000
	x 20%	x 15%	x 10%
	= 12,000	= 9,000	= 6,000
Fixed cost	9,500	6,000	3,750
Profit	2,500	3,000	2,250

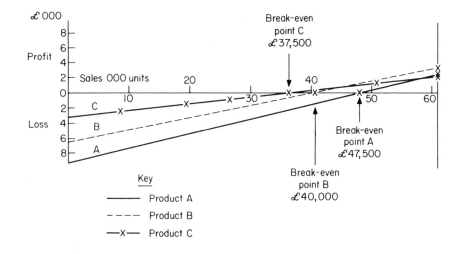

Figure 6.2

	Product A	Product B	Product C
Information from the graph			
Break-even point	47,500	40,000	37,500
Margin of safety	12,500	20,000	22,500
Profit at estimated sales	2,500	3,000	2,250
Fixed cost	9,500	6,000	3,750

Comment

From the above information, Product A is more vulnerable to loss of profits in the event of reduced sales than Products B and C. Fixed costs are high in the case of Product A. The point at issue is the reliability of the estimated sales figure because at 60,000 units, Product B is the most profitable product.

Management facing the problem mentioned in the question would require further information before a satisfactory decision could be made, e.g., the factor that may be used to the limit to optimise profit in relation to investment to be made by the business.

6   The total costs to be plotted on the scattergraph:

Year	Sales £		Profit before tax £		Total cost £
1	64,400	–	12,600	=	51,800
2	56,000	–	7,700	=	48,300
3	75,600	–	19,600	=	56,000
4	70,000	–	16,800	=	53,200
5	67,200	–	15,400	=	51,800

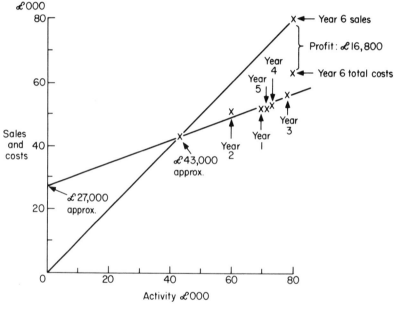

Figure 6.3

The conclusions that can be drawn from the graph are as follows:
(a) The margin of safety in Year 6 will be reduced which will have the effect of raising the break-even point from its figure of approximately £43,000.
(b) The Year 6 profit is below the level of profitability shown on the graph by the trend lines. Costs in relation to sales for Year 6 have increased.
(c) Fixed costs are approximately £27,000.

7 The required profit graph (Figure 6.4):

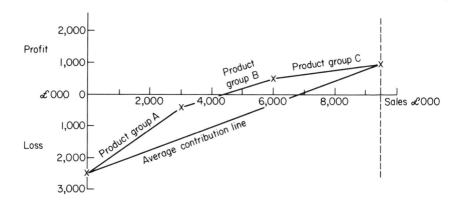

Figure 6.4

8 (a) Budgeted profit:

	Company 1	Company 2	Company 3
	£	£	£
Sales	20,000	20,000	20,000
Variable cost	15,000	12,500	10,000
Contribution	5,000	7,500	10,000
Fixed costs	3,000	5,500	8,000
Profit	2,000	2,000	2,000

(b) Budgeted break-even point in units $= \dfrac{\text{fixed cost}}{\text{Contribution per unit}}$

	Company 1	Company 2	Company 3
	$\dfrac{£3,000}{£0.50}$	$\dfrac{£5,500}{£0.75}$	$\dfrac{£8,000}{£1}$
	= 6,000 units	= 7,334 units	= 8,000 units

(c) (i) Budgeted margin between break-even point and budgeted sales:

	Company 1	Company 2	Company 3
	units	units	units
Budgeted sales	10,000	10,000	10,000
Break-even point	6,000	7,334	8,000
	4,000	2,666	2,000

(ii) Total capacity $= \dfrac{10{,}000}{80} \times 100 = 12{,}500$ units

	Company 1	Company 2	Company 3
(iii) $\dfrac{\text{(i)}}{\text{(ii)}} \times 100$	$\dfrac{4{,}000}{12{,}500}$	$\dfrac{2{,}666}{12{,}500}$	$\dfrac{2{,}000}{12{,}500}$
	$\times 100$	$\times 100$	$\times 100$
	$= 32\%$	$= 21\%$	$= 16\%$

(d) The 10% deviation in sales is 1,000 units. The impact on profits is plus or minus 1,000 x the contribution per unit for each company:

	Company 1	Company 2	Company 3
	$1{,}000 \times$	$1{,}000 \times$	$1{,}000 \times$
	£0.50	£0.75	£1.0
	$= £500$	$= £750$	$= £1{,}000$

Comment
The highest margin of safety belongs to Company 1 followed by Companies 2 and 3. This means that the drop in sales is not so serious in terms of profitability for Company 1 as compared with Company 3. On the other hand, the increase in sales brings a marked improvement in profits for Company 3 as soon as the break-even point is passed because Company 3 has the highest break-even point; Company 1 having the lowest break-even point.

9   (a) Variation in sales: £43,000 − £39,000 = £4,000
        Variation in costs: £37,600 − £34,800 = £2,800
        i.e., for every £10 variation in sales there is a variation in costs of £7.
        Using Year 1 figures: $\dfrac{£39{,}000}{£10} \times £7 = £27{,}300$

        Fixed cost = £34,800 − £27,300 = £7,500

   (b) P/V ratio $= \dfrac{\text{Contribution}}{\text{Sales}} \times 100$

        $= \dfrac{£39{,}000 - £27{,}300}{£39{,}000} \times 100$

        $= 30\%$

   (c) Break-even point $= \dfrac{\text{Fixed cost}}{\text{Contribution}} \times \text{Sales}$

$$= \frac{£7,500}{£11,700} \times £39,000$$

$$= \underline{£25,000}$$

(d) Margin of safety = Sales − break-even point
         Year 1   £39,000 − £25,000 = £14,000
         Year 2   £43,000 − £25,000 = £18,000

Assuming that the varied range of products mentioned in the question include products of varying contribution per unit, the profit/volume ratio may be improved apart from increasing selling prices or reducing costs by varying the sales mix in favour of the products with the greatest contribution per unit.

10   The chart required (Figure 6.5):

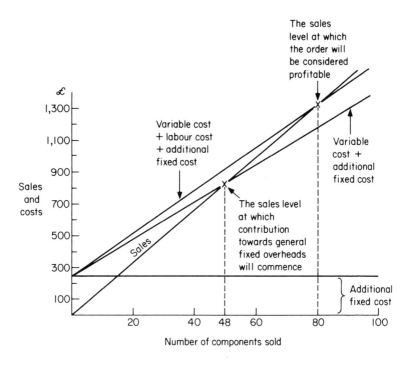

The sales level at which contribution towards general fixed overheads will commence = 48 units. The sales level at which the order will be considered profitable = 80 units.

70

11 (a) Break-even point $= \dfrac{\text{Fixed cost}}{\text{P/V ratio}} = \dfrac{£1,010,000}{£2,020,000} \times £4,000,000$

$= \underline{£2,000,000}$

(b) *Sales proposal A*

	£
Reduction in selling price per unit:	10.00
Less 5%	0.50
	9.50

	units
Increase in sales volume:	400,000
Add 12½%	50,000
	450,000

£

Profit calculation

Sales: 450,000 x £9.50 =   4,275,000

Prime cost:

Per graph: £2,610,000 − £1,010,000 = £1,600,000

$\dfrac{£1,600,000}{400,000} \times 450,000 = 1,800,000$

Variable costs other than promotion commission:

Per graph:

	£	£	£
		2,990,000	
Less	1,010,000		
	1,600,000	2,610,000	380,000
		2,930,000	
		2,730,000	200,000
			180,000

$\dfrac{£180,000}{400,000} \times 450,000 =$ 202,500

Brought forward	2,002,500	
Promotional commission:		
5% of £4,275,000	213,750	2,216,250
Contribution		2,058,750
Less fixed costs		1,010,000
Profit		1,048,750

Sales proposal B

	£
Reduction in selling price per unit	10.00
Less 10%	1.00
	9.00

	units
Increase in sales volume	400,000
Add 25%	100,000
	500,000

	£	£
Profit calculation		
Sales: 500,000 x £9.00 =		4,500,000
Prime cost:		

$$\frac{£1,600,000}{400,000} \times 500,000 = \qquad 2,000,000$$

Variable costs other than promotional commission:

$$\frac{£180,000}{400,000}\text{xx } 500,000 = \qquad 225,000$$

Promotional commission:		
5% of £4,500,000 =	225,000	2,450,000
Contribution		2,050,000
Less fixed costs		1,010,000
Profit		1,040,000

(c)   Quantity to be sold:

$$\frac{\text{Contribution under Proposal A}}{\text{Contribution per unit under Proposal B}}$$

Contribution per unit under Proposal B:

	£
Selling price	9.00
Less marginal cost	4.90
	4.10

Quantity to be sold under Proposal B to achieve the profit disclosed by Proposal A:

$$\frac{£2,058,750}{£4.10} = 502,135 \text{ units}$$

(d)   Providing the limitations of cost-volume-profit analysis are borne in mind, the technique is useful as a profit planning tool assisting management to understand the significance of their plans. The detailed study of cost-volume-profit relationships prompted by the application of the technique is particularly valuable because this analysis can go beyond the simple relationships that are the basis of the assumptions depicted on the break-even chart.

12   (a)   The underlying assumptions usually made in the use of cost-volume-profit analysis data for profit planning and cost control are:
  (i)   The constant price per unit of sales
 (ii)   The constant variable cost per unit over the anticipated range of operations
(iii)   That fixed costs will be fixed for the anticipated range of operations
(iv)   That the sales mix will be maintained
 (v)   That each factor considered is dependent of changes in other factors
(vi)   That efficiency is constant over the range of operations
(vii)   That total costs can be divided into their fixed and variable elements.
         The fact that these constant factors are not necessarily applicable means that without care the information produced could be misleading. This problem is, to a large extent, overcome by restricting one's attention to a limited range of activity where the relationships implied in the assumption given above are likely to be applicable. If error is introduced it is not likely to mislead management in the information given.

(b)   The formulae required:

(i)   The level of sales in £s to obtain a given profit =

$$\frac{\text{Given profit} + \text{Fixed cost}}{\text{P/V ratio}}$$

(ii) The sales volume in units needed to maintain the current profit given a reduction in selling price =

$$\frac{\text{Total contribution prior to price reduction}}{\text{New P/V ratio as a result of the price reduction}} \div \frac{\text{New selling price}}{\text{per unit}}$$

(iii) The sales volume in units required to maintain the current profit after an increase in fixed costs =

$$\frac{\text{New fixed cost} + \text{Profit prior to the increase in fixed costs}}{\text{Contribution per unit}}$$

7 Funds Analysis

1   Funds analysis is important because the technique makes possible an assessment of the quality of the company's financial management. The statements produced explain:

(i)   The use of the profits in the business

(ii)   Why working capital may be reduced in the period although profits have increased

(iii) The possible need to gain additional finance to purchase fixed assets although the profits and depreciation in the period are greater than the cost of the fixed assets

(iv)   What has happened to the provision of additional funds such as proceeds from the sale of fixed assets or new capital introduced.

In addition, funds analysis facilitates the planning for the future: long-term planning with the help of the sources and applications of funds statement, and short-term planning with the help of the cash flow statement.

The profit statement indicates the excess of revenue and other income over expenses and losses in the period and as such includes items like depreciation which does not require the use of working capital. Depreciation, therefore, is not deducted in calculating the working capital change in the period. The depreciation charge reduces profit and the fixed asset to which it relates. A funds and cash flow statement only measure changes in the working capital or cash of the period. All expenses are deducted from revenue in the profit statement to calculate the profit or loss for the period.

2   The possible belief that a cash budget is not required is not taken to imply that accountants are not interested in cash flow information. On the contrary, the control of the cash position is of vital importance and this may seriously affect other plans for the business.

Although it is possible to calculate the cash position as a residual figure in a planned balance sheet, the better method as an alternative to the receipts and payments basis is the sources and applications of funds statement, calculated from the profit for the year.

It is usual to divide the cash statement for management into two parts:
(a) Increase in cash available
(b) Reduction in cash available.

Section (a) begins with the depreciation for the year added back to the operating profit. An increase in creditors or a decrease in stocks and debtors may be supplemented by proceeds from shareholders and/or proceeds from the sale of fixed assets. Section (b) includes increases in stocks and debtors, payments of tax and dividends and the cost of additional fixed assets.

The net result of parts (a) and (b) will give the net increase or decrease in cash.

3   Liabilities are paid in cash and this requirement is met by the company's credit account at the bank or the extension limit allowed by the bank, if the company operates on a bank overdraft, cash in hand, cash receipts from debtors, and possibly, short-term investments available for quick realisation. These are the liquid assets of the business and are part of the working capital of the company which reduces in liquidity as the production cycle is considered.

The cash received from debtors has only arrived after a credit period has elapsed; the finished goods available for sale may have been in store for some time; work-in-progress in all its stages of production will represent cash investment as also raw material. These assets are not available to meet the debts and obligations of the business.

When a business has a full order book, the optimism generated by the market opportunities and good business climate can blind management to the fact that the increased business requires increased investment in working capital and that the cash receipts lag behind the cash expenditure. It is unfortunate that a company may have a good product which sells well and provides the company with full employment of resources and good profits, yet collapse owing to a liquidity problem. This is usually because the financial control has been weak and the cash flow time-lag not recognised adequately.

4 (a)		Period 1	Period 2
$\dfrac{\text{Average working capital employed}}{\text{Average daily sales}}$	$=$	$\dfrac{£260,500}{£5,000}$	$\dfrac{£239,000}{£6,000}$
Working capital equivalent to the number of days sales		52	40

Working capital turnover has increased.

(b)	$\dfrac{\text{Receivables}}{\text{Average daily sales}}$ =	*Period 1* £235,000	*Period 2* £330,000
		£5,000	£6,000
	Number of days credit	47	55
	$\dfrac{\text{Inventory}}{\text{Average daily sales}}$ =	£134,500	£144,000
		£5,000	£6,000
	Inventory equivalent to the number of days sales	27	24
	$\dfrac{\text{Current assets}}{\text{Current liabilities}}$ =	£417,000	£483,000
		£156,500	£244,000
	Current ratio	2.7:1	2:1
	$\dfrac{\text{Liquid assets}}{\text{Current liabilities}}$ =	£276,000	£332,000
		£156,500	£244,000
	Liquid ratio	1.8:1	1.3:1

(c)   Comments on the apparent financial position of the company:
  (i)   The collection period for accounts has increased and appears to be rather high.
 (ii)   The reduction in stock levels is generally a good trend.
(iii)   The current and liquid ratios are generally considered to be at reasonable levels although there is insufficient information to be certain of this. These ratios are decreasing and the cash balance has dropped significantly. The company appears to be financially sound at the moment but the trend should be watched in the future.
 (iv)   Current liabilities have increased. This figure should be investigated to ensure that the increased credit taken is not detrimental to the interests of the business.

5

A.B. Stores Ltd

Cash Budget – 3 months ended 31st August 19....

See note		£000	£000	£000
	Opening cash balance			1,100
	Add receipts			
	From customers:			
	Cash sales	5,500		
(i)	Credit sales	5,250	10,750	

		£000	£000	£000
(ii)	From associated company:			
	Loan repayment		150	
(iii)	Proceeds from the sale of			
	fixed assets		150	
(iv)	From debenture holders		1,500	12,550
				13,650
	Less payments			
(v)	To suppliers		7,900	
(vi)	For wages and expenses		2,100	
(vii)	For taxation		500	
	For dividends		625	
	For debenture interest		75	
	For assets purchased		2,000	13,200
	Closing cash balance			450

Workings		£000
(i)	Receipts from credit sales customers	
	Opening debtors' balance	2,070
	Add credit sales	7,000
		9,070
	Less closing debtors' balance	3,820
		5,250
(ii)	Loan repayment	
	Opening balance	175,000
	Closing balance	25,000
		150,000

(iii)		£000
	Proceeds from the sale of fixed assets	
	Fixed assets at cost – opening balance	21,250
	Add purchases	2,000
		23,250

	£000	£000
Brought forward	23,250	
Less closing balance	22,750	
Assets sold at cost		500
Depreciation on fixed assets –		
opening balance	4,950	
Add depreciation for the quarter	600	
	5,550	
Less closing balance	5,150	400
Book value on assets sold		100
Add profit on sale of assets		50
		150

(iv) Debenture issue receipts

		£000
Closing balance		3,000
Opening balance		1,500
		1,500

(v) Payments to suppliers

		£000
Opening creditors' balance		2,220
Add purchases:		
Cost of sales	8,050	
Add closing stock	4,330	
	12,380	
Less opening stock	4,130	8.250
		10,470
Less closing creditors' balance		2,570
		7,900

(vi) Payments for wages and expenses

		£000
Per profit statement		2,350
Add opening balance – other creditors		385
		2,735

	£000	£000
Brought forward		2,735
Less closing balance – other creditors		630
		2,105
Add closing balance – prepayments		75
		2,180
Less opening balance – prepayments		80
		2,100

(vii) Payment for taxation

	£000	£000
Opening balance		1,775
Add tax provision		600
		2,375
Less closing balance		1,875
		500

6   (a)

*Working Capital Flow Statement
for the current year*

	£000	£000	£000
Sources of Working Capital Funds			
Net profit after tax for the year	20		
Amount not involving a flow of funds			
Depreciation	8	28	
Issue of debentures		65	
Proceeds from the sale of fixed assets		10	103
Disposal of Working Capital Funds			
Purchase of additional fixed assets		30	
Dividends		10	40
Increase in Working Capital			63

		£000
	Workings	
(i)	Net profit after tax for the year	
	Per profit and loss account	23
	Less profit on disposal of fixed assets	3
		20
(ii)	Proceeds from the sale of fixed assets	
	Cost of assets sold	10
	Less depreciation to date of sale	3
		7
	Add profit on disposal	3
		10

(iii)	Increase in working capital			
	Working capital	*Current assets*	*Current liabilities*	
	At end of the year	184	66	118
	At beginning of the year	121	66	55
				63

(b) Liquid assets include cash, temporary investments held in place of cash and sundry debtors. These assets are cash or near cash in the sense that they can be converted to cash currently at their balance sheet amounts. A liquid asset flow statement shows changes in these items in the period; a cash flow statement, changes in cash only.

(c) The purpose of these statements is to describe the sources from which additional funds were obtained and the use made of funds available. The changes between the figures shown in two consecutive sets of financial accounts are explained identifying significant movements for user attention.

7	*XY Trading Co. Ltd – Cash Flow Budget*			
Note		*June*	*July*	*August*
		£	£	£
	Opening balance	16,000	1,150	(10,250)
(i)	Add receipts from customers	79,750	97,300	109,500

		June £	*July* £	*August* £
	(A)	95,750	98,450	99,250
	Less payments			
(ii)	To suppliers	73,600	67,200	74,880
	Capital expenditure	–	20,000	–
(iii)	For other expenses	21,000	21,500	22,700
	(B)	94,600	108,700	97,580
	Closing balance (A−B)	1,150	(10,250)	1,670

Workings

(i) Debtors to credit sales ratio (May): $\dfrac{£14,000}{£35,000} \times 100 = 40\%$

	June £	£	*July* £	£	*August* £	£
Opening debtors		18,000		35,500		40,000
Add sales on credit		80,000		80,000		90,000
		98,000		115,500		130,000
Less closing debtors						
(see note (a))	3,500		8,000		8,000	
(see note (b))	32,000	35,000	32,000	40,000	36,000	44,000
Accounts settled		62,500		75,500		86,000

Notes

(a) July: 10% of £35,000 = £3,500
  July and August: 10% of £80,000 = £8,000
(b) June and July: 40% of £80,000 = £32,000
  August: 40% of £90,000 = £36,000

	June £	July £	August £
Discounts taken			
In respect of the month's credit sales:			
Credit sales for the month	80,000	80,000	90,000
Less 25% where settlement made in the following month	20,000	20,000	22,500
	60,000	60,000	67,500
Less 20% where customers do not pay in time to obtain discount	12,000	12,000	13,500
	48,000	48,000	54,000
Discount	5% of £48,000 = £2,400	5% of £48,000 = £2,400	5% of £54,000 = £2,700
In respect of the previous month's credit sales:			
Credit sales for the month	35,000	80,000	80,000
Less 75% where settlement made in the previous month	26,250	60,000	60,000
	8,750	20,000	20,000
Less 20% where customers do not pay in time to obtain discount	1,750	4,000	4,000
	7,000	16,000	16,000
Discount	5% of £7,000 = £350	5% of £16,000 = £800	5% of £16,000 = £800
Accounts settled	62,500	75,500	86,000
Less discounts taken in respect of the month's credit sales	2,400	2,400	2,700
	60,100	73,100	83,300

		June £	July £	August £
	Brought forward	60,100	73,100	83,300
	Less discounts taken in respect of the previous month's credit sales	350	800	800
	Cash received from credit sale customers	59,750	72,300	82,500
	Cash received from cash sale customers	20,000	25,000	27,000
	Receipts from customers	79,750	97,300	109,500
(ii)	Sales	100,000	105,000	117,000
	Less profit mark-up (see note (a))	33,333	35,000	39,000
	Cost of sales	66,667	70,000	78,000
	Add closing stock (see note (b))	60,000	60,000	60,000
		126,667	130,000	138,000
	Less opening stock	50,000	60,000	60,000
	Purchases	76,667	70,000	78,000
	Less discount at 4%	3,067	2,800	3,120
	Payments to suppliers	73,600	67,200	74,880

Notes
(a) 50% on cost is $33\frac{1}{3}\%$ on selling price
(b) £90,000 less $33\frac{1}{3}\%$

(iii)	Fixed expenses	14,000	14,000	14,000
	Less depreciation	3,000	3,000	3,000
		11,000	11,000	11,000
	Variable expenses	10,000	10,500	11,700
	Payments for other expenses	21,000	21,500	22,700

8 (a) *Cash Flow Statement for the year ended* ....

Note		£	£	
	Increase in the cash resources available			
(i)	Profit before taxation	80,050		
	Depreciation for the year added back	49,000	129,050	
(ii)	Proceeds from the sale of fixed assets		10,000	
(iii)	Proceeds from the sale of trade investments		19,800	
(iv)	Increase in creditors		7,875	
(v)	Reduction in stock		14,400	
	Reduction in investments		3,550	
	Reduction in bills receivable		3,250	
			187,925	(A)
	Reduction in cash resources available			
(vi)	Increase in debtors		27,910	
(vii)	Redemption of preference shares		2,000	
	Repayment of loan		20,000	
(viii)	Purchase of assets		116,890	
(ix)	Payment of tax		31,687	
(x)	Payment of dividend		19,963	
			218,450	(B)
	Net reduction in cash resources (A − B)		30,525	
	Net reduction in cash resources		30,525	
	Less change in the cash balance in the period:			
	Opening cash balance	500		
	Closing cash balance	425	75	
	Increase in the bank overdraft		30,450	

Workings		£	£
(i)	Profit before taxation		77,500
	Add loss on disposal of plant		
	Book value	5,050	
	Sale value	2,500	2,550
			80,050
(ii)	Proceeds from the sale of fixed assets		
	Land and buildings		
	Opening book value	100,330	
	Closing book value	92,830	7,500
	Plant and machinery		2,500
			10,000
(iii)	Proceeds from the sale of trade investments		
	Opening book value		35,550
	Closing book value		15,750
			19,800
(iv)	Increase in creditors		
	Closing book value		160,375
	Opening book value		152,500
			7,875

(v) Reduction in current assets	Opening book values £	Closing book values £	Difference £
Stock	175,150	160,750	14,400
Investments	8,050	4,500	3,550
Bills receivable	5,750	2,500	3,250

(vi) Increase in debtors	£
Closing book value	280,000
Opening book value	252,090
	27,910

(vii)		*Opening balance* £	*Closing balance* £	*Difference* £
	Redeemable preference shares	40,000	38,000	2,000
	Loans	180,000	160,000	20,000
(viii)	Purchase of assets			
	Plant and machinery			
	Closing balance at cost		569,950	
	Opening balance at cost	475,000		
	Less disposals at cost	15,800	459,200	110,750
	Loose tools			
	Closing valuation	1,870		
	Opening valuation	1,230	640	
	Add depreciation		2,500	3,140
	Goodwill:			
	Opening balance		15,000	
	Closing balance		18,000	3,000
				116,890
(ix)	Payment of tax			
	Opening balances (£32,000 + £41,000)			73,000
	Add taxation provision			30,500
				103,500
	Less closing balances (£30,500 + £41,313)			71,813
				31,687
(x)	Payment of dividend			
	Opening balance			10,650
	Add dividend provision			24,030
				34,680
	Less closing balance			14,717
				19,963

(b)   Comment on the statement prepared in (a) above:
 (i)   A large increase in the bank overdraft has taken place and it is unfortunate that the repayment of the loan has been necessary.
(ii)   A large increase in debtors has taken place and these should be investigated to ensure that extended credit is not being taken.
(iii)   An increase in the goodwill suggests the takeover of another company and this may account for at least a part of the large increase in the assets in the period.
        The turnover of capital is an area where further investigation might disclose opportunities for improving the company's profitability.

9   To: Managing Director   Date . . . .
       From: Accountant
                Accounts Accuracy and Finance Provision
I have examined the management accounts prepared and supplied to you and I am satisfied that they are reasonably accurate.

(a)   *Reconciliation of the management accounts' profit with the bank overdraft movement*
The best way to explain the reason why a profitable period is producing an increased bank overdraft is to show the cash flow movement as a reconciliation statement:

Reconciliation Statement
Four weeks ended ....

	£000
Operating profit per the management accounts	5
Depreciation added back	3
	8
Increase in creditors	1
Proceeds from sale of fixed assets	2
Increase in cash resources	11
Increase in stock	5
Increase in debtors	2
Cost of additional fixed assets	10
Reduction in cash resources	17
Increase in the bank overdraft	6

(b) *Improving the financial position*

Before seeking external finance to support our profitable operations which are planned to increase and, therefore, increase the pressure on our financial resources; it is proposed that greater efforts should be made to conserve our use of funds in the business. An examination of the working capital position suggests that the following action should be taken:

(i) Control stocks more effectively. This should begin with the detailed scrutiny of raw material stocks to: eliminate obsolete stock; reduce stock variety which is not necessary; increase stock turnover; and obtain a better service from suppliers.

Work-in-progress levels should be examined in relation to production programmes and an attempt should be made to reduce finished goods stocks to amounts more closely allied to sales requirements.

The general aim should be to reduce stocks of all types.

(ii) Control debtors more effectively. With financial stringency many companies are taking advantage of weak credit control and we have noticed a marked increase in the number of companies extending the credit period as long as possible. We have already taken steps to follow up debtors who are not settling their accounts as promptly as we would wish.

Signed . . . .

10   To: Board of Directors   Date . . . .
       From: Management Accountant

Control of Working Capital

I have examined the control of company working capital as requested and the following measures are proposed:

Stock control

Our stock turnover rate on raw materials is 6:1 (annual purchases of raw materials of £330,000: stock of raw materials, £55,000) and two months' stocks does not appear an unduly high figure but an investigation should be carried out to ascertain:

(a) The possibility of standardisation of raw material requirements
(b) The stock items held for longer periods than appears warranted by their usage rate
(c) The extent of possible deterioration and obsolescence in stock
(d) The relationships with suppliers and acceptable lead times
(e) The calculation of economic ordering quantities so that the costs of carrying stock are matched against ordering costs to optimise stock levels.

The stock turnover rate on finished goods is approximately 17:1 (annual cost of sales of £1,000,000: stock of finished goods, £60,000) and this figure appears to be a good turnover rate. Nevertheless, an investigation should be carried out to ascertain:

 (i) The extent to which finished goods stock levels may be reduced without the serious risk of stock-cuts damaging customer goodwill
 (ii) The need for such a wide range of stock in relation to the supplies our competitors can provide
(iii) The period variation that can be arranged as seasonal patterns affect supply and demand.

Debtors control
The debtors at £125,000 is not an unreasonable figure at this time of the year because action on the follow-up of overdue accounts has been increased; but the bad debts pattern this year shows the need to review our credit policy in relation to the opening of credit accounts. The various stages in cash collection procedure are being reviewed and it is suggested that our terms of sale and discount policy might be examined with advantage.

Cash control
The £10,000 cash balance appears to be low. Current liabilities of £200,000 are to be met by cash and near cash items (debtors) of only £135,000. For a limited period this may not be serious but a cash flow statement on a receipts and payments basis, projected into the future, is a useful means of establishing regular monthly control and anticipating cash problems.

Signed . . . .

11   *The meaning of overtrading*
Overtrading exists when the level of business is in excess of the funds available to transact that business and in an extreme case the company may be forced out of existence. A profitable company with increasing trade can find itself short of funds owing to the increased working capital required for stock and trade debtors.

The extreme situation may not arise but over-trading could seriously affect profits as attempts are made to increase cash by selling products at reduced prices or delaying investment opportunities.

The methods that may be used to reduce the working capital cycle include:
(a) Improved methods employed for raw materials stock control.
Raw material stocks may be reduced by reviewing slow moving items or obsolete parts.
(b) Standardisation of materials required for products produced.

(c) Improved buying by the adoption of economic ordering quantities and shortening the lead times on deliveries. Better quantity discounts may be obtainable from suppliers able to grant improved terms of trade.

(d) Improved production control to cut down work-in-progress.

(e) Standardisation of products produced.

(f) An attempt to relate more closely stock production with sales requirements. The aim is to reduce finished goods stock.

(g) Improved credit control procedures and the follow-up of outstanding accounts with possibly the offering of attractive discounts to obtain the prompt settlement of debts.

(h) Extend the credit period with suppliers where this can be negotiated.

12 (a) Profits will vary with the changing interest charges reflecting the fluctuating bank overdraft in the periods when cash balances are converted to deficits and vice versa. In addition to changed profit figures in the balance sheet, significant changes in working capital will be recorded. The cash balances will change as described in the case; and debtors will reduce and creditors increase as the effects of the financial policy changes are reflected in the planned figures produced. Stock figures will show large reductions.

(b) The details described are only possible plans for the company. The advantage of the procedure described is that alternative policies can be considered, and their effects traced through the cash flows generated, without actually putting the procedure into practice with possible disruption and disadvantage to the company. With the proposals described, management can decide on the best course of action and act accordingly.

(c) The sales and factory managers are likely to emphasise the following points:

(i) Reduced volume in production runs and the less orderly control of factory production

(ii) The possibility of stock problems in the form of finished goods not being produced sufficiently in advance of sales needs

(iii) Supply difficulties owing to suppliers being reluctant to grant extended credit

(iv) The effect of competition may be increased owing to potential customers being able to obtain their requirements from competitors willing to grant better terms

(v) Possible personnel problems in the factory as a result of varying the production rate each control period.

8 The Managerial Control Process

1   The purpose of the cost control procedure is to ensure that the resources of the business are used in accordance with the objectives of the business. For example, if an objective of the business is to obtain a 15% profitability return on sales, costs as a component of this ratio will need to be controlled within the limits necessary to secure the profit level in relation to sales satisfactory to the management.

This implies that a standard of performance can be established against which the actual performance may be judged and that an individual manager in the organisation will be held accountable for the costs to be controlled.

The procedure adopted to secure cost control is:

(a)   Identify the managers responsible for sectional costs in the business
(b)   Ascertain the appropriate standard to judge the performance of the manager in controlling his costs
(c)   Fix the cost level to be achieved for a defined period
(d)   Ensure that a means exists to check on costs being incurred
(e)   Identify the extent and reason for costs being different from the cost level agreed and report the result of these inquiries to the manager in sufficient time for him to take corrective action where appropriate.

The techniques that may be employed to obtain cost control include budgetary control and standard costing and an effort may be made to reduce costs. Costs may be reduced in two ways: (i) reducing costs for a given volume of activity to the level considered appropriate for efficient performance; and (ii) increasing the volume of activity for a given level of cost.

Efficient business management includes cost control, as outlined above, with the emphasis placed on the accountability of the individual manager.

2   The essential aspects of a buiness control system are the main features of the managerial control cycle:

(a) Forward planning
(b) Ascertaining the actual results achieved
(c) Comparing the actual results with the plans and evaluating the performance of the company
(d) Provision of information to managers to assist them in controlling performance against the plan and possibly modifying plans to achieve the objectives of the business.

The first step in the situation outlined in the question is to ascertain the facts and given the cost control deficiency presumably cost levels are not planned, frequent checks are not made on actual costs, and relevant information for cost control not supplied to management.

The main matters to be introduced, therefore, to make good the systems deficiencies are:

(a) Recognising defined areas of responsibility for costs, obtain plans with cost levels incorporating appropriate standards for comparison.
(b) After the approval of the plans submitted, provide a procedure to obtain actual costs on the same basis as the plans submitted.
(c) Interpret variations between actual and planned costs to indicate to management the areas in need of their attention.
(d) Review control procedures in sectional cost areas: material, labour and overheads. If the procedures are weak in supporting the control activities described, progressively strengthen these procedures.

3   The nature and scope of the managerial control process involves the establishment of plans relating the responsibilities of managers to the policies established to meet the objectives of the business, and the continuous comparison of actual with planned results as a basis for managerial control action.

In the above outline, the organisation structure of the business is relevant to the control process since responsibilities are delegated to many managers in defined areas of company performance. Control is only possible where managers, possessing the authority in line with the responsibility undertaken, are accountable for the activity performance in the areas for which they are responsible. When planning takes place, the centres of responsibility will be governed by the organisation structure of the business.

Detailed planning is usually short term. The short-term detail is provided in the context of long-term plans to secure the objectives which may only be possible of achievement if a long enough view is taken. The control aspect is developed through the day-to-day monitoring of actual performance against the plan and the differences interpreted for the benefit of management.

When comparisons are made between actual and planned results, advantage is taken of the principle of management by exception which is the practice of drawing to the attention of management the factors that require their attention. Management has limited time available and they are not concerned with activities that are going according to plan and, therefore, not requiring their attention. They are concerned with activities not going according to plan and, therefore, needing managerial attention. Reports produced for management that isolate the latter aspects of the performance of a responsibility centre are of particular value.

4   The management of a company is delegated to many managers at various levels of management in the business and a segment of the organisation controlled by a manager is termed a responsibility centre. Where the accounting system prepares and reports information applicable to the responsibility centre, and therefore relevant to the specific needs of the manager, the term 'responsibility accounting' may be used. The extent of the information reported varies according to the responsibilities of the individual manager. If the manager is only responsible for costs, reports information will be limited to costs; if the manager is responsible also for revenue, costs and revenue information may be given. If the manager is also responsible for assets employed in his centre, return on investment information may also be supplied.

From the above outline, the matters that must be decided before such a system is introduced are:
(a)   The definition of areas of responsibility
(b)   The allocation of authority to enable the manager to take the necessary executive action appropriate to his job
(c)   The nature of the manager's responsibility
(d)   The type of information needed by the individual manager to enable him to control his segment of the business
(e)   The relationship of each segment report to the overall reporting system to provide a comprehensive reporting service to management.

5   Terms used in the statements are interpreted as follows:

Predetermined objective
For effective management, there is the need to determine the objectives of the business and define these objectives in terms that all managers can understand and act upon.

Predetermined policies
Also for effective management there is the need to define the policies to be followed to achieve the objectives fixed. These policies are usually fixed in

relation to the following areas of the business: (a) production; (b) marketing; (c) financial management; (d) personnel.

The achievement of the objectives of the business through the application of the defined policies is accomplished by managers exercising their responsibilities in an organisation. The procedures enable the plans to be communicated and activities are checked by the comparison of actual results with planned performance.

The managerial control process described forms the background to the techniques of budgetary control and standard costing. An attempt is made in the planning phase to quantify the objectives laid down to serve as the basis for the financial comparison between the actual and the plan, when performance is assessed. The reporting to management of this financial information is the feedback into the control system to correct unsatisfactory tendencies in company performance. The corrective action necessary is a managerial responsibility.

6   The production control department is initially concerned with planning in the decision on what machines are to be used; when they are to be used; and what operations are to be carried out to provide the manufactured product. The quality checks will similarly be planned and the work of the related departments co-ordinated, such as material control and inspection, to ensure that there is an even flow of work completed to the required standard to meet production targets.

All this planning information is part of the overall plans for the business to be quantified and costed. The management accountant will be responsible for gathering these plans and piloting them through the committees where his advice will be sought regarding the financial implications of the proposals submitted.

When the plans have been approved, it is the responsibility of the production control department to ensure that the plans are achieved. The contribution the management accountant can make in this area is to provide control information. This control information is primarily of a financial nature but so much quantity data is fed into the management accountant's department it is not unusual to produce reports using this data relevant to the work of the production control department, e.g., machine utilisation, labour efficiency, stock and quality control statistics.

The management accountant is also involved with related departments keeping financial records concerned with, for example, material control. In this way the management accountant serves as an important link to co-ordinate production control and quality control with other activities of the business.

7   In the manufacturing sections of the business, a large part of the product cost is variable to the product. The product specification itself determines the quantities and costs of the elements incurred in manufacture and, therefore, control of actual expenditure is facilitated. In the non-manufacturing sections of the business the costs are principally non-variable and it is difficult to select a unit against which such costs can be measured.
    The principal problems of financial control are as follows:

(a)   The level of cost incurred in non-manufacturing sections of the business is at the discretion of management according to policies laid down by top management. The policies may be easily changed and costs reduced but that does not necessarily mean that the level of cost has been controlled effectively.

(b)   There is difficulty in deciding what the level of expenditure should be, e.g., advertising cost.

(c)   Financial control may be regarded in this area as a check on expenditure to a permitted level in the accounting period preferably, showing a reduction. Improvement in performance may be secured in some situations by increasing rather than reducing the non-manufacturing costs. It is difficult making an accurate control assessment.

    The control of non-manufacturing costs is possible by greater reliance on the experience and personal judgement of the manager responsible for authorising expenditure.

8

Control system	Features involved in selecting the control system	Information necessary to operate the control system
(a) No intervention by the manager until a breakdown of the process occurs (the deterministic system)	The ability to incorporate in the system a control mechanism to maintain the process operating efficiently and effectively until breakdown occurs	Feedback of data to indicate the departure from automatic operation

(Table continued on facing page)

Control system	Features involved in selecting the control system	Information necessary to operate the control system
(b) Periodic interven-tion by the manager for the purpose of adjusting or otherwise influencing the process (the probabilistic system)	The stages of the system inter-dependent on each other	Factors affecting the probability that each stage will be achieved as required
(c) Intervention based on the inform-ation obtained from the process (the adaptive system)	The ability to fix stand-ards of performance	Supply of information in the same form as the standard fixed for comparative purposes

9   Cost control involves fixing:
(a)   Responsibility centres in relation to which costs may be identified
(b)   The authority of specific individuals for costs
(c)   Standards of good performance
(d)   The classification of costs to enable relevant information to be identified
(e)   The reporting of the relevant information as feedback in the control process
(f)   Plans for profit improvement.
        Items (a), (b), (c) and (f) are not primarily an accounting process although items (c) and (f) need accounting support. Item (a) may be significantly affected by accounting method. Items (d) and (e) require management support.
        The closing sentence is valid as a general statement but it may be necessary to use cost information to control operations. Control of operations is an essential element of cost control procedures.

10   The three other departments whose assistance would be required by the management accounting department in the planning and control of material costs are:

(a) *The production control department*
This department would supply details of material usage and production details to enable materials cost to be ascertained for products produced. Departures from planned material cost levels will be ascertained with the help of this department.

(b) *The inspection department*
This department is responsible for checking the quality of materials purchased and would supply information to enable suppliers' invoices to be passed for payment as being valid costs for material supplied per orders raised with suppliers.

(c) *The buying department*
This department, which is responsible for purchasing the materials requisitioned according to requirements, would also supply information to enable suppliers' invoices to be checked for payment. Control information on material costs would also be provided where planned material purchase prices are not achieved.

An accounting function in relation to material control requiring the assistance described above is the financial accounting for material stocks. The value of material receipts and issues representing movements in stock levels require reconciliation and discrepancies explained.

11

Statement made	Relevance to the managerial control process
Company 1	
'Problem was to get the basic information'	A vital requirement for control purposes. The accountant should assist with the provision of financial information.
'difficult to . . . understand the costs involved'	The point here is the interpretative phase.
'costs involved to substantiate my case'	The financial aspect is usually the profit impact on the company.
'the accountant . . . in opposition to everybody else'	By reputation the accountant is cautious but the ideal is a co-operative team effort rather than one member being regarded as in opposition to others.
'using management control techniques'	Budgetary control and standard costing.

(Table continued on facing page)

Statement made	Relevance to the managerial control process
'A large organisation can go badly wrong and managers not be aware . . . '	The communication phase.
'rapid response to changing situations'	Good feedback in the control process.
'get the facts behind evidence of something going wrong'	The basis for subsequent action and possible revision of plans.

Company 2

'must be considerable delegation'	Work delegated must be controlled.
'discuss policies'	A vital decision phase for top management. After setting the objectives of the business it is necessary to define the policies by which those objectives can be reached.
'other people are employed to deal with the detail'	The organisation structure supporting the managerial control process. (The activities of the business distributed among the personnel employed and the interrelationships established as a result of these responsibilities.)
'judgement on the expert advice given'	Sufficient expert advice being available to enable management to make valid judgements.

Company 3

'exercise considerable personal initiative'	This is possible with maintained control within the framework of agreed plans.
'Management is a team effort'	Integration of managers' efforts in the planning and control phases.
'planning ahead for about five years'	Long-term planning.
'setting detailed targets'	Short-term planning.
'make sure that the plans are achieved'	The element of risk is greater in long-term planning. Short-term plans are more likely to be achieved.

(Table continued overleaf)

Statement made	Relevance to the managerial control process
'The shorter the chain of command the quicker things get done'	Importance of communication.
'add to the team elements that were missing such as financial management'	Financial management of a high order needed in management control.

12 The following constitutes good management in terms of management style:

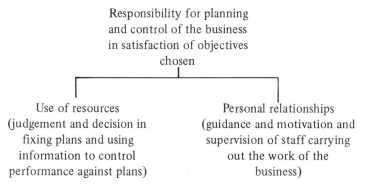

Responsibility for planning
and control of the business
in satisfaction of objectives
chosen

Use of resources
(judgement and decision in
fixing plans and using
information to control
performance against plans)

Personal relationships
(guidance and motivation and
supervision of staff carrying
out the work of the
business)

Regarding each factor, managers vary in their attitude, some placing greater emphasis on the technical aspects of their work as compared with the personnel function. A balancing of these values fixes the managerial style. A manager may have a false impression of his own practice and the assessment mentioned in the case serves to aid the managerial control process by:
(a) The classification of good management practice
(b) The fixing of the standard by which performance may be judged
(c) The assessment of performance against the standard
(d) Improvement in management practice by optimisation of the elements of good management.

The improvement in management practice (decision-making, direction and control) should be reflected in the results of the business.

9 Business Objectives

1   A business policy is a company's decision to be continually applied to repetitive problems, providing the conditions that formed the basis of the decision have not changed. An objective is a company goal to be used to guide the company managers in managing the business. Both terms are linked in the management control process where managers implement policies to accomplish objectives. A policy is a general statement and an objective a specific statement of intent. For example:

> A policy statement: to distribute the products of the company nationally
> An objective: to establish distribution facilities in a regional network so that company products will be distributed throughout Great Britain by the end of 19..

Policies have a curious relationship in company operations because they appear to have a primary role in moving from the general to the specific yet arise out of and reflect company objectives.

When considering the establishment of a new policy or the alteration of an existing policy the following action should be taken:

(a)   Obtain relevant factual data regarding the need for the policy
(b)   Review the proposed policy in relation to existing objectives
(c)   Consider the best policy from possible alternatives by reviewing likely outcomes of applied policy
(d)   Decide on the policy to be applied and its effective date.

2   The principles applicable to the formation and use of company objectives as an essential feature of the management control process are:

(a)   *Acceptability*
Managers should understand that they are expected to attain the objectives applicable to their responsibility in the organisation. The best results are

likely to be achieved where the objectives are framed in such a way as to be acceptable to all personnel responsible for implementing them.

(b) *Attainability*
Objectives should be realistic. They should be possible of attainment under efficient operation of existing or proposed facilities and they should be attainable within a reasonable period. The balancing of long- and short-term objectives is particularly important in this context.

(c) *Motivation*
Co-operative effort is so necessary to efficient management that any attempt made to secure the required result at all levels will produce significant results. The motivation should be at the highest level incorporating social and spiritual ideals not measured in monetary terms.

(d) *Simplicity*
A multiplicity of objectives for any one manager will clearly work against their attainment and the more simply the objectives can be stated the better.

(e) *Communication*
Top management must be aware not only of the results they would like to see achieved but also of the factors which may assist or hinder their subordinates in achieving those results. This involves a high level of communication between top management and other managers.

3   The methods that may be used by a company to communicate its objectives to managers include:

(a) *Personal discussion*
The greater the personal contact between managers, the greater the likely effectiveness of the communication of objectives.

(b) *Through planning instructions*
As managers are asked to submit their plans, the background basis for their deliberations is given in the form of corporate objectives appropriate to the individual manager's own responsibilities.

(c) *In committee*
In this method, the related managers for specific objectives are brought together. Where co-ordinated discussion is desirable this method is useful.

(d) *By internal memo or other written form*
A written objective facilitates interpretation to the extent that there is less room for subsequent argument about the nature of top management's intentions.

(e) *Through internal training courses*
This is a useful opportunity to bring to the attention of managers on courses what the company is seeking to do and why.

Lack of understanding of the objectives of the business is a serious deficiency in many companies and once the objectives are established, every effort should be made to communicate them to staff as effectively as possible.

4   The requirements for company success that should be incorporated in business objectives include:

(a) *The growth in profit*
There should always be the attempt to identify the growth markets where the business can increase its profit.

(b) *Return on investment stability*
It is not sufficient to aim for high profit margins unrelated to investment.

(c) *Flexibility*
The ability to respond to change in the interests of the business such as the need to change products and processes.

(d) *Co-ordination*
The results of individual responsibility centres linked to provide the overall result for the business.

(e) *Key result identification*
Vague objectives do not identify the changes that must be made and the action required by specific managers.

(f) *An ambitious commitment*
Managers with a low expectation will not be motivated to high performance.

(g) *Realism*
A recognition of managerial capacity and external factors that may govern the future of the business. In this context, for success the company should seek to capitalise on its own strengths and competitor weakness.

5   The questions that should be asked in trying to define the overall objectives of the business are as follows:
(a)   What is our business?
(b)   What could the business be?
(c)   What should the business be?
(d)   What, if anything, needs to be done by the business to change from its present position?

(e)   How long will it take to effect the needed changes in the business?

(f)   What will be the cost of the business changes?

(g)   What could result in terms of future growth, business stability, and profit return from the business changes?

(h)   What are the main areas of business activity?

(i)   What will be the most significant limiting factors affecting the business?

(j)   How can the limiting factors best be deployed and improved in order to optimise profit return and stability in the longer term?

(k)   Which are the main areas of cost?

(l)   To what extent can each of these really be considered fixed or variable during times of trade boom or recession, if there is the wish to maximise our profit return over the long term (say, five to ten years)?

(m)   What must be the company basic policies towards financing and towards the employment of people?

(n)   What must be the company plans, policies, strategies and tactics in the short term?

6   Answers to this question will vary according to the student's practical experience. One example, using the process plant manufacturing industry is given below.

The key features of this industry affecting the setting of objectives are as follows:

(a)   *The cost structure of the company*

A feature of these businesses is that material costs can be as much as 45% to 50% of total costs and labour costs 40% to 45% of total costs. Control objectives should be concentrated on these major cost areas.

(b)   *The demand pattern of the company*

There are wide fluctuations in demand in this industry which cause wide variations in unit costs. Objectives should be concentrated on activity costs and profits within the framework of longer-term plans, policies and strategies of the business.

(c)   *Marketing information provision difficulty*

It is difficult in this industry to obtain reliable information on markets, market size and trends. Unless information in this area is reliable it is foolish for a company to develop and pursue long-term objectives which do not have an inbuilt flexibility.

(d)   *Company difficulties in obtaining a balanced workload*

In this industry there can be major problems in trying to obtain at all times a balanced workload between the various operations. This can frequently cause wide variations in the utilisation of labour and equipment and consequently in unit costs.

Although much may be done to improve matters it is necessary in this industry to accept that it will never be possible to resolve this problem completely. Cost effectiveness objectives may, therefore, be pursued by: (i) identifying the potential 'bottleneck' operations where capacity cannot be expanded quickly; and (ii) taking action to expand the capacity in these areas to a point which, though uneconomic for those areas alone, will more than repay the extra cost by the increase which can result in the total throughput of the factory.

(e)   *Inflexibility of labour*
Specialisation of labour within the industry has prevented or reduced the flexibility and interchangeability of staff. The objective in this area should be to gain the co-operation of employees for greater flexibility.

7   The changes in the company's business environment that affect the choice of objectives include the following:

(a)   *Market changes*
Customer needs change which may affect sales volume, sales mix, product type and product quality. Total demand may be increasing or declining and to profit from these changes product planning, sales promotion, and sales distirbution should be reviewed using techniques, such as market research, to aid the process. Sales pricing will also need review in relation to the effect on unit profit and the volume of sales.

(b)   *Technical changes*
New materials and methods of manufacture may significantly affect the company position in the industry. A company that does not change its methods of manufacture or use the new materials may be faced with declining markets for its products. An attempt to keep ahead of competitors may involve clear objectives in research and development.

(c)   *Economic changes*
The economic changes not only in the UK but in other areas of the world cannot be ignored by any company. A good economic climate may lead to a buoyant business; a poor economic climate may mean a struggle for the company. The business must have a planning discipline to ensure company stability in an insecure economic environment.

(d)   *Sociological changes*
A change in population or personal affluence can also affect the company.

An examination of sociological trends is the best basis for a company response to these changes.

(e) *Political changes*
The increasing influence of government in the affairs of business mean that company objectives must be fixed in this context particularly where a change of government means political policy changes.

8   A planning system involves decision-making by managers regarding the future course of the business. Control involves guiding the company towards its predetermined objective by means of predetermined policies and planning decisions.

A key factor in the control process is the need to determine the objectives of the business and define these objectives in terms that all managers can understand and act upon. When these objectives are fixed, the policies may be defined so that when followed the objectives may be achieved.

The cost control system is made operational by the attempt to achieve the objectives of the business by managers exercising their responsibilities in the organisation. The procedure enables the plans to be communicated and activities checked by comparison of actual results with planned performance.

An overall objective such as a 15% return on capital employed may be expressed in specific objectives for profitability and turnover of capital. The breakdown of the profitability objective, for example, will identify specific areas for cost control. A specific objective may be to restrict the cost level in a defined segment of the business. To give direction and purpose to management activity it is essential to stipulate the objectives for the business.

9   The following policy considerations are relevant to the automation decision:

(a) *The maintenance of volume production (capacity use policy)*
With automation the increased capital cost involves an increased fixed cost commitment. If volume drops, significant losses will be incurred.

(b) *The stability of the production programme (capacity use policy)*
With automation it will not be as easy for the production management to respond to seasonal variations in operations.

(c) *The repair of equipment (maintenance policy)*
The reliability of the expensive equipment will assume a greater importance.

(d) *Output control (production control policy)*
Work assignment and results achieved will be different with increased automation.

(e) *Product standardisation (product policy)*
With automation, greater economy is secured from standardised operations.

(f) *Stock considerations (stock policy)*
The business may need to consider increased stocks of work-in-progress and finished goods.

(g) *Selling ability (sales policy)*
Presumably the sales revenue expected from the products to be manufactured by the new equipment will cover the anticipated costs to the extent that profitability will be satisfactory.

(h) *Redundancy (redundancy policy)*
The semi-skilled labour released will be declared redundant and the treatment of this staff must be considered.

(i) *Future staff requirements (manpower policy)*
The type and number of staff of other grades and their particular skills required may change.

10   The management accountant can assist management in determining the general price strategies for the company by investigating:
(a)   The possible need for alternative price policies
(b)   The relevant facts necessary to making a pricing decision
(c)   Cost changes resulting from policy changes that may be considered
(d)   The likely long- and short-term effects of a change in pricing policy
(e)   Product trends in terms of volume and profitability.

The cost information which should be made available to the marketing management function is as follows:
(a)   The variable cost and profit per unit of product for each type of product
(b)   The return on assets employed in manufacturing product groups
(c)   The expected changes in profitability arising from different pricing policies that may be adopted including sales mix
(d)   Order size profitability data giving the variation in profits from meeting small orders
(e)   Cost-volume-profit data relationships
(f)   The likely effects on profitability of possible changes in advertising costs

(g)   Distribution costs

(h)   Sales administration costs.

11   It is true that the major objectives of business are usually orientated to profits. To survive, a business requires profits for satisfactory returns to investors and to finance future growth. The old aim of profit maximisation has given way to the earning of satisfactory profits over the long term. This long-term aim is usually expressed in the plans for the business at a level fixed on the basis of experience and judgement of what can reasonably be expected in the future.

   The large company cannot restrict its objectives — it should recognise multiple responsibilities which must be discharged if the business is to remain successful. The key result areas described in the case have evolved by answering the basic question which the General Electric Company in America asked as a criterion for identifying assessments of subsidiary company performance: 'Will continued failure in this area prevent the attainment of management's responsibility for advancing General Electric as a leader in a strong competitive economy, even though results in all other key areas are good?'

   A successful company aims to increase its share of the market by manufacturing products efficiently to acceptable standards and developing new products to meet a market need. Its objectives in these areas cannot be met without good industrial relations, managers committed to good performance and of the required calibre to make this possible. Ethical conduct extends company responsibilities outside the business to include public responsibility and the need to cultivate an image that will enhance the future of the company. Essentially, all these requirements return to the need for profitability on financial investment over a long period but general management divisional responsibility covers other aspects, detailed in the case, that should be considered in the appraisal system.

12   The background conditions that should be provided for a management-by-objectives scheme are:

(a)   Top management support and the personal involvement of managers in setting objectives

(b)   A guidance framework supplied to managers to enable them to put forward plans that are in the long-term interest of the business

(c)   An advice service available to managers to assit them in preparing their proposals, particularly assessing the profit impact of their plans

(d)   The intention to analyse critically proposals for action submitted by managers

(e)   A good information service not only to provide data to meet requirement (c) above but also to facilitate performance review

(f) The authority passed to managers necessary to enable them to discharge the responsibilities covered by the proposals approved.

The initial action taken by managers includes the following:

(a) Identify the key result areas vital to good performance in the job

(b) Assess the standard of performance to judge the effectiveness of performance in each key result area

(c) Identify what could be done to achieve a higher standard in each key result area

(d) Establish priorities and the action that could be taken in the planning period to improve performance

(e) Agree with senior management specific proposals for action identifying what is to be done, when it is to be done and who must take the action required

(f) Assess the control information required to measure the results achieved.

The subsequent action that should be taken by managers includes the following:

(a) Obtain the control information reporting on action taken

(b) Check that results anticipated have been achieved, or are in the process of being achieved, in accordance with the stage timing agreed

(c) If the results anticipated have not been achieved, question why not and decide what action can be taken to put matters right

(d) Take the action necessary in consultation with colleagues affected.

10 Budgetary Control (1)—a Management Control Technique

1   To: Chairman   Date . . . .
     From: Management Accountant
                The Purpose and Nature of Budgetary Control
     The brief requested on the above subject is as follows:

The budgetary control technique
The technique which embraces all activities of the business and serves to support the key aspects of the management control process is budgetary control. The plans for the business expressed in financial terms relate the managerial responsibilities of executives to policy requirements. When these plans or budgets are compared with actual results for the period, the differences may be analysed to indicate the areas requiring corrective action to restore the business on course.

The relationship between forecasting and planning
A forecast is a probable event and in the planning stage it is necessary to prepare forecasts of probable courses of action for the business in the future. Arising from these forecasts, plans or budgets are prepared for the future operation of the business so that it may achieve its objectives.

Factors to be considered in relation to forecasting and planning
The essential factors for effective forecasting and planning are as follows:
(a)   Clear objectives should be established
(b)   Top management should support the planning process
(c)   The use of available techniques to ensure that forecasts are as realistic as possible, e.g., market research
(d)   The correct choice of the budget period; forecasts are often long term and detailed plans are usually short term
(e)   A recognition of responsibility for forecasting, planning and control
(f)   Clear instructions to executives to assist them in their job of preparing forecasts and budgets

(g) The scrutiny and discussion of submitted forecasts and budgets, and where necessary, explanations given to managers of changes made

(h) The use of approved budgets as an essential feature of the management control process.

The value of the budgetary control technique
The technique relates the overall objectives to specific managers. Management is in the position of anticipating business problems and provided with a tool to judge their detailed effects on the organisation. Co-ordinated managerial activity is facilitated to solve complex problems that demand the approach that budgetary control provides.

Signed . . . .

2   The principal implication in the argument presented is that because conditions change a company can avoid forward thinking. This is not so – the planning may be rudimentary but business decisions are made on assumptions regarding the future. Also implied is the view that the differences between the actual and planned situation cannot be used to advantage and the discipline of formal planning brings no benefits to the business.

The points to be made to the manager should include:

(a) Where the budget is not achieved in one section of the activities of the business, its implications on planned results in other sections of the business may be indicated.

(b) The extent and nature of changes in conditions, as measured by the comparison with budgets, can assist in identifying remedial action to be taken to correct unsatisfactory performance.

(c) Some aspects of changing conditions can be incorporated into the budgetary procedure, e.g., changes in the volume factor allowed for in the flexible budget.

(d) Conditions may change but the existing budget can be the basis for future policy and the revision of current policy.

(e) Not all aspects of company operation significantly change in the short term.

(f) The use of budgetary control is a tool of management operating within and making use of the managerial control cycle. This cycle applies whether or not budgetary control is practised.

3   The possible difficulties inferred in the statement are:

(a) The belief that no member of the organisation can anticipate what will happen in the future with the degree of accuracy required for forward estimating.

(b) The inadequacies of the present control system to serve as a guide for future planning. Many small businesses are particularly weak in the financial control area.

(c) A fear that management's authority may be undermined; in particular, the accountant having too important an influence on line management.

(d) A reluctance to get too involved in other managers' problems and an inadequate understanding of the interrelationships that should exist between departments.

(e) Lack of knowledge of the factors for co-ordinated activity.

(f) The belief that the budget criteria may be used to increase the pressure on managers to a level of efficiency considered unreasonable.

(g) The belief that the friendly atmosphere of the small organisation may be replaced by inter-departmental conflicts and bad feeling.

In general, a reluctance to plan ahead will be evident and the inexperience of managers in forward planning will result in significant errors in the early stages of introducing budgetary control. These results may be used by managers to prove their earlier arguments against the system.

4   The activity level reasonably expected by the business in the budget period is an important figure in the budgeting process. Where the principal budget factor is sales, an accurate assessment of sales volume gives the following budgetary approach:

	£	
Budgeted sales	—	
Deduct budgeted variable costs	—	The variable costs of producing the possible sales
Budgeted contribution	—	
Deduct budgeted fixed costs	—	
Budgeted profit	—	

It is usually difficult to estimate sales accurately but the attempt must be made based on an examination of the market using available techniques such as market research and available information such as salesmen's reports.

If the budgeted profit, calculated as above, is inadequate as a return on capital employed, it will be necessary either to reduce costs, to increase the turnover of capital or to improve sales revenue. After allowing for any planned adjustment of stock, a check is made on the ability of the factory to meet the estimated demand for each product.

If sales are the limiting factor, it is possible that there may be unused productive capacity.

5   The action programme approach is based upon programmes produced by individual managers with the expectation that their action, as described in their personal plan of action, will usually result in improved profits. As might be anticipated, the number of possible action programmes may be greater than the facilities available to carry them out and selection of the best programmes for a particular period is necessary.

Each action programme is aimed to achieve selected objectives for the specific manager and because there may be various methods of achieving such objectives, selection of the best method should be made.

Proposed plans are submitted to senior management for approval and, when approved, the sum total of the action programmes determine the profit improvement that is to be made as a result of management action. This is not the total profit (or loss) to be made by the company – a certain profit level would have been reached in any case simply through the momentum of the firm. The budgeted profit for the budget period may, therefore, be expressed as follows:

	£	
Profit on the basis of the current year's operation	–	
Add/Deduct the effect of action programmes originated in the current year on operations for the budget year	–	Known as the carry-over effect
	–	
Add/Deduct the effect of environment factors affecting the business in the budget year not experienced in the current year	–	
	–	
Add/Deduct the effect of action programmes originated in the budget year	–	After allowance for the carry-over effect
Budgeted profit	–	

6   A factor whose influence must first be assessed in order to ensure that the functional budgets are reasonably capable of fulfilment is known as the principal budget factor. The factor may be customer demand, manufacturing facilities, a shortage of materials or skilled labour and possibly cash.

If there is a limit on, for example, manufacturing facilities this will affect the other budgets because unless output can be increased in some other way, the limited manufacturing facilities will dictate the sales to be made. Other ways of increasing the output could include:

(a)   The subcontracting of component manufacture and assembly facilities extended into the manufacturing area previously used for the manufacture of the components
(b)   Extended use of existing facilities by means of overtime or extended shift working
(c)   Plant improvements.

In summary, because the principal budget factor is a limiting factor on budgeting, any attempt to increase the factor effect will reduce the restrictions on the sectional budgets to be produced.

7   A budget may be set at high or low levels of attainment. If the former, the budget will be difficult to attain; if the latter, it will be easy to attain. With an easy budget, variances between actual and budget are likely to be favourable or low unfavourable differences. With a difficult budget variances may be expected to be unfavourable.

The aim of a high level of attainment is to encourage better performance since pointers for improvement are continually revealed. If a manager is continually faced with unfavourable variances he may be discouraged in his efforts and the level of attainment adopted, far from proving an incentive, may prove to be a disincentive to better performance.

The level of attainment adopted should be capable of achievment with reasonable effort. The level of attainment usually incorporated in the budget is a realistic figure for the budget period: one that is reasonably attainable in the conditions that are expected to exist in the budget period although there should be an element of incentive to be a challenge to management.

Two levels of attainment may be fixed. Using sales as an example, one sales figure may represent the minimum level beyond which the sales are not likely to fall; the other fixed at a higher level which the company hopes to achieve. The idea behind this double budget is to fix a level which can be used for judgements of risk and cash flow with a certainty not matched by the higher level used for operating control.

8   Companies normally develop their short-term plans in relation to long-term forecasts. The long-term forecast may be for a period of three to five years, not in great detail, because of the uncertainties involved, but in sufficient detail to serve as a sound guide for short-term budgeting. The short-term plan is usually for a year corresponding to the financial year of the business. Deciding factors are the seasonal nature of the business, the manufacturing cycle, the effort necessary to prepare the budget and the reliability of the estimates made. The type of budget might also affect the budget period chosen. For example, capital expenditure needs to be planned on a long-term basis whereas other budgets are more realistically considered in the short term. A cash budget is a good example of the latter category.

     For control, management require information on a more frequent basis than the budget period. To enable comparative information to be extracted from the budget for period control, the budget is analysed by control periods. The frequency of these control periods depends on the extent effective action can be taken as a result of interpreting the information provided. Some budgetary data may be required weekly, four-weekly, or monthly according to the report frequency required by management for control purposes.

9   Budgets need to be reviewed, co-ordinated and changed in preparation and this procedure takes time. The length of time taken to prepare the budget varies according to the size of the business, the detail required, and the necessity to co-ordinate with other plans. For example, the long-term planning may advance the starting-point of the process to as much as six months for a three-year plan and two months for a one-year plan from the start of the budget year.

     The prepared budget needs to be approved as a commitment for the business in advance of the period to which it relates. To achieve this target time, the times for individual budgets to be completed must be specified. Also specified must be the order to be adopted for the various budgets to be constructed, reviewed, co-ordinated and changed, as necessary.

10   The reasons why the advantages usually claimed for budgetary control are not achieved are:

(a)   Staff regard the technique as a pressure instrument rather than a procedure to assist the executive to do a better job.
(b)   Because the technique is so closely identified with the management control process, executives imagine that the technique can replace management. There is no substitute for good management.
(c)   The motivation may be misplaced. For example, managers may be

satisfied with budget performance when better performance is possible and could reasonably be attained if low levels of attainment had not been agreed in the budget.

(d)   The checking of estimates may be difficult and it is sometimes forgotten that budgets are estimates given in the context of defined anticipated conditions that can change.

(e)   The required degree of management co-operation may not be obtained and top management support may also be inadequate.

(f)   Where managers know that the figures they submit for budgeting purposes will subsequently be used as a measure of their efficency, there is built in the system an incentive to submit estimates that are not too demanding on their performance.

(g)   The supporting accounting system may not be sufficiently effective.

(h)   There may be deficiencies in the organisation structure of the business.

(i)   Forecasting may be practised too far into the future before appropriate techniques have been developed.

(j)   Not enough time may be allowed for the system to be developed and managers gain the necessary experience to use the technique to maximum advantage.

Budgetary control can be a powerful technique in supporting the executives of a business in achieving objectives but this is dependent upon the quality of management. It also depends on the attention given to motivating staff to react favourably to the discipline the technique imposes.

11   (a)   Few people will not tend to raise objectives to change particularly when the proposed change is likely to reflect upon their own performance. There is also a reasonable feeling of opposition to be expected from executives who believe that changes made will reduce their responsibilities and status in the business.

The case refers to the senior executives usually working together as a team and it is necessary to preserve this harmony. The case describes areas where discontent will quickly destroy this co-ordinated activity. If any one member has a dominent personality (e.g., the sales manager) disagreements can be more severe in their effect. The closer all executives can be in working out the problems of budget installation and practice the better.

One way of avoiding some friction is to emphasise budget objectives and stipulate that the system will support organisation responsibilities. This can be done if there is no intention to alter responsibilities on budget installation because it is believed that the present organisation is sound. If executives feel less vulnerable they are likely to be more amenable   to change

116

and make a constructive contribution to installation problems.

The managing director should acknowledge the personality considerations of his executives and use his personal knowledge to distinguish between points which are genuine points of concern and matters which are merely reflections of the opposition of the manager to the new system. A concentration on the former category of queries with a sincere attempt to convince executives that their views are valued as a contribution to running the business efficiently will be rewarded by better personnel relationships.

(b)   The easy answer would be to terminate the employment of the executive concerned with the company but this action should not be taken unless all other avenues have been explored without success.

The point made under (a) above regarding the identification of genuine matters for concern is particularly important. The sales manager's worry about the impossibility of assessing sales might be a genuine difficulty demanding education in forecasting techniques. It would be far better to give the executive concerned this education than terminate his employment because of his alleged non-co-operation.

It should be remembered that all executives will need to feel their way and in the early stages of budget installation many estimates will be unrealistic and almost useless as control figures.

Reasoned persuasion of executives to co-operate in installing the system is the action that should be taken, always pointing to the value of the system to the executive personally.

12   (a)   Expenses should be analysed in detail although the way the budgets have been prepared in this case renders them of doubtful value. Some checking at operating company level seems to have been carried out because it is stated that some items were considerably above budget. This observation seems at variance with the statement that the budget was fixed at the lowest possible figure. There is room for improvement in the budgetary procedure on this point.

Would the provision of the increased detail be such a big job? It seems unlikely and when the increased value of the detail is considered, surely this would outweigh the cost of the increased clerical work.

(b)   The criticisms of the present system are as follows:
  (i)   In the case, budgeting appears to be from the top downwards. Budgeting should be from the bottom of the management hierarchy upwards. Lower levels of management and subsidiary companies should submit their plans to headquarters. Unless budgeting is approached in this way, control is not as effective as it can be.

(ii)   Operating company potential does not appear to have been investigated. Company budgets appears to be allocated activity. It would be useful to ascertain the possible effective return on capital resources in each unit.

(iii) The budgeted level of attainment appears to be a course assessment and is in need of greater refinement.

(iv)   Is the budget available at the start of the budget year? This question is prompted by the statement that opening stocks are taken from the last trading statement. If the budget is available at the start of the budget year, the opening figures would not be available in time from that source. The budget should be available at the start of the budget year.

(v)   It is difficult to understand what use this budget can be to control company activities. In the case, if there are variances in control periods, how may these be interpreted for effective action? The detail is not available for this purpose.

11 Budgetary Contol (2)—Budget Type Aspects

1   An approved budget should not be changed without good reason. Changes in circumstances since the budget was prepared will take place continually, but a distinction must be made between:

(a)   Actual and budget variations which arise in the normal course of business but do not affect the budget
(b)   Changes in the basic conditions upon which the budget was based.

In the first case, the variations, or variances as they are usually called, will be revealed by the periodical returns for management. It is necessary to analyse the causes of such variations so that immediate action may be taken to remedy any wrong tendencies. In the second case, the budget as a measure of current efficiency would be of restricted value if it was not altered.

Changes such as activity levels can be accommodated by the flexible budget. Where continuous budgeting is practised, the short control periods covered by each successive stage of the budgeting process help to keep the budget at a resalistic level of performance.

If budget amendments are considered essential, it is desirable to ensure that the system does not develop into a means of covering up inefficiency on the part of managers. On the other hand, the analysis and explanation of variations can become an irksome task where the budget is not realistically compiled and maintained. To preserve the balance between these partially conflicting requirements, no amendment should be allowed without reference to the budget committee.

Amendments should be submitted to the budget committee for their approval on a form designed to show:
(a)   The budget period concerned
(b)   The budget heading
(c)   The effective dates of the change
(d)   The budget figure already approved and the recommended revised budget amount

(e)   The reasons for submitting the budget amendment

(f)   The signature of the official responsible for originating the budget amendment form.

A budget amendment form incorporating the above requirements is illustrated below (Figure 11.1):

BUDGET AMENDMENT FORM	No.		
BUDGET PERIOD _____ BUDGET CENTRE _____			
Budget heading	Budget figure approved	Amended budget figure	Reasons for amendment
	£	£	
EFFECTIVE DATES:			
SIGNATURE _____ DATE _____			
COMMENTS BY BUDGET COMMITTEE:			

Figure 11.1

2   To: Managing Director   Date . . . .
      From: Management Accountant
           Operating Statement and the Flexible Budget

The operating statement produced based on a budget of 400,000 units is misleading because the actual level of activity is 460,000 units. Actual costs for 460,000 units are being compared with budgeted costs for 400,000 units. A more meaningful comparison is to produce a return where both sets of figures are on the basis of 460,000 units. Such a return is shown below.

Operating Statement for the period ....

	Flexible budget		Actual		Variance	
	£	£	£	£	£	£
Sales		448,500		450,500		2,000
Less cost of sales						
Factory:						
Material	132,250		134,650		(2,400)	
Labour	92,000		88,000		4,000	
Expenses	67,200		71.000		(3,800)	
		291,450		293,650		(2,200)
		157,050		156,850		(200)
Sales expenses	56,000		62,550		(6,550)	
Administration						
expenses	45,000	101,000	42,500	105,050	2,500	(4,050)
Profit		56,050		51,800		(4,250)

The extent of the misleading information shown in the present statement is now apparent. All variances shown on that statement are significantly different from the true position. In most cases the variances are reversed in their effect.

The clear advantage of producing the statement, showing actual compared with the flexible budget, suggests that the budgetary control system could be altered to incorporate flexible budgeting so that an improved information service may be provided.

Signed . . . .

Workings	£
(a) Sales: 460,000 x £1 =	460,000
Less sales rebate: 2½%	11,500
	448,500

(b) Factory costs:

Material $\dfrac{460,000}{400,000}$ x £115,000 = £132,250

Labour $\dfrac{460,000}{400,000}$ x £80,000 = £92,000

Expenses:
Variable: $\dfrac{460,000}{400,000}$ x 80% of £60,000 = £55,200

Fixed: 20% of £60,000 = £12,000

£67,200

(c) Sales expenses:
Variable: $\dfrac{460,000}{400,000}$ x 80% of £50,000 = £46,000

Fixed: 20% of £50,000 = £10,000

£56,000

3   Effective planning and control implies the provision of plans that have been the subject of scrutiny and approved as a commitment for the marketing management; the supply of budgetary reports of actual performance for comparison with the plan; an analysis of differences revealed with an indication of corrective action to be taken and such action taken. In this context, the usual forms of sales analysis and their purpose are as follows:

Sales Analysis	Purpose
(a) Location – territorial division	Market coverage
(b) Product and product group	Product profitability and relationship to associated product statistics
(c) Customer type – according to credit terms: cash, credit and HP sales	Market coverage

(Table continued on facing page)

Sales Analysis	Purpose
(d) Customer type — according to channel of distribution: wholesaler, retailer or final customer	Market coverage
(e) Sales representative	Performance assessment and incentive payment
(f) Order size	For review of order size profitability and discount policy

Overall, the various forms of analysis will give the marketing manager information for directing marketing effort and reviewing performance.

4 (a) A sales budget should be based on a sound sales forecast that is realistic for the business in the future trading period. To be realistic, the sales manager should:

(i) Recognise information gained by staff on the likely sales pattern in the future
(ii) Study existing sources of information such as past sales statistics
(iii) Relate associated policy decisions to expected sales, e.g., pricing policies
(iv) Consider the effect of advertising and other sales promotional aids
(v) Consider the relative profitability of individual products to secure the best product mix
(vi) Obtain information regarding: future economic conditions affecting the business; and competitors' share of the market and strategy
(vii) Attempt to balance short-term activity with long-term objectives
(viii) Assess the likely impact of new products.

Market research may be used to supplement external information noted above. Before the sales budget can be finalised, the production capacity relative to stock levels should be considered.

(b)

	Product A	Product B	Product C
Trend in sales	Volume declining	Volume increasing	Volume increasing
Price movement	None	Reducing	None
Trend in sales value	Reducing	Increasing	Increasing
This year's actual compared with budget:			
(i) Volume	Declined	Declined (reducing steadily, quarters 2, 3 and 4)	Maintained and improved in quarter 3
(ii) Sales value	Declined	Declined	Declined
(iii) Price per unit	Same	Reduced	Reduced
This year's P/V ratio	8%	20%	20%
This year's contribution to labour cost	$33\frac{1}{3}\%$	100%	150%

Recommendation to the budget committee
Product A. Further investigation to assess the future of this product. On the basis of the information given a poor prospect.
Product B. Try to increase the product price to the former level.
Product C. This is the best product and the attempt should be made to increase the sales of this product.
General. Examine costs with a view to their reduction and assess the profitability of the products on the basis of future costs.

5   (a)   Predetermined material costs per product:

Material	Unit price £	Products P1 £	P2 £	P3 £
M1	0.50	—	0.50	1.00
M2	0.20	0.20	—	0.40
M3	0.25	0.50	0.25	—

(Table continued on facing page)

Material	Unit price £	P1 £	P2 £	P3 £
			Products	
Brought forward		0.70	0.75	1.40
M4	0.15	0.30	0.30	0.15
		1.00	1.05	1.55

(b)

(i) *Production Budget for the year ended 31st December 19 ....*

Units: 000

Products

	P1	P2	P3	
Closing stocks — finished goods	10	15	30	
Add sales	52	58	75	(Note A)
	62	73	105	
Less opening stocks — finished goods	5	10	15	
Production	57	63	90	

(ii) *Production Cost Budget — Director Material*
year ended 31st December 19 ....

Raw Material	P1	P2	P3	Total	
Department 1					
M1	—	35,000	100,000	135,000	
Department 2					
M2	12,000	—	42,000	52,000	
M3	30,000	17,500	—	47,500	
				99,500	
Department 3					
M4	18,000	21,000	15,000	54,000	
Grand total				288,500	(Note B)

125

Purchasing Budget – year ended 31st December 19 ....

Units: 000

Materials

	M1	M2	M3	M4	
Closing stock –					
raw material	40	30	20	50	
Add production	270	260	190	360	(Note C)
	310	290	210	410	
Less opening stock					
– raw material	30	40	10	60	
To purchase	280	250	200	350	*Total*
Purchasing cost (£)	140,000	50,000	50,000	52,500	292,500 (Note D)

Workings

Products

		P1	P2	P3
(A)	Budgeted sales in units:	$\dfrac{£260,000}{5}$	$\dfrac{£580,000}{10}$	$\dfrac{£450,000}{6}$
		= 52,000 units	= 58,000 units	= 75,000 units
(B)	Material issued to production:			
	Good production	57,000	63,000	90,000
	Add rejects	3,000	7,000	10,000
		((5/95)×57,000)	((10/90)×63,000)	((10/90)×90,000)
	Material issue in units	60,000	70,000	100,000

	Material issue at cost	Above figures for each department multiplied by the cost per material unit

(C) Material issued to production in units (000):

	Raw material			
	M1	*M2*	*M3*	*M4*
P1	–	60	120	120
P2	70	–	70	140
P3	200	200	–	100
	270	260	190	360

(D) Purchasing cost: Purchase figures in units for each raw material multiplied by the cost per material unit.

6   The cash forecast on **pages 128/9**.

Workings	*January* £	*February* £	*March* £
(a) Cash receipts			
Sales: November	54,000		
December	240,000	72,000	
January	216,000	108,000	32,400
February		252,000	126,000
March			360,000
	510,000	432,000	518,400

(b) Cash receipts			
Obsolete stock – cost			30,000
Profit margin: $\frac{2}{3}$ × £30,000 =			20,000
Selling value			50,000
Disposal value: $\frac{1}{2}$ × £50,000 =			25,000

(c) Cash payments			
Purchases:			
Next 3 months sales	1,560,000	1,620,000	
Required stock level			
(60% of sales)	936,000	972,000	

	January £	February £	March £
Stock at beginning of month (£840,000 − £30,000)	810,000	936,000	
Stock sold in the month (60% of sales)	216,000	252,000	
	594,000	684,000	
Stock level required	936,000	972,000	
Monthly purchases	342,000	288,000	

(d) Cash payments
Variable expenses:

	January £	February £	March £
Paid in current month (70%)	25,200	29,400	42,000
Paid in following month (30%)	24,000	10,800	12,600
	49,200	40,200	54,600

(e) Cash payments
Bank loan interest:

	January £	February £	March £
Loan outstanding at beginning of month	280,000	260,000	240,000
Interest paid at $\frac{1}{2}$%	1,400	1,300	1,200

Brown & Co. Ltd Cash Forecast – three months ended 31st March 19 ....

		January £	February £	March £
Cash balance (deficiency) at beginning of the month		100,000	51,400	(33,100)
Cash receipts				
Sales		51,000	432,000	518,400
Obsolete stock		25,000	—	—
	(A)	635,000	483,400	485,300

		January £	February £	March £
Cash paymenets				
Purchases		370,000	342,000	288,000
Fixed expenses (excluding depreciation)		100,000	100,000	100,000
Variable expenses		49,200	40,200	54,600
Rates		–	–	25,000
Special advertising costs		–	10,000	15,000
Equipment		3,000	3,000	3,000
Taxation		40,000	–	–
Bank loan:				
Principal		20,000	20,000	240,000
Interest		1,400	1,300	1,200
	(B)	583,600	516,500	726,800
Cash balance (deficiency) at end of the month	(A–B)	51,400	(33,100)	(241,500)

7   (i)   *Cash Budget – six months ended 30th June 19 ....*

		January £	February £	March £	April £	May £	June £
Opening balance		2,000	1,200	(600)	11,200	(5,000)	(4,500)
Add receipts from customers		10,000	10,000	10,000	15,000	25,000	25,000
	(A)	12,000	11,200	9,400	26,200	20,000	20,500
Add subscription by the chairman				38,100			
				47,500			
Payments							
Creditors		8,000	9,000	13,000	27,000	20,000	20,000
Salaries		2,000	2,000	2,000	2,875	3,000	3,000
Fixed assets		–	–	20,000	–	–	–
Rent		–	–	500	–	–	500
Other expenses		800	800	800	1,325	1,500	1,500
	(B)	10,800	11,800	36,300	31,200	24,500	25,000
Closing balance (A–B)		1,200	(600)	11,200	(5,000)	(4,500)	(4,500)

(ii) *Budgeted Trading and Profit and Loss Accounts*
for six months ended 30th June 19 ....

	£		£
Opening stock	9,000	Sales	125,000
Add purchases	109,000		
	118,000		
Less closing stock	18,000		
Cost of sales	100,000		
Gross profit carried forward	25,000		
	125,000		125,000
Rent	1,000	Gross profit brought	
Salaries	15,000	forward	25,000
Other expenses	6,900		
Depreciation	1,750		
Net profit carried forward	350		
	25,000		25,000
Balance carried forward	11,900	Balance brought forward	11,550
		Net Profit b/f	350
	11,900		11,900

Budgeted Balance Sheet as at 30th June 19 ....

	£	£	£	£
Fixed assets at cost			45,000	
Less depreciation to date			7,750	37,250
Current assets				
Stock		18,000		
Debtors (2 months sales)		50,000	68,000	
Current liabilities				
Trade creditors (one				
month's purchases)		20,000		

	£	£	£	£
Brought forward		20,000		37,250
Accruals	375			
Expenses	375	750		
Bank overdraft		4,500	25,250	
Working capital				42,750
Capital employed				80,000

Represented by
Issued share capital:

			£	£
Opening balance			30,000	
Additional capital subscribed			38,100	68,100
Revenue reserves: profit and loss				
account balance				11,900
				80,000

Workings	January £	February £	March £	April £	May £	June £
(a) Payments to creditors – based on purchases:						
Sales at cost (sales minus 20% of sales)	8,000	12,000	20,000	20,000	20,000	20,000
Add closing stock	10,000	11,000	18,000	18,000	18,000	18,000
	18,000	23,000	38,000	38,000	38,000	38,000
Less opening stock	9,000	10,000	11,000	18,000	18,000	18,000
Purchases	9,000	13,000	27,000	20,000	20,000	20,000

(b) Salary payment for April	£
Salary for April	3,000
Less payment made in May: $\frac{1}{8} \times$ £3,000	375
	2,625
Add payment outstanding from March: $\frac{1}{8} \times$ £2,000	250
	2,875

(c) Payment of other expenses excluding rent for April	
Other expenses for April	1,500
Less payment made in May: $\frac{1}{4} \times$ £1,500	375
	1,125

		£
Brought forward		1,125
Add payment outstanding from March: $\frac{1}{4} \times £800$		200
		1,325

(d) Depreciation for six months ended 30th June

10% of £25,000 = £2,500	$\frac{1}{2} \times$ £2,500 =	1,250
10% of £20,000 = £2,000	$\frac{1}{4} \times$ £2,000 =	500
		1,750

8   (a)

A.B. Rubber Co. Ltd
Budgeted Profit Statement – year ended 30th November 19 ....

Note			Grade 1 £	Grade 2 £	Grade 3 £	Total £
(i)	Sales	(A)	50,000	42,000	44,000	136,000
(ii)	Marginal cost of sales					
	Opening stock – finished goods		2,960	2,323.5	3,450	8,733.5
	Add production cost:					
(iv)	Material cost		34,638	28,380	31,297.5	94,315.5
(v)	Labour cost		2,510	2,600	2,340	7,450
			40,108	33,303.5	37,087.5	110,499
(vi)	Less closing stock – finished goods		3,108	2,323.5	2,587.5	8,019
		(B)	37,000	30,980	34,500	102,480
	Contribution	(A–B–C)	13,000	11,020	9,500	33,520
(vii)	Contribution per block		5.2	5.51	4.75	

		£
Less fixed costs		
Factory		6,500
Selling		3,600
Administration		2,100
	(D)	12,200
Profit	(C–D)	21,320

(b)   *Budgeted Cash flow Statement – year ended 30th November 19 ....*

Note		£	£	£
	Bank overdraft – opening balance			8,000.5
	Add sources of funds			
	Profit	21,320		
	Add depreciation	1,700	23,020	
(viii)	Increase in trade creditors		1,344	
(ix)	Decrease in stocks		469.5	24,833.5
	Less applications of funds			16,833
(x)	Increase in trade debtors		1,500	
	Capital expenditure		2,500	4,000
	Closing cash balance			12,833

Sufficient cash will be available to meet the additional capital expenditure due early in December 19 ....

(c)   *Budgeted Balance Sheet as at 30th November 19 ....*

Note		£	£	£	£
	Fixed assets				
(xi)	Land and buildings		10,000	–	10,000
	Equipment		18,000	7,200	10,800
			28,000	7,200	20,800
	Working capital				
	Current assets:				
	Stock: Raw material	8,285			
	Finished goods	8,019	16,304		
	Trade debtors		17,000		
	Cash		12,833	46,137	
	Current liabilities:				
	Trade creditors			7,880	38,257
	Capital employed				59,057
	Represented by				
	Share capital				25,000

	£	£
Brought forward		25,000
Reserves: General reserve	10,000	
Profit and loss account	24,057	34,057
		59,057

Workings

(i) Sales:
Grade 1   2,500 x £20 = £50,000
Grade 2   2,000 x £21 = £42,000
Grade 3   2,000 x £22 = £44,000

(ii) Opening stock: finished goods:

Valuation per 100 unit block

	Grade 1	Grade 2	Grade 3
Direct materials			
E156	50 x £0.12 = £6.00	50 x £0.12 = £6.00	–
E157	60 x £0.13 = £7.80	63 x £0.13 £8.19	60 x £0.13 = £7.80
E158	–	–	55 x £0.15 = £8.25
	£13.80	£14.19	£16.05
Direct labour cost			
Department 1	2 x £0.40 = £0.80	2½ x £0.40 = £1.00	2½ x £0.40 = £1.00
Department 2	$\frac{1}{3}$ x £0.60 = £0.20	½ x £0.60 = £0.30	$\frac{1}{3}$ x £0.60 = £0.20
	£14.80	£15.49	£17.25
	200 x £14.80 = £2,960	150 x £15.49 = £2,323.5	200 x £17.25 = £3,450

(iii) Production (blocks):

	Grade 1	Grade 2	Grade 3
Sales	2,500	2,000	2,000
Add closing stock	210	150	150
	2,710	2,150	2,150

134

	Grade 1	Grade 2	Grade 3
Brought forward	2,710	2,150	2,150
Less opening stock	200	150	200
	2,510	2,000	1,950

(iv) Material cost:
Grade 1 2,510 x £13.80 = £34,638
Grade 2 2,000 x £14.19 = £28,380
Grade 3 1,950 x £16.05 = £31,297.5

(v) Labour cost:
Grade 1 2,510 x £1.00 = £2,510
Grade 2 2,000 x £1.30 = £2,600
Grade 3 1,950 x £1.20 = £2,340

(vi) Closing stock – finished goods:
Grade 1 210 x £14.80 = £3,108
Grade 2 150 x £15.49 = £2,323.5
Grade 3 150 x £17.25 = £2,587.5

(vii) Contribution per block:
Grade 1 £13,000 ÷ 2,500 = £5.20
Grade 2 £11,020 ÷ 2,000 = £5.51
Grade 3 £9,500 ÷ 2,000 = £4.75

(viii) Purchases:

	E156 units	E157 units	E158 units
Raw materials consumed:			
Grade 1	125,500	150,600	–
Grade 2	100,000	126,000	–
Grade 3	–	117,000	107,250
	225,500	393,600	107,250
Add closing stock	23,000	18,000	19,500
	248,500	413,600	126,750
Less opening stock	20,000	20,000	22,000
	228,500	395,600	104,750
	x £0.12	x £0.13	x £0.15

	E156	E157	E158
Total	= £27,420	= £51,428	= £15,712.5

$$\frac{\text{Total}}{\text{£94,560.5}}$$

Closing balance — trade creditors $\frac{1}{12}$ × £94,560.5 = <u>£7,880</u>

	£
Closing balance — trade creditors	7,880
Opening balance — trade creditors	6,536
Increase in trade creditors	1,344

	£	£	£
(ix) Opening stocks			16,773.5
Closing stocks			
Finished goods		8,019	
Raw materials:			
E156 23,000 × £0.12 =	2,760		
E157 20,000 × £0.13 =	2,600		
E158 19,500 × £0.15 =	2,925	8.285	16,304
Decrease in stocks			469.5

	£
(x) Closing trade debtors $\frac{1}{8}$ × £136,000 =	17,000
Opening trade debtors	15,500
Increase in trade debtors	1,500

	£
(xi) Depreciation on equipment	
Per opening balance sheet	5,500
Add depreciation charge for the year	1,700
	7,200

	£
(xii) Profit and loss account	
Opening balance	2,737
Profit for the year	21,320
Closing balance	24,057

9   (a)   The chief work of the budget cmmittee is:
  (i)   To offer advice to managers responsible for preparing budgets
 (ii)   To co-ordinate budget activity with special responsibility for reconcil-
         ing the views of executives where their plans overlap and agreement
         is necessary to govern the preparation of other associated details, e.g.,
         the agreement of sales levels in relation to production activity
(iii)   To receive sectional budgets and scrutinise the plans as a basis for any
         revisions that may be necessary
 (iv)   To make recommendations to the board of the company regarding the
         consideration and approval of the master budget
  (v)   To review routine budgetary reports on actual performance as a basis
         for recommendations for managerial action that is considered necessary.

(b)   As secretary to the budget committee the main duties undertaken
would include:
  (i)   The calling of committee meetings and the issue of the agenda with
         supporting papers needed by committee members
 (ii)   The taking of minutes and the issue of advice regarding the conduct of
         the meetings
(iii)   The selection of committee members for specific budgets and possibly
         additional members where specialist advice is necessary
 (iv)   The provision of general advice to all members of the committee on
         technical factors affecting budget preparation
  (v)   The fixing of preparatory procedures.

(c)   The contents of a budget manual may include the following:
  (i)   System objectives — the objectives of the system and the way the
         system will operate
 (ii)   Business objectives — the objectives to be achieved by the business in
         the budget period in relation to its long-term plans
(iii)   Company policies — the policies adopted by the business to operate
         in the budget period
 (iv)   Organisation structure and responsibilities — the organisational struc-
         ture and responsibilities of specific personnel for aspects of the
         budgetary procedure
  (v)   Budget timetable — details of when sections of the budgetary procedure
         are to be completed
 (vi)   Sectional budget preparation — specific instructions on the preparation
         of each sectional budget
(vii)   Master budget procedure — the procedure for preparing the master
         budget
(viii)   Budget review — the procedure for the review of submitted plans

(ix)   Budgetary reports – the statements to be produced for management

(x)   Accounting procedure – the related accounting routines to be observed

(xi)   Report review – the procedure for the review of budgetary reports.

10   (a)   The master budget summarises sectional budgets that may be classified into two types: (i) the operating budget; and (ii) the financial budget.

The former is associated with the trading and profit and loss statement; the latter, the balance sheet. This simplified classification requires subsidiary analysis in most companies and the analysis should follow management control requirements. Review comments are difficult to standardise because (i) limited development of sectional budgeting may be practised; and (ii) specific areas may assume greater significance in some businesses than in others.

Where there is limited development of the system the overall advantages of budgetary control are unlikely to be secured. If significant expenses are not made the subject of separate analysis, the degree of detail required for control may not be obtained.

The types of budgets tend to follow the functional analysis of costs and should be related to specific managerial responsibility centres. The fact that budgets may be produced that cross responsibility boundaries, e.g., product cost budgets, means that for control purposes a distinction must be made between the two types because the latter are unsuitable for control without appropriate analysis.

The activity level may have greater relevance to certain sectional budgets than others and for this reason a flexible budget may be used for overhead. If an alternative type of budget is used, the fixed budget, misleading variance information may be produced for management.

Some budgets have a greater long-term effect than others, e.g., capital expenditure and research and development, and the fact that commitments may have been made in earlier years means that short-term planning flexibility may be restricted for sections of the master budget.

Co-ordinating the sectional budgets is a complex operation because the detailed plans may not be in balance when consolidated into an overall picture. This is particularly the case regarding the cash requirements of sectional budgets which in all other respects may be satisfactory. The adjustment of detailed budgets as necessary for co-ordinated planning must be carried out with care and skill.

(b)   In the planning stage the sales, production and finished goods stock levels need to be co-ordinated. Although the budgeting process usually begins with the sales forecast, there is no point in converting this into a sales plan if production facilities allowing for movements in finished goods stock levels, cannot meet the expected sales demand. To meet expected improved sales levels, capital expenditure to increase facilities may be planned but before these increased resources are available the current budget period may have expired.

A well-balanced manufacturing plan is essential for efficient use of production facilities and fluctuating production activity can materially affect costs. The close relationship of sales to production means that significant reductions of sales from the plan may mean significant reductions of production or the build-up of finished goods stock. In some organisations it is very difficult to plan sales accurately and significant differences between actual and budget may be unavoidable. This variation will affect the funds required for working capital and the planned changes in resources may add to cash requirements. Timing of cash movements is crucial where there are changing sales and the possible change in production levels is being considered.

As mentioned in section (a), where activity levels change the use of a flexible budget providing varying cost levels for a range of possible activities may be useful.

11 (a) Interpretative comments that may be provided include:
  (i) For the financing factors:
    (1) Explanation of the factors which have determined the judgement of the likely position of key balance sheet items at the year end
    (2) Outlining the significance of major deviations from the original plan and the major reasons why such deviations exist
    (3) Outlining the actions taken by management to overcome significant deviations, to maximise the use of cash resources and to minimise the cost of funds.
  (ii) For the classified capital expenditure:
    (1) An explanation of all major variations in estimated actual expenditure from amounts approved
    (2) The nature of the projects being carried forward to future year(s) and, if not in accordance with the submission to the board, the delays which caused the carried forward amounts
    (3) Explanation of the significant additions to and deletions from the original current year plan.
  (iii) For the significant environmental factors:
    The impact of these factors on sales, expense or assets.

In summary, the emphasis should not be on what has been done, or what should have been done in the current year, but on:

(1)   Summarising variances from the current year's planned results
(2)   Establishing the major reasons for these variances from planned results
(3)   Assessing the effect on the future year(s) of management decisions and programmes only partially effective in the current year
(4)   Determining the further action which should be taken in the budget year.

(b)   Interpretative comments that may be provided include:
  (i)   For new product introductions:
        (1)   The purpose of each major project and its relationship to product line strategy
        (2)   Summarising the impact of the programme on the present product line
        (3)   Outlining the impact of the new products on future years' performance
        (4)   Outlining alternative plans considered for the introduction, particularly those designed to cover the possibility of delays in availability or competitive action.
  (ii) For price factors:
        (1)   The reasons for the price changes
        (2)   The timing and level of management by which key decisions in each programme will be taken
        (3)   Company pricing strategy relative to competition.
 (iii) For sales:
        (1)   The significance of changes in sales in the classifications and the trend of total sales
        (2)   The competitive pressure on sales.
  (iv) For supply requirements:
        (1)   The significance of any major changes in supply requirements
        (2)   Reasons for any major changes in the planned source of production, the impact of these changes and possible alternative plans for the source of production to meet changes in demand
        (3)   Reasons for finished stock changes, if any, from the current year
        (4)   Any known major changes in requirements or source of production for the year following the budget period.
  (v)   For utilisation of production capacity:
        (1)   The significance of past trends in available capacity and the cost of additional capacity
        (2)   Summary of the capital expenditure planned for capacity

additions in the budget year and subsequent years

    (3)   Reasons for significant differences between effective and available capacity

    (4)   The method by which capacity has been calculated.

(vi) For the effect of production level on manufacturing costs:

    (1)   The reasons for increases in expense at each level of production, indicating whether the changes in level of expense follow automatically from changes in programme or whether they will occur only as a result of a management decision on production levels spread over a period; the additional expense required to support the change

    (2)   The level of authority required for key decisions to implement the changes in the programme.

(vii) For manpower:

    (1)   The reasons for changes in the numbers of staff of each type including any significant change in grade

    (2)   Programmes developed to increase the effectiveness of staff or to reduce their numbers.

12   (a)   The steps I would take in establishing budgetary control in this case are:

  (i) Ascertain the structure of the organisation and managerial responsibilities

 (ii) Ascertain the objectives of the business

(iii) Identify managerial requirements to assist them in the budgeting process

(iv) Fix the control period

 (v) Assess the budgeted level of attainment

(vi) Prepare a timetable to be met and the stages of introduction for the system

(vii) Identify the supporting requirements from the accounting system

(viii) Prepare instructions to executives to assist them in their job of preparing the budgets

(ix) Design the control reports to be issued.

The difficulties that may be encountered in introducing the system are:

  (i) Bad accounting system support

 (ii) Poor management and faulty organisation structure

(iii) Obtaining the background statistics required

(iv) Lack of co-operation in the budgeting process

 (v) Poor management understanding of what is required

(vi) Obtaining the degree of co-ordination necessary

(vii) The lack of information on objectives

(viii) Reluctance of staff to commit themselves to plans for the future and the feeling that it is impossible to predict the future

(ix) Expectation of too much from the technique in the early stages of its introduction.

It is assumed in the case that top management support would be available.

Attempts to overcome the above difficulties would include:

(i) Not introducing the system until the accounting support is of a reasonable standard

(ii) Insisting on a reasonable stage-by-stage introduction of the system

(iii) Emphasising the managerial aspects of the system and the manager's responsibility for its effectiveness

(iv) Modification of the organisation structure as necessary

(v) Undertaking an educational programme to enable executives to appreciate the key features of the system and what is required of them.

(b)

MANUFACTURING STATEMENT PERIOD ENDED						
	This period			To date		
	Actual	Budget	Variance	Actual	Budget	Variance
	£	£	£	£	£	£
Analysis of prime cost						
Prime cost factory overhead						
Total factory cost Work-in-progress variation						
Factory cost of goods completed						

Figure 11.2

TRADING AND PROFIT & LOSS STATEMENT
PERIOD ENDED ....

	This period			To date		
	Actual	Budget	Variance	Actual	Budget	Variance
	£	£	£	£	£	£
Net Sales Less cost of sales						
Gross profit Less operating expenses						
Add/Deduct Non-operating items						
Net profit before tax Taxation						
Net profit after tax						

Figure 11.3

FACTORY COSTS STATEMENT
PERIOD ENDED ....

	This period			To date		
	Actual	Budget	Variance	Actual	Budget	Variance
	£	£	£	£	£	£
Analysis by (a) Fixed/variable costs (b) Controllable/ uncontrollable costs (c) Function						
Totals						

Figure 11.4

(Similar returns for administration, selling and distribution costs)

BALANCE SHEET AS AT			
	Actual	*Budget*	*Variance*
	£	£	£
Fixed Assets			
Analysis			
Working Capital			
Analysis			
Net Assets			
Represented by:			
Share Capital			
Capital Reserves			
Revenue Reserves			
Loan Capital			
Long-term Deferred Liabilities			

Figure 11.5

	CASH RETURN

PERIOD ENDED ....

	Actual	Budget	Variance
	£	£	£
Opening balance of cash receipts			
Analysis			
Payments			
Analysis			
Closing balance of cash			

Figure 11.6

ACCOUNTING AND BUSINESS CONTROL

12 The Acquisition of Long-Term Resources

1   The need for a system of capital expenditure control in a business may be demonstrated by considering the following:

(a)   Most capital projects involve the company in a significant outlay of cash which has a marked effect on the use of funds in the business.

(b)   Capital expenditure usually means a definite commitment decision which cannot be reversed without a substantial loss.

(c)   Current expenditure is incurred in the short term where a manager's judgements about the future are fairly reliable. Capital expenditure decisions are made relative to a longer time-scale and the longer the period, the less reliable the forecasts made.

(d)   Management ability is stretched to the limit with some projects demanding an awareness of all relevant factors and their measurement and evaluation where appropriate.

(e)   Management talent and funds are often limited and the use of these resources should reflect an awareness of the priorities appropriate to the business. Information on priorities relative to proposed capital expenditure proposals is necessary.

(f)   The completion of a project may take some time and, without adequate control information, costs may be exceeded by a significant amount.

The objectives that should be met by a capital expenditure system are:

(a)   The investment of funds in projects meeting the objectives of the company

(b)   The recognition of all relevant factors regarding proposed investments to ensure that as far as possible correct decisions are made

(c)   The carrying through of approved projects to a successful conclusion or the modification of projects as necessary

(d)   The effective control of project cash flows in relation to overall cash availability and use.

146

2   The essential features of a capital expenditure control system are as follows:

(a)   An understanding by key personnel of the importance of the need for effective capital expenditure control
(b)   A recognised level of responsibility for project approval
(c)   The ability of those submitting projects to state their case adequately (a standard form for project proposals may be used)
(d)   A knowledge on the part of the management accountant on how to evaluate a project from the financial point of view so that adequate advice can be given to management
(e)   An understanding by those responsible for decision-making of the techniques involved in point (d) and their significance
(f)   A good communication system for capital expenditure decisions and their implications at all levels of management to be understood
(g)   A good accounting control and reporting procedure as a check on approved projects.

3   The criteria recommended when considering alternative investment opportunities should include the following:

(a)   Do the investment opportunities being considered relate to the long-term objectives of the business?
(b)   Will the alternative investment opportunities give the return required by management using the DCF technique of investment appraisal?
(c)   Are the risks and uncertainties regarding the future of the project at an acceptable level?
(d)   What are the preferences relating to the alternative investment opportunities being considered?
(e)   The weighting of the arguments put forward in favour of or against a proposal so that the relative value of these arguments may be determined
(f)   Are the assumptions on which the projections have been based valid?
(g)   What non-quantifiable factors are relevant and what weighting must be given to these factors?

The problems in applying the above criteria would include the following:

(a)   Identifying investment opportunities of value to the business
(b)   Estimating the future regarding possible investment opportunities with reasonable accuracy
(c)   Giving due weight to all factors affecting the investment decision.

147

The formula for the evaluation of a capital expenditure project by the discounted cash flow method is as follows:

$$P = \frac{S_n}{(1 + i)^n}$$

where
- P = the sum of money originally invested
- S_n = the accumulated value of a sum of money invested at compound interest over a given period of time
- i = the interest rate for each compounding period as a percentage
- n = the number of compound periods.

The above formula is obtained from the compound interest formula:

$$S_n = P(1 + i)^n = P = \frac{S_n}{(1 + i)^n}$$

Example

Calculate the amount to be invested in a project at the start of year 1 to yield £1,338 at the end of year 5 at a compound interest rate of 6%.

$$P = S_n \frac{1}{(1 + i)^n}$$

$$= £1,338 \frac{1}{(1 + 0.06)^5}$$

$$= £1,338 \times \frac{1}{1.06} \times \frac{1}{1.06} \times \frac{1}{1.06} \times \frac{1}{1.06} \times \frac{1}{1.06}$$

$$= £1.000$$

Therefore, if the investment was £1,000 and the cut-off rate for projects was 6% and the future cash flow at the end of year 5 was greater than £1,338 the return on the project must be greater than 6% – a favourable investment. This gives the formula:

Net present value (NPV) = Discounted present value of future cash flows at the cut-off rate – Investment cost

Where the result is positive, the investment is favourable.

4   The capital expenditure proposal evaluation is inaccurate for the following reasons:

(a)   Part of the capital cost of the asset is the installation cost of £1,000. This should not be included in the annual operating costs.

(b)   The saving in overheads has been assessed by the use of an arbitrary percentage. It is unlikely that savings in overhead would total £3,750 and they should be estimated with greater care on the assumption that the investment is made.

(c)   The loss on the old machine of £11,000 has nothing to do with the assessment of the new project because this is an existing commitment unaffected by future decision.

(d)   Taxation has been ignored in the evaluation.

(e)   The time value of cash flows has not been recognised in the submission.

   Factors (a) to (d) should be incorporated in a new proposal and a DCF calculation made to recognise point (e).

5   (a)   Payback period = the number of years it will take the company to recover its original investment = <u>2 years</u>.

(b)   Rate of return on original investment

$$= \frac{\text{Average profit per year}}{\text{Original investment}} \times 100$$

$$= \frac{£400,000 \text{ less depreciation} \div 5}{£200,000} \times 100$$

$$= \underline{20\%}$$

(c)   Rate of return on average investment

$$= \frac{\text{Average profit per year}}{\text{Average investment}} \times 100$$

$$= \frac{£400,000 \text{ less depreciation} \div 5}{£200,000 \div 2} \times 100$$

$$= \underline{40\%}$$

(d)   Discounted cash flow:

Year	Cash flows of the project £	Net present value £	Calculation
0	(200,000)	(200,000)	
1	100,000	90,909	£100,000 ÷ 1.1
2	100,000	82,645	£90,909 ÷ 1.1
3	80,000	60,106	£82,645 ÷ 1.1 × $\frac{4}{5}$
4	80,000	54,642	£60,106 ÷ 1.1
5	40,000	24,837	£54,642 ÷ 1.1 × $\frac{1}{2}$
	200,000	113,139	

Present value of £1 = $1/(1 + i)^n$ = for the end of year 1: 1/1.1. It is assumed that the cash flow is received at the end of each year.

6   (a)   The return in cost savings is £4,000 for 5 years. Referring to the table: present value of an annuity of £1 where i = 13% and 14% with n = 5 years:

i	Discount factor		£
13%	3.517	x £4,000 =	14,068
14%	3.433	x £4,000 =	13,732
			336

Interpolating: $\dfrac{£14,068 - £14,000}{£336}$ x 14% − 13% = 0.2

Discounted rate of return: 13 + 0.2 = 13.2%

(b)   Reference to the table for present value of an annuity of £1 where i = 12% and n = 5 years gives a discount factor of 3.605.
    The level of annual saving necessary to achieve a 12% DCF return is:

$$\frac{£14,000}{3.605} = £3,884$$

(c)   Reference to the table for present value of an annuity of £1 where
i = 10% and n = 5 years gives a discount factor of 3.791.
   The present value of the cost savings in 5 years at a 10% return =

	£
£4,000 × 3.791 =	15,164
Investment	14,000
Net present value	1,164

7   For both methods, the cash inflows and outflows are identified by time
periods for the life of projects and these are then discounted to their present
values.
   In the NPV method, the discounting process uses the project cut-off
rate and when the present values of the cash inflows and outflows are related
the result is an excess or deficiency of the present value of the inflows over
the outflows. If there is an excess, the rate of return for the project is greater
than the cut-off rate. If there is a deficiency, the rate of return for the
project is less than the cut-off rate.
   In the IRR method the discount rate is the one that calculates the
present values of the cash inflows and cash outflows to the same figure. The
discount rate used is the rate of return for the project.
   Both methods can rank projects in order of preference and by this
means investment priority may be indicated. With the NPV method the
preferred projects are those with the greatest NPV. With the IRR method the
preferred projects are those with the highest return.
   The order of priorities by the two methods will not necessarily be the
same. A variation in the cut-off rate used for the NPVmethod will produce a
different result because of the varied pattern of the cash flows. At a low
cut-off rate projects with greater cash flows towards the end of their life will
have highest present values than would be the case with a higher cut-off rate
and vice versa.
   The assumption of reinvestment at the discount rate is also a feature of
the DCF method and there is a greater likelihood of this being realistic at
lower interest rates. This point favours the use of the NPV method.

8 (a) The big disadvantage of the return on investment method is that it ignores the time value of money and this factor is important if the life of the investment is as shown in this case.

The pay-back method also ignores the time value of money although, if funds are short, management may be influenced by the speed with which the money is returned to the business.

Conceptually, the DCF method is to be preferred because it is the only method that recognises the time value of money. The investment is usually made at the beginning of the year (assumed in this case) and cash inflows occur over a period of time. This factor should be considered.

It is useful to use the pay-back period in conjunction with the DCF method.

(b) It is true that the taxation factor is uncertain but there are many uncertainties regarding project appraisal and it is unwise to ignore such a significant item. With taxation effects included in the figures an appraisal preference can be changed.

The accountant's view is widely held and some authorities take the view that this is the reason why attempts by government to influence investment policy by tax allowances has only had limited effect. It would be interesting to have the accountant's views on the uncertainties surrounding the cash flow estimates for future years. The accountant approves of the DCF technique. Many managers do not favour its use on the grounds that it is a scientific approach to figures whose accuracy must be in doubt and, therefore, the exercise is not worth the effort.

(c) The DCF method should be used after tax, discounting the tax effects as well as the other cash flows given in the case. On the facts of the case, one is unable to state a preference not only because of this point but because of the influence of non-measurable factors which seem in doubt. The non-measurable factors may have greater importance in the decision and the factory manager suggests in this case that this is so. An attempt should be made to test his judgement in this area, a managerial matter, and then consider the project taking all factors into account.

9   (a)   Cash flow input per year:

Machine A	Machine B
48 hours x 50 weeks = 2,400 hours	48 hours x 50 weeks = 2,400 hours
2,400 x 1.25 pieces per hour = 3,000 pieces	2,400 x 3.2 pieces per hour = 7,680 pieces
Changeover loss = 10% of 3,000 = 300 pieces	Changeover loss = 40% of 7,680 = 3,072 pieces pieces
Loss for other causes = 10% of 3,000 = 300 pieces	Loss for other causes = 10% of 7,680 = 768 pieces
3,000 − 300 − 300 = 2,400 pieces	7,680 − 3,072 − 768 = 3,840 pieces
2,400 x £1 = £2,400	3,840 x £1 = £3,840

Net present value of cash flows (reference to the table for the present value of an annuity of £1 where i = 7% and n = 10 years):

Machine A		Machine B	
Inputs:	£	Inputs:	£
£2,400 x 7.024 =	16,858	£3,840 x 7.024 =	26,972
Output	10,000	Output	20,000
	6,758		6,772

Preference on the basis of the above information: Machine B.

(b)   Other economic factors which should be taken into consideration before a final decision is made include the following:
(i)   Taxation
(ii)   The ability to sell the increased production
(iii)   Availability of the necessary finance to obtain the new machinery.

10   (a)   *Interpretation of the revised planned programme of work in relation to the original plan*
      The work was originally expected to take 52 weeks and this time was shortened to 44 weeks with the same planned expenditure of £100,000. It is anticipated, therefore, that expenditure will rise more steeply than under the original plan.
Interpretation of actual expenditure and commitments in relation to the revised plan
      An anticipated expenditure of approximately £32,000 was planned at the end of week 16 whereas actual expenditure and commitments so far incurred amount to £50,000. Funds are being used at a more rapid rate than planned.

(b)   Further information required would be as follows:
(i)   What stage of work has been reached at the end of week 16?
(ii)   What further costs are planned to be incurred to complete the work as originally planned?
(iii)   Will the job be completed by week 44 or will the job be completed at an earlier or later date?
(iv)   What is the planned pattern of expenditure between week 16 and the completion date?

(c)   I would take the following action:
(i)   Check with management that they are satisfied with the answers under (b).
(ii)   Check the profitability of the proposal under the revised plans and obtain management approval of any variations in profitability.
(iii)   Check cash availability for any variation in payments from the original plans submitted. If any cash problems are revealed as a result of these changes, attempt to resolve these problems as necessary.

11   Net present value calculation based on revised estimates:

Year	Cash flows of the project				Net present value of project		
	Most likely result £	Opti- mistic estimate of result £	Pessi- mistic estimate of result £	Discount factor i = 20%	Most likely result £	Opti- mistic estimate of result £	Pessi- mistic estimate of result £
1 (i)	(5,000)	(5,000)	(5,000)	0.833	(4,165)	(4,165)	(4,165)
2	(1,250)	(1,000)	(1,500)	0.694	(868)	(694)	(1,042)
3	(1,250)	(1,000)	(1,500)	0.579	(724)	(579)	(869)
4	(3,000)	(2,400)	(3,600)	0.482	(1,446)	(1,157)	(1,735)
5	(9,500)	(7,600)	(11,400)	0.402	(3,819)	(3,055)	(4,583)
6	3,000	3,600	2,400	0.335	1,005	1,206	804
7	7,000	8,400	5,600	0.279	1,953	2,344	1,562
8	10,000	12,000	8,000	0.233	2,330	2,796	1,864
9	9,000	10,800	7,260	0.194	1,746	2,095	1,397
10	12,000	14,400	9,600	0.162	1,944	2,333	1,555
	21,000	32,200	9,860		(2,044)	1,124	(5,212)
		(ii)	(iii)	(iv)		(ii)	(iii)

Workings
 (i)   The £5,000 is actual expense for the year
 (ii) This column is the most likely result plus 20% for years 2 to 10
 (iii) This column is the most likely result minus 20% for the years 2 to 10
 (iv) Assuming cash flows at the end of each year — reference to the table
        for the present value of £1 where i = 20%.

Advice to the board
The most likely DCF return on the complete project is below the required
20% but this is inclusive of design expenditure which has already been
expended and, therefore, has no bearing on future activity. The projected
activity gives a net present value of £2,121 (£4,165 − £2,044) — the most
likely DCF return of over 20%. Management should continue the project
providing there is effective control to achieve this result or improve on it.
The pessimistic estimate gives a clear warning that without this control the
return will drop below 20%.

12   The system to ensure accurate cost ascertainment of capital expenditure would include the following:

(a)   The identification of each capital expenditure project by a number
(b)   A capital expenditure cost sheet established for each job passing

through the civil and plant engineering sections

(c)   The identification of costs directly incurred on the capital work on basic documents and records

(d)   The recording of the costs ascertained in (c) above on the cost sheet mentioned in (b) above

(e)   A decision made on the treatment of overheads and the amount, if any, added to the direct costs for the project.

The system to ensure adequate cost control of capital expenditure would include the following:

(a)   The use of project sanction procedure which would provide the following cost control data: (i) Estimated costs for each element of cost and (ii) Planned completion times and costs for each stage of the work to be checked

(b)   The provision of the costs incurred on the job as each stage is completed with certification that the job has been completed to the required standard for each stage

(c)   The comparison of the results ascertained in (b) with the planned costs given in (a)

(d)   The period reporting of the results with an indication to management of unsatisfactory performance

(e)   Where applicable, the revision of the control data in (a) as a result of management decision and the future use of this data for subsequent stage cost control.

13 Use of Resources (1)—Material Control

1   (a)   The faults in the system were as follows:
Mr Leak was not adequate for his job
Lack of security
Inadequate control over documentation
No checking carried out on a continuous basis
No review of goods for disposal
Lack of co-ordination between the production and stores departments
Unnecessary purchasing
Storekeeping of a poor standard
Clerical work inefficient
Pricing system inadequate
Old Hezekiah unsuitable.
Mr Leak was not wholly responsible for the following reasons:
He was left to himself
Poor staff support
Co-ordination was outside his control.

(b)   The other advantages that would accrue from the installation of a good
stock control system are as follows:
Physical stocks checked regularly with the book figures and differences
        investigated — a moral check
Causes of differences may be currently eliminated
Minimum investment of funds in stock
Buying more systematic
Efficient storage
Obsolescence at the minimum
Stock turnover at the maximum
Extent of wastage owing to physical causes can be assessed and these
        may be reduced
More efficient stock handling

Reduced costs of operation
Provision of accurate information for management.

(c) I would introduce a new system by:
Appointing a stock controller and requesting Mr Leak to concentrate
      on purchasing
Appointing a new storekeeper
Fixing a timetable for implementation
Preparation of new instructions and forms
Staff training
Stock-taking on the implementation date to establish opening balances
Stage-by-stage introduction of improvements in the system.

2   It is agreed that the proper control of inventories can make a substantial contribution to the efficiency of a business for the following reasons:

(a) Material cost is a significant item with many companies and if inventories are taken to include all stocks — work-in-progress and finished goods as well as raw material — their high value adds to the importance of this point

(b) Funds are limited in most businesses and a good control of inventories will ensure that excess funds are not tied up in stocks

(c) Production efficiency is directly related to supplies being available when required and to the required quality

(d) Sales efficiency is directly related to ensuring customer satisfaction with, for example, prompt deliveries, i.e., goods in stock ready for despatch when required

(e) Store costs can be considerable and if proper control of stock is maintained these costs may be minimised, e.g., low stock losses and economical procedures.

The control measures that may be applied include:

(a) The determination of sound stock control objectives and policy

(b) Effective co-ordination between related departments and the stores department, e.g., buying and production

(c) The planning of all activity affecting stocks preferably through the medium of budgetary control

(d) Effective reporting of areas requiring managerial attention so that effective performance may be obtained

(e) The application of a perpetual inventory system in conjunction with continuous stock checking

(f) The fixing of realistic stock limits.

3   The areas where control is possible include the following:

(a)   *Design*
Costs may be controlled by: (i) ensuring the design of the product does not demand a higher quality of material than necessary; and (ii) substituting, wherever possible, alternative materials which though they do not reduce quality, cost less, require a smaller initial quantity of material or require less processing.

(b)   *Specifications*
Ensure adequacy so that losses of material not incurred and inspection delayed.

(c)   *Ordering*
The requisitioning in advance in sufficient time to ensure that orders can be placed to the best advantage and quantities purchased should not be too large or too small.

(d)   *Stores*
Costs may be controlled by: (i) the careful checking of goods with all documents to avoid loss; (ii) inspection should be neither too lax nor too strict; (iii) effective stores security to reduce opportunities for theft; and (iv) operation of perpetual inventory system to help to reduce stock losses.

(e)   *Use of material*
(i) The returning of unused materials to store; and (ii) the comparison of actual use with planned use to identify differences, and institute corrective action where necessary.

(f)   *Handling*
Careless handling at any stage can cause damage to materials.

(g)   *Scrap reclamation*
Where possible, materials should be reclaimed from defective work.

4

	The movement	Controlled by
(a)	Receipt of raw material from the supplier's warehouse to the stores department	Supplier's transport or transport contractors
(b)	Raw material issues to production	Production control department

(Table continued overleaf)

	The movement	*Controlled by*
(c)	Production of components	Factory department manufacturing the components
(d)	Components to stores	Production control and stores departments
(e)	Issue of components to assembly department	Production control department
(f)	Assembly of components to finished products	Assembly department
(g)	Finished products to finished goods stores	Production control and stores departments
(h)	Despatch of finished products to the customer	Transport department

5   (a)   Cash discounts received are usually regarded as 'other income' but some companies consider that additional control information is provided if cash discounts receivable are deducted from other inputs making up purchase cost. The example to follow indicates the additional control information provided.

Data:
Materials purchased at a value of £100
Cash discount obtainable if the purchase invoice is paid within the agreed payment term: £5

Accounting entries:
Stores account debtied with £95
Trade creditors account credited with £95
If the creditor is paid promptly:
    Trade creditors account debited with £95
    Cash credited with £95 (payment to supplier)
If the creditor is paid outside the discount period:
    Trade creditors account debited with £95
    Cash discounts not obtained debited with £5
    Cash credited with £100 (payment to supplier)
    (the £5 entry is the control information).

(b)   Wastage which occurs prior to materials being issued to production is usually treated as works overhead on the basis of an authorised write-off document. Normal wastage cost may supplement the issue cost direct to production. Abnormal wastage should not be regarded as a production cost but be written off to profit and loss account.

6

	Method	Advantages	Disadvantages
(a)	Specific cost	Costs specifically identified with the material used for production	(i) Need to main the identification of the cost with the specific stores item (ii) Difficult to apply with small items and the rapid turnover of stock
(b)	Weighted average cost	Averages the costs to products where prices are fluctuating	A new average price must be calculated with each new purchase
(c)	FIFO cost	(i) An actual cost (ii) Assumes the usual usage sequence	(i) Similar products manufactured in the same accounting period may be charged different material issue costs (ii) Changing unit costs can make the calculation complex and time-consuming when stock turnover is frequent
(d)	LIFO cost	(i) An actual cost (ii) Products are costed at the most recent prices	As (c) above with the addition that LIFO is not favoured by the Inland Revenue
(e)	Standard cost	(i) A standardised cost (ii) Easier clerical procedure (iii) Relates to the standard costing technique (iv) Prompt price variance reporting	The fixing of a realistic standard where prices are fluctuating

(Table continued overleaf)

161

Method	Advantages	Disadvantages
(f) Replacement cost	Recognises current price levels	(i) Reconciliation of stores records difficult (ii) Not favoured by the Inland Revenue
(g) Inflated cost	Identifies the added factor with its related cost item: material cost	Usually more convenient to treat the added factor as works overhead

7   The blanks in the accounts are completed with the following figures:

(a)   Total of material A units: 200
(b)   Total of material A value: £110
(c)   Total of material B units: 410
(d)   Value of material B returns: £10

The return of 10 units of stock has been valued at original cost rather than the inflated value of £10.5 to prevent an excessive charge for wastage to jobs carried out on 28th December. By this procedure, the £10.5 debited to jobs in progress will only have been credited with £10, the remaining £0.5 being cleared from work-in-progress by a debit to works overhead.

(e)   Total of material B value: £450
(f)   Value of issues of material A on 6th December: £62

	£
100 units	50
20 units	12 (£60/100 x 20)
	62

(g)   Value of issues of material A on 26th December: £15

$$\frac{£60}{100} \times 25 = £15$$

(h)   Value of the balance of material A carried forward: £33 (55 x £0.6)

$$£110 - (£62 + £15) = £33$$

(i)   Wastage in units of material B: 20
$$410 - (100 + 140 + 150) = 20$$
(j)   Value of issues of material B on 12th December: £105
$$100 \times £1 = £100 + 5\%$$
(k)   Value of issues of material B on 28th December: £153.3

	£
100 x £1 =	110.0
30 x £1.2 =	36.0
	146.0
Add 5%	7.3
	153.3

(l)   Value of the balance of material B carried forward: £180
$$150 \times £1.2 = £180$$
(m)   Value of the waste of material B: £11.7
$$£450 - (£105 + £153.3 + £180) = £11.7$$

Stores Control Account

	£
1st December Balance brought forward	250
31st December Creditors	300
Work-in-progress	10
	560
31st December Work-in-progress	335.3
Works overhead	11.7
Balance carried forward	213.0
	560.0

8   (a)   In the LIFO method of pricing materials issued, the purchase costs for the last materials received are used for the first issues made and where a series of purchases have taken place the purchase cost inputs are used for issue costs in reverse order. The LIFO method does not assume a cost flow identified with the materials issued. By this method, the issue costs are the most recent costs and products are costed at current price levels if purchases have been recently made or if the stock has been held for some time, material prices are not rising rapidly.

163

Stock values as a residual amount will be priced at the oldest input costs and in a period of rising prices this will mean that the value of stock is understated. If current prices reduced stock, valuations would be over priced as a residual value and would need adjustment to a more realistic value.

(b)   *Stores Ledger Card – Component B 1716*

Date	Reference	Receipts		Issues		Balance	
		Units	£	Units	£	Units	£
1st November	Balance					100	30
5th November	Requisition 8131			30	9	70	21
7th November	Requisition 8379			50	15	20	6
11th November	Goods received note 319	50	16			70	22
18th November	Requisition 8479			40	12.8	30	9.2
21st November	Requisition 8516			20	6.2	10	3
25th November	Goods received note 817	80	28			90	31
28th November	Requisition 8694			60	21	30	10

9   (a)   The considerations affecting an annual stocktaking in a medium-sized engineering concern are as follows:
(i)   Timing of the stores check to be carried out and the sectional activities
(ii)   Personnel selection for the various tasks to be performed
(iii)   Preparation of stock-taking instructions covering detailed procedure and the instruction of personnel selected
(iv)   Preparation of forms with as much information in advance as possible
(v)   Stores department preparation in advance.

(b)   The advantages which might accrue to the company if a system of perpetual inventory and continuous stock-taking were adopted include:
(i)   The elimination of the annual stock-taking with the disruption that is caused by that procedure
(ii)   A greater degree of confidence in stock figures throughout the year
(iii)   Variable stock-checking may be adopted. The more expensive or vulnerable items may be checked more frequently.
(iv)   Greater control over losses and the standard of storekeeping and clerical work. Discrepancies may be easier to resolve.
(v)   A deterrent to pilferage since stock check dates for particular items of stock are not known in advance.

10   (a)   The possible reasons for the differences between physical stock, bin card and stores ledger account balances are as follows:
(i)   Clerical errors on the bin card, stores ledger account and supporting documentation
(ii)   Storekeeping errors such as incorrect issue, placing items in the wrong bin or container and not checking that all stock movement is supported by appropriate documentation

164

(iii) Stock losses owing to pilferage, breakages, evaporation and deterioration. Where these can be anticipated an incorrect assessment of them.

(b) *Treatment of the difference between the balance in stock and on the bin card*
  (i) Check the bin card with the stores ledger account
  (ii) Adjust, as necessary, and if the physical stock now agrees with the bin card the matter is resolved. If not, investigate the difference between the balance in stock and the stores ledger account.
  Treatment of the difference between the balance in stock and in the stores ledger account
  (i) Check the bin card with the stores ledger account
  (ii) Adjust, as necessary, and if the physical stock now agrees with the stores ledger account the matter is resolved. If not:
     (1) Check stock loss calculations, where appropriate, e.g., normal wastage
     (2) Check for clerical errors (see (a)(i) above)
     (3) Check for storekeeping errors (see (a)(ii) above).
  Treatment of discrepancies after investigation
A stock shortage report would be completed which should be authorised by an official who should be satisfied that all appropriate action has been taken. Stock balance corrections would then be made using this form as the authority.

11   The following reports on the subject of stock may be submitted to top management:

(a) Stock levels by principal classifications with an indication of:
  (i) The state of the stock, e.g., if an investigation has been carried out on slow moving items, an indication of the situation and proposed action
  (ii) The value of the stock, e.g., any indication of funds lying idle owing to over-investment or the reason why values have been allowed in excess of planned levels
(b) Supply problems
(c) The relationship of issue requirements to future stock needs
(d) Stock losses with a note of exceptional items and the action taken
(e) Stock turnover ratios, e.g.,

$$\frac{\text{Stocks of raw materials}}{\text{Monthly consumption}} \quad \text{or} \quad \frac{\text{Cost of sales}}{\text{Average stock}}$$

Reports to top management should be brief, indicating an overall picture and emphasising the departures from plans where corrective action is necessary.

12   To: Managing Director   Date: . . . .
     From: Management Accountant
          The Introduction of a Stores Accounting System
Following the preliminary investigation, which established the need for a stores accounting system and its justification in terms of cost, this report outlines the important aspects of the procedure that should be introduced.

(a)   *Forward planning*
An assessment should be made of material requirements, and stock levels. Stores policy should also be decided.

(b)   *Security*
Stores should be recognised as the valuable resource they are and adequate accommodation equipment, staffing and procedures should be adopted to ensure that unauthorised access to stores is not allowed.

(c)   *System documentation*
The description of the detailed procedure to deal with the recording of existing stocks and the following stock movements:
  (i)   Stores receipts
  (ii) Stores issues.
Associated factors should be included in this procedure:
  (i)   Purchasing routine
  (ii)   Inwards inspection
  (iii) Stores return
  (iv)   Stores transfer
  (v)   Stock checking.
       Forms should be designed and stationery quantities required estimated.

(d)   *Staff and equipment*
An assessment of staff requirements and equipment is necessary.

(e)   *Staff training*
All staff will need instruction in the new procedures to be adopted including those outside the stores and clerical departments who will use the system.

(f)   *Initial introduction of the system*
The following points should be covered:
  (i)   Appointment of staff
  (ii) Choice of the implementation date

(iii)   Stock-taking on the implementation date to establish opening balances.

(g)   *Information provided by the system*
The important information required will be provided by the system as follows:
(i)   Stock levels and date of stock – stores ledger sheets
(ii)   Value of stock – stores ledger sheets and stores control account
(iii)   Supply problems – purchase requisition/order analysis
(iv)   Stock issues – stores requisitions
(v)   Stock losses – stock shortage reports.

(h)   *Future developments*
Your decision is awaited on implementation of the above system when a suitable timetable can be agreed.

Signed . . . .

14 Use of Resources (2)—Labour Control

1

Gross Pay Calculations – Week 34

	X (£)	Y (£)	Z (£)	Note
		Craftsmen		*Note*
Basic wages	19.20	21.60	24.00	(i)
Overtime	2.56	4.50	–	(ii)
Basic plus overtime	21.76	26.10	24.00	
Bonus	7.50	9.00	–	(iii)
Gross pay	29.26	35.10	24.00	

Workings

(i)

$40 \times £0.48 = £19.2$ $40 \times £0.54 = £21.6$ $40 \times £0.60 = £24.0$

(ii)

Hours works	44	46	40
Basic hours	40	40	40
Overtime hours	4	6	Nil
Hours at time-and-a-third	4	4	
Hours at time-and-a-half		2	
	4	6	

Overtime payment

$4 \times £0.64 = £2.56$ $4 \times £0.72 = £2.88$
$2 \times £0.81 = £1.62$
$£4.50$

Time in hours that
should have been
taken to do the work
passing inspection:

Tudor model	$7 \times 5 = 35$	$6 \times 4 = 24$	$8 \times 3 = 24$
Regency model	$10 \times 3 = 30$	$9 \times 5 = 45$	$9 \times 2 = 18$
	65	69	42

Time taken to do the
work passing inspection:

Week 34: hours worked	44	46	40
Less time carried forward to week 35	7	8	3
	37	38	37
Add time worked in week 33 brought forward	8 45	7 45	5 42
Time saved	20	24	Nil
Bonus hours	15	18	
Bonus	15×£0.50 = £7.50	18×£0.50 = £9.00	

2   To: Directors, XY Engineering Co. Ltd   Date: . . . .
From: Management Accountant
Labour Cost Control – Alpha Factory

The essentials of a labour cost control system are as follows:

(a)   The determination of planned levels of expenditure on labour preferably included in a budgetary control procedure

(b)   The determination of standards of performance in terms of the use of
labour on the work to be completed

(c)   The ascertainment of actual costs and time spent on work performed

(d) The comparison of (c) with (a) and (b) and the ascertainment of causes of significant discrepancies

(e) The reporting of the information identified in (d) to management to enable corrective action to be taken, where necessary.

Work study is essential for the establishment of meaningful labour standards and begins with an examination of the way in which the work is done. When the method of doing the work has been approved, the value of the work content of production tasks and their associated features can be assessed to form the labour standard.

Analysis of the labour variances may disclose inefficiency owing to the use of poor quality labour. Detailed investigation can show the effect on costs of associated factors such as production problems: faulty equipment, low quality material, etc. This analysis explains the difference between the time that should have been taken to do the work and the actual time taken.

Signed ....

3   Production is the output of the manufacturing unit which may be measured in quantity and/or value.

Productivity is the effectiveness of the use of the labour and two bases that may be used for direct labour are:

(i) A comparison of the number of hours taken to do a job with the hours that should have been taken for that work

(ii) A comparison of the number of hours staff were available for work with the time staff were engaged productively for the business.

Using the figures given in the question, the following results indicate the effects of:

(a) *A 10% increase in production*

	Existing situation	Proposed situation
Production in units	10,000	11,000
Labour hours	5,000	5,500
	£	£
Production costs		
Direct material	8,000	8,800
Direct labour	2,000	2,200
Factory overhead – variable	3,000	3,300
Factory overhead – fixed	4,000	4,000
	17,000	18,300

(b)   *A 10% increase in the productivity of direct labour*   *Proposed*
                                                                      situation
        Existing situation as in (a) above
        Production in units   11,000
        Labour hours   5,000
                                                                         £
        Production costs
            Direct material   8,800
            Direct labour   2,000
            Factory overhead – variable   3,000
            Factory overhead – fixed   4,000

                                                                      ────────
                                                                       17,800
                                                                      ════════

4   The main classes into which remuneration and incentive systems can
be divided are as follows:

Type of system	*Examples*
(a) Weekly wage incentive systems (individual and group); workers earnings and direct labour costs vary:	
(i) In the same proportion as output	Straight piece rate
(ii) Proportionately less than output	Barth, Bedaux, Halsey and Rowan systems
(iii) Proportionately more than output	Higher piece rate
(iv) In proportions which differ at different levels of output	Accelerating premium, Gannt, Emerson, Merrick and Taylor systems
(b) Longer term individual system	Measured day work
(c) Long-term collective systems:	
(i) Those based on standard production or added value	Priestman or Scanlon systems
(ii) Those based on profits	Profit sharing and co-ownership

(Table continued overleaf)

171

Type of system	Examples
(d) Systems not directly dependent on production:	
(i) Those based on personal assessment	Merit rating, high day rates, attendance bonuses and length of service awards
(ii) Those supplementary to production	Quality and waste bonuses.

5   Profit sharing is a financial incentive scheme where all workers receive a bonus as an addition to wages and salaries based on a fixed percentage of profits achieved. The main criteria for implementing such a scheme are as follows:

(a)   The belief that the bonus given in this form will increase the productivity of labour and encourage good industrial relations.

(b)   Because all workers share the bonus, the belief that labour control is sufficiently effective to ensure that general work standards are maintained. If this criterion is not observed good workers may not be motivated to give good performance when they see less industrious staff receiving the same bonus.

(c)   The ability to agree with labour representatives the profit figure to adopt and its calculation as a basis for bonus payments.

(d)   The ability to provide the quality of working environment necessary to provide profits.

These criteria are difficult to meet for the following reasons:

(a)   Poor quality management

(b)   Profitability is primarily a management responsibility

(c)   Profits may not be obtained

(d)   It may be difficult to prevent poor workers not obtaining the same bonus as the best workers

(e)   Payment of the bonus may be delayed in relation to the period to which it refers

(f)   Poor communications between management and workers and trade union distrust of profit-sharing schemes.

To implement a profit-sharing scheme successfully, the aim should be to try to overcome these difficulties in meeting the criteria given.

6   Job evaluation is the technique that may be used to fix a points rating regarding the extent to which identified job characteristics are applicable to work undertaken.

Merit rating assesses the extent to which the individual matches the points rating for the work undertaken.

The distinguishing feature in the two techniques is that job evaluation measures the relative labour worth of the jobs to be done. Merit rating measures the individual's ability in doing the work.

The steps to be taken to apply job evaluation are as follows:

(a)   Identify the job characteristics applicable to the work to be undertaken. Examples are: skills, responsibilities, effort, training and education and physical effort required.

(b)   Assess the importance of each job characteristic by a points rating relative to the maximum number of points that may be awarded for that factor.

(c)   Total the points awarded for each job for all job characteristics considered.

(d)   Grade the jobs according to the job values identified in the above procedure.

7   There is considerable evidence that the complications arising from the use of some incentive schemes have caused some managements seriously to question their value. It is true, however, that financial incentive schemes are being successfully used in industry and their success can be traced to the specific identification of company needs and a realistic assessment of objectives; the choice of a scheme relevant to those needs; the thorough preparation and proper introduction of the scheme; and supporting management providing the quality of working environment necessary to apply the procedure with confidence.

A significant point in the case is the good labour relations enjoyed by the company and whatever the decision taken, great care should be taken to prevent these relationships deteriorating.

It should be possible to:

(a)   Ascertain the facts regarding many of the points made on both sides of the argument

(b)   Profit from the experience of similar companies operating incentive schemes.

In addition to providing this information, it should be established whether the company is losing staff to these other cmpanies because of their inability to secure bonus additions to their basic pay.

The following points are relevant to the case:

(a)   In group bonus schemes the poorer workers share the same bonus payments as good workers in the group and the possible action of the individual significantly to affect his personal bonus may be limited

(b)   Quality standards should be capable of enforcement whether an incentive system is introduced or not

(c)   If a scheme is introduced great care should be taken in the setting of standards.

After the inquiries suggested, unless a clear benefit to the company is anticipated, the introduction of the incentive scheme should be deferred — profit and control improvements being sought by other means. If a group scheme is to be adopted, the factors for successful introduction outlined in the opening paragraph should be applied.

8   (a)   The purpose of financial incentive schemes is to increase the productivity of labour in whatever section of the business the labour is engaged.

(b)   The points implied in the situation described are as follows:

  (i)   Managers will be motivated to sell products with the highest selling prices

 (ii)   The products with the highest selling prices will not necessarily be the most profitable products

(iii)   Service is being neglected presumably because staff are being encouraged to maximise their time in increasing the sales turnover figures

(iv)   Branch conditions for selling appear to vary widely.

     Proposals for improvement would include the following:

  (i)   An assessment of the area selling conditions and the fixing of realistic selling quotas, bearing in mind the relative profitability of the various products and sales outlets

 (ii)   The payment of the bonus on attaining the sales quotas providing a satisfactory level of service is given to customers.

9   The following factors need to be examined if a wage structure revision is contemplated:

(a)   An assessment of whether the reason given at the leaving interview is the true reason for leaving

(b)   What are the levels of remuneration for equivalent type jobs in the locality?

(c) The cost of the labour turnover for this particular reason

(d) An assessment of the amount of the increase in remuneration necessary to keep trained staff

(e) A comparison of the increased cost under (d) with the cost calculated in (c)

(f) The ability to obtain new trained staff of the quality required in the locality

(g) The effect on other staff of any adjustment to remuneration for the employees affected by the labour turnover — for example, other wage rates may need adjustment.

10   (a)   An outline labour analysis is shown below (Figure 14.1):

LABOUR ANALYSIS											
WEEK ENDED											
Document Reference	COST UNIGS						COST CENTRES				Totals
	Job Codes						Departmental Codes				
	Hrs	£	Hrs	£	Hrs	£	£	£	£	£	£	£

Figure 14.1

The reconciliation between the costs directly assigned to jobs and the wages paid would be secured by the end columns where indirect labour costs would be identified with cost centres. A description column may identify the reason for the cost centre cost. Wages paid should agree with the 'totals' column.

175

(b)   The principle determining whether or not the overtime premium is charged to a job is the cause of the overtime worked. If overtime is worked to enable the company to complete its production programme, there is no justification for charging the overtime premium to the specific job, just because in the order of the work performed that job is completed in overtime. If the job is completed in overtime on the basis of specific customer instructions a specific charge of the overtime premium to the job should be made. Normally, the overtime premium is charged to works overhead.

11   The following information should be provided to management each control period to keep it fully informed about the labour factor in the business:

(a)   Gross labour costs analysed by cost centres and departments compared with budgeted amounts
(b)   Overtime payments analysed by departments
(c)   Bonus payments analysed by departments
(d)   Staff numbers leaving analysed by cause and labour turnover cost
(e)   Manpower estimates and actual numbers employed by control categories
(f)   Labour related cost levels compared with budget for the following expenses:
      (i)   Employee benefits on wages and salaries
      (ii)   Employee relations
(g)   Labour idle time analysis analysed by department and cause
(h)   Labour efficiency statistics for each department: hours taken to produce work in relation to the time that should have been taken to do the work.

12   (a)   The routine character of the work in the office does appear to be the central issue and the difficulty may be eased by:
 (i)   Mechanisation
 (ii)   Reallocation of work from other departments
 (iii) The use of juniors or older staff.
      Some reorganisation would be inevitable with suggestions (i) and (ii). Where juniors were employed, the routine character of the work may lead to discontent if the junior was very intelligent and had potential to make a better contribution to the work of the department. Even in this situation, the work could be considered as a step to higher grade work in the future.

(b)   Labour turnover cost would be assessed by calculating the associated costs concerned with:

176

(i)   Recruitment, selection and training

(ii)   Production efficiency losses.

Costs may be analysed into:

(i)   Preventive costs

(ii)   Replacement costs.

Preventive costs may be considered, the application of personnel policies designed to foster good industrial relations, and terms and conditions of employment that would encourage staff to stay with the organisation.

Replacement costs cover (i) and (ii) above, some of these being relatively easy to calculate such as separate training establishments. Others are more difficult such as the inefficiency of new staff engaged as replacement labour.

The full cost of labour turnover is difficult to calculate because it is impossible to measure such factors as the loss of good employees who might not apply for employment with the company, owing to the bad record of the organisation in keeping its staff.

15 Use of Resources (3)—Expense Control and Depreciation Methods

1   Accountants are paying attention to investment decisions because of the long-term nature of the decision and the consequencies of entering into a commitment that may be costly to the business if withdrawal is necessary. Such decisions not only can affect the way in which the business is carried on for a considerable period but the amounts involved may be substantial. It is right, therefore, that accountants should provide advice to management on the financial implications of their likely courses of action in this area.

Paying attention to the provision of capital investment decision advice does not mean that the accountant should ignore the responsibility to provide advice in connexion with day-to-day operations. Cost effectiveness must be established in respect of current resources: men, machines and money. This implies the use of performance standards (cost standards, flexible budgeting and return on investment) that are sufficiently relevant to isolate weaknesses in the utilisation of plant, labour and materials. These standards should be built into the management control system to motivate management to eliminate expected losses in efficiency.

2   (a)   The information that may be recorded in the asset register for each asset includes the following:
  (i)   The asset description and identification reference
 (ii)   The asset location and location reference
(iii)   Details regarding the cost of the asset
 (iv)   Asset changes, e.g., locations, additions and sale information
  (v)   Data regarding the asset to:
         (1)   Support accounting routines, e.g., depreciation and book value calculations
         (2)   Assist in the review of machine efficiency, e.g., repair and maintenance costs
         (3)   Support other procedures, e.g., insurance arrangements.

(b)   Only sections of the report are quoted in the case and presumably the report did state the objectives to be met by the system. If not, these objectives should be specified. In the absence of this information, it is impossible to judge whether the proposed system meets the requirements of management.

It is apparent that extensive documentation is planned and when any system is contemplated the significant generation of paperwork should be viewed with suspicion. Paperwork should be kept to the minimum consistent with meeting the requirements fixed for the system.

The case does not quote the reasoning behind the centralisation of the asset registers at head office. The reasoning might be in the original report. If not, it should have been included so that management could assess whether the reasoning was sound and centralisation of recording justified. It may be justified, but local recording could reduce paperwork.

3   Where property in the company is owned and rented, the ascertained costs for operating units may need some adjustment so that comparability is possible. The unit where property is rented will have a rental charge included in its costs. The unit where property is owned can be made comparable by including in its costs an estimated rent for the facilities. This estimated figure is sometimes described as notional rent and when profits per the financial accounts are compared with profits per the management accounts, the latter profit figure will need to be increased by the notional rent to achieve profit reconciliation. An alternative course of action to achieve comparability of costs could be to eliminate the rent charge from the unit in rented accommodation but the former course of action is preferable to include all costs relevant to the use of facilities.

Where a company is not large enough to have several comparable units under its control, a notional rent may still be included in costs to enable the business to take advantage of interfirm comparison arrangements either through a trade association or the Centre for Interfirm Comparison.

A difficulty is to fix the estimated rent for owner-occupied property. If the rent of comparable property is available there is no problem. Otherwise, the professional opinion of a surveyor may be required.

4   Production control is concerned with producing the planned production, to the required quality and type, when required and at acceptable cost. This action should be achieved with the minimum investment of funds in stock.

Effective production control can make a valuable contribution to the financial control of the business in the following ways:

(a) Assisting the planning function regarding the provision of materials and other resources such as labour and equipment

(b) Assisting the planning function with the planned use of resources, e.g., scheduling, routing and operations planning

(c) Facilitating the optimum use of resources to enable fixed costs to be recovered on expensive machinery and equipment

(d) Facilitating production operations so that expensive delays are reduced to the minimum

(e) Recognising cost relationships concerned with long production runs as compared with small batches or single unit production

(f) Facilitating the introduction of new products and phasing out old products

(g) Facilitating the introduction of new production methods and the phasing out of old methods or the use of old machinery

(h) Keeping production and delivery dates to satisfy customers

(i) Keeping minimum stocks consistent with meeting production demands and delivery schedules

(j) The control machinery being available to report unsatisfactory tendencies regarding performance against the plan and take corrective action, where necessary.

5   A defective production report of the type shown in Figure 15.1 may be used.

The figures obtainable from the form in Figure 15.1 with reference to defective work would be: (a) the cost prior to rectification; and (b) the additional costs concerned with rectification.

The cost prior to rectification would be credited to work-in-progress account and debited to defective production account to recognise that the work has been taken out of production. The additional costs concerned with rectification would be charged to the defective production account.

Work-in-progress or finished goods would be debited with the normal cost of the rectified job according to its condition, and the credit for this amount would be to defective production account.

The balance on the defective production account would be charged to factory overhead for the department responsible for the rectification costs.

6   (a)   It is true that a provision for depreciation does retain funds in the business that may have been distributed as dividends but the replacement decision, if indeed an asset is replaced, is a matter unrelated to the

DEFECTIVE PRODUCTION	Date: . . . .

JOB OR ITEM REJECTED:	Job Number	REASON FOR REJECTION:
		SIGNED INSPECTOR

ACTION TO BE TAKEN:

ACCOUNTS OFFICE	SCRAP		RECTIFICATION	
		£		£
WORK-IN-PROGRESS ADJUSTMENT			COST PRIOR TO RECTIFICATION	
	Cost			
			RECTIFICATION COSTS:	
SCRAP/DEFECTIVE PRODUCTION RECORDS	Scrap value		Material Labour Overhead	

Figure 15.1

depreciation provision. The financial transaction concerned with asset purchase may be at a price level unrelated to original cost and a different asset may be acquired.

The provision for depreciation does not provide funds for the replacement of assets in the way described in the statement.

(b) Some factors affecting the provision for depreciation calculation may result in a loss in value of an asset, e.g., wear and tear and obsolescence, but the depreciation charge is a cost allocation not a measure of value. In inflationary times, the value of the assets may increase and the book value of assets (original cost less depreciation to date) is not likely to agree with the current value of assets.

It is most unlikely that the £4,000 mentioned in the statement represents the decrease in value of the plant and machinery.

7 (a) If obsolescence is excluded from the definition of depreciation, the following description may be used:

Depreciation is the deterioration in fixed assets arising from use and the effluxion of time.

(b) Obsolescence is the loss of value of a fixed asset through technical and market changes. This loss may be owing to improved machinery coming onto the market which renders the older equipment uneconomic or uncompetitive. It can also arise where demand drops or ends for the product manufactured from the equipment.

It is usual, where possible, to include obsolescence in depreciation and the provision for depreciation in the accounts of the business may be calculated by the following methods:

(i) *The straight-line method*

In this method, the annual provision for depreciation is calculated as follows:

$$\frac{\text{Cost of asset } - \text{ Residual value}}{\text{Expected life}}$$

Given the cost of the asset as £5,000, residual value 'nil' and the expected life of the asset 5 years, the annual provision for depreciation would be:

$$\frac{£5,000}{5} = £1,000 \text{ per year}$$

At the end of the five years the book value of the asset will be nil (£5,000 original cost less £5,000 accumulated depreciation).

(ii) *The reducing balance method*

In this method, a fixed percentage is written off the reducing book value of the asset each year. The formula for the calculation of this percentage is:

$$i = 100 - 100 \sqrt[n]{\dfrac{\text{Residual value}}{\text{Cost of asset}}}$$

Assuming the cost of the asset is £5,000 and the residual value £840 at the end of year 5, the percentage is:

$$i = 100 - 100 \sqrt[5]{\dfrac{\text{£840}}{\text{£5,000}}}$$

$$i = 100 - 100 \sqrt[5]{0.168}$$

$$i = 100 - 100\,(0.7)$$

$$i = 30\%$$

The provision for depreciation for each year is calculated as follows:

Year	Asset book value at beginning of year £	Provision for depreciation £	Asset book value end of year £
1	5,000	1,500 (30% of £5,000)	3,500
2	3,500	1,050 (30% of £3,500)	2,450
3	2,450	735 (30% of £2,450)	1,715
4	1,715	515 (30% of £1,715)	1,200
5	1,200	360 (30% of £1,200)	840

Two methods where funds are provided at the end of the anticipated life of the asset by the setting aside of the provisions for depreciation are:

(i) *The sinking fund method*

In this method, if the depreciation charge is invested at 10% and subsequent depreciation provisions plus interest received are invested at 10%, the investment value at the end of the life of the asset is expected to be the original cost of the asset. For this illustration, taxation and investment charges and market price fluctuations have been ignored, and the asset at an original cost of £5,000 is assumed to have a five-year life with a residual value of nil. The annual provision for depreciation is calculated as follows:

$$\frac{\text{Cost of asset}}{\substack{\text{Reference to Table 3, Appendix B} \\ \text{in the main text where n = 5 and} \\ i\ =\ 10\%}} = \frac{£5,000}{6.105} = £819 \text{ per year}$$

The £5,000 at the end of five years is calculated as follows:

Year	Annual provision for depreciation £	Interest received at 10% of the previous end of year balance				Total invest- ment £
		Year 2 £	Year 3 £	Year 4 £	Year 5 £	
1	819	–	–	–	–	819
2	819	82	–	–	–	901
3	819	82	90	–	–	991
4	819	82	90	99	–	1,090
5	819	82	90	99	109	1,199
						5,000

(ii) *The endowment policy method*
To secure £5,000 at the end of 5 years in this method, an insurance company is approached to issue an endowment policy maturing in five years time at a value of £5,000. The annual premium is the annual provision for depreciation.

8 (a) The plant and machinery account for this asset would be debtied with £15,000. The accumulated depreciation account for this asset at the end of year 5 would be credited with £5,000.

On the basis of a 10-year life, the depreciation per year is £1,500 and the accumulated depreciation to the end of year 5 should be £7,500 (5 × £1,500).

The adjustment required would be:
(i) Debit 'Adjustment to depreciation for previous years' account with £2,500
(ii) Credit 'Accumulated depreciation account – plant and machinery' with £2,500.

(b)   The office equipment account for this asset would be debited with
£500.   The accumulated depreciation account for this asset would be
credited with £400.
    The adjustment required would be:
  (i)   Debit 'Loss on sale of fixed assets' account with £50
 (ii)   Debit the purchaser's account with £50
(iii)   Debit 'Accumulated depreciation account – office equipment' with
        £400
(iv)   Credit 'office equipment' account with £500.

9   (a)   Reference is made to the depreciation policies quoted in the case
as follows:

Policy 1
Agreed. The earlier disposal may arise because of obsolescence owing to
changed technology and it would be an unfair charge against current production. There is the point that it could be argued that product costs were
understated in earlier periods but whether any adjustments are worth while
to earlier cost records is debatable.
Policy 2
Agreed. If the amount of the write-off is significant this could have an
adverse effect on current costs and this should be avoided since the excess
write-off arises because depreciation in earlier periods was understated.
Policy 3
Agreed for financial accounts purposes. For product costing purposes,
depreciation should continue to be charged in the costing records although
the amount should reflect the revised asset life, i.e., recognise that earlier
charges were higher than they should have been because the asset life was
underestimated.
Policy 4
Not agreed. It is unlikely that no depreciation is taking place because the
asset is not being used. There is depreciation owing to the effluxion of time.
It could be argued that excess depreciation is possible because the lack of
use may be an indication that obsolescence is possible.

(b)   The action I would take regarding the depreciation rate problem
would be:
  (i)   Check the basis on which the Trade Association rates have been
        calculated
 (ii)   Compare these findings with the basis adopted by company engineers
(iii)   Where a difference in the basis is identified reassess the conclusions
        reached and amend the company detail as necessary.

In the case, it is noted that the company is manufacturing a new range of products and using the latest technical equipment. Company engineers may not be aware of reduced asset lives on the new equipment as compared with the plant and machinery used in other parts of the group.

It is also noted that the factors mentioned by the company engineers in their assessment do not include loss owing to the effluxion of time. This should be included in the assessment of depreciation rates.

10   The term 'research and development ocst' includes the following:

(a)   Research cost — the cost of seeking new or improved products, applications of materials or methods

(b)   Development cost — the cost of the process which begins with the implementation of the decision to produce a new or improved product or to employ a new or improved method, and ends with the commencement of formal production of that product or by that method.

Examples of various types of research and development are as follows:

(a)   Fundamental research or basic technological study

(b)   Applied research leading to the development of a new product, process or equipment

(c)   Market research to determine potential demand, quality, price range and related commercial studies

(d)   Development of the product or process into commercial production

(e)   Improvement research involving study of an existing product to improve its design, performance, quality, serviceability, durability or its appearance.

11   To: Industrial Engineer   Date: . . . .
     From: Management Accountant
              Cost Ascertainment and Cost Control Aspects of
                    Research and Development
The following procedure is outlined for your consideration:

Review of submitted projects
It is suggested that research and development proposals are submitted on project sanction forms which may be designed to secure answers to the following questions:

(a)   To what questions is the research to provide the answers?

(b)   What is the value of the information to be obtained and how is it to be applied?

(c)   What are the references to relevant reports or other literature?

(d)   Has any exploratory work been done which may indicate lines along which further investigation may proceed?

(e)   What preliminary ideas have been formed as to the procedure to be followed with the research?

(f)   Are there any customers who would co-operate in experimental work?

Appropriate estimated costs of the research would be included on such a project sanction form and after consideration of the objective of the research work, the timing of research, limits set for particular project research costs, and the probability factor as to the success of the project, a decision would be made.

Cost ascertainment of approved projects
On the basis of approved projects, work would commence and each project would be allotted a project number. This number would be used to identify all relevant costs which would be accumulated and reported to management for control purposes.

Control of research and development projects
Subsequent control of research and development project costs would be facilitated by actual costs being compared with estimates at each significant stage of research according to the agreed research programme. Timing of work done would also be checked against estimates and an assessment made at each significant research stage that the remainder of the research programme is likely to be achieved. Where this is not the case, plans may be reviewed to cover the possibility that it is desirable for the company to close down a particular research project that promises little prospect of achieving its objectives.

Further information
Further information may be supplied should you wish to consider these suggestions in greater detail.

Signed ....

12   Help can be given to the company managers in the following form:

(a)   Information given to indicate the importance of credit control, e.g., if the company net profit percentage is 4% and a bad debt of £400 is incurred, the company has lost its profits on sales to the value of £10,000.

(b)   Taking an active part in fixing selling policies that may affect debt collection, e.g., fixing the maximum acceptable level of bad debts to achieve the sales required.

(c)   Keeping in close touch with sales staff regarding credit limits and specific customer difficulties. The credit policy should be reflected in standard procedure and documentation.

(d) Advice regarding the use of mercantile agencies and taking bad debts insurance.

(e) Providing a prompt invoicing and sales accounting routine.

(f) Regularly inspecting ledger balances and taking action to recover debts promptly. Lists of customer debts may be referenced to action to be taken or taken regarding bad/slow payers.

16 Investment Results

1   The features of a cost reduction programme where drastic action is required to prevent a business going out of existence are:

(a)   The need for speedy action. This has the effect that phased action may take too much time and cost reduction activity may be severe, e.g., extensive redundancy of staff.
(b)   The removal of the less profitable segments of the business. Given management attention they may have growth potential but the business cannot cover the development stages.
(c)   The taking of decisions on the minimum of information. Effort must be concentrated on the main problems.
(d)   The emphasis on liquidity and decisions calculated to improve the available funds that are usually short when a business is in difficulty.
(e)   The co-operation of the key personnel that are likely to respond to the challenge of the situation and make the best possible contribution to the turn-round in the fortunes of the business.

When a business is in a more prosperous position the approach to cost reduction can be less drastic and more positive. For example:

(a)   Phased action is possible and redundancy may be avoided by:
    (i)   Using the labour released for the increased work-load arising from business expansion
    (ii)   Stopping recruitment to allow wastage to match the reductions in the labour force required
(b)   The ascertainment of cost information in sufficient detail to serve as a basis for profit improvement emphasis
(c)   The involvement of all personnel in profit improvement programmes with the initiation of proposals to educate staff to be cost conscious
(d)   Training programmes initiated to enable staff to gain new skills as required by changes that may be necessary

(e)   Incorporating the targets for profit improvement in long-term
        objectives.

2   The management accountant can assist in cost reduction programmes
as follows:

(a)   *Before the cost reduction programme is defined*
Information may be provided regarding areas of thegreatest potential saving,
and product and departmental profitability calculations may be investigated
in greater detail.

(b)   *During the course of a cost reduction programme*
Assessments may be made of proposed savings. Additional information may
be compiled as required, e.g., the financial effects of plant utilisation. Special
cost investigations may be requested, e.g., the effect of idle capacity. The
monitoring of pilot schemes for cost reduction can be useful to assess the
full financial effects of extended application.

(c)   *After a specific cost reduction programme has been applied*
The use and extension of appropriate control measures, e.g., the budgetary
control technique. Where routine control measures are not applied, spot
checks and special cost investigations may be required.

3   Where to place the profit improvement emphasis in the cost sector is
a question answered by cost analysis in terms of total cost, high cost, functional cost and controllable cost.

Total cost
The minimum breakdown of cost should follow the conventional pattern of:
        The cost of raw materials and components
        Direct labour cost
        Factory overhead cost
        Administration cost
        Selling and distribution cost.
        Further subjective analysis may be necessary and the overheads divided
into the fixed, variable and semi-variable cost categories.
        Apart from the need to relate cost initiation to product cost for the
development of the cost reduction programme, cost ascertainment is an
essential tool for the evaluation of cost reduction proposals.
        In costing systems, abnormal costs are not included in product costs.
From the cost reduction point of view they should not be ignored. Such
costs are classified as abnormal because they should not arise under normal
operating conditions but in the average business abnormal items appear each

year. A good example in process industries is waste. An examination of all waste can be a rewarding exercise for cost reduction personnel.

The sources of high costs
To recognise items that account for the highest cost is an important phase in cost reduction analysis. The reason for this is that it is normally easier to obtain a substantial cost saving from such items than obtain an equivalent cost reduction from a low product cost element. This concentration on high costs should not obscure the fact that a few savings of small amount may make a substantial cost reduction in total.

Functional cost analysis
Control of cost is secured by the identification of costs with cost or expense centres. Such a centre represents an activity of the business where responsibility should be clearly defined. To associate cost reduction possibilities with the individual, responsibility centre analysis is necessary and the subjective analysis is developed by the objective analysis of cost.

Controllable cost analysis
All the costs of a responsibility centre may not be influenced by one manager. Cost or expense analysis is the preliminary step to the analysis of functional costs between controllable and uncontrollable classifications. Cost reduction emphasis should be placed on the controllable costs for a particular level of responsibility.

4   (a)   The key factor in this case was the involvement of top management, not only in their support for junior executives but in ensuring that they were personally committed as well as lower levels of management.

In large organisations, the avoidance of personal contact means that people rely to an increasing extent on the exchange of correspondence which increases the origin and flow of paperwork. In the case it was recognised that personal contact must be increased to reduce the paperwork.

Any established organisation has a series of procedures that become fixed for the future unless someone in that organisation reviews the existing methods and procedures to ensure that they can be justifiably continued in th changing environment of the business. Marks and Spencer Ltd made this assessment and decided that many of its systems could be discarded because they were obsolete.

Throughout the profit improvement programme, Marks and Spencer Ltd considered their staff and it will be noted that the benefits of their scheme were shared with the staff and customers. The reduction in prices increased the company's volume of sales considerably increasing profits further form the profit improvement programme.

Many organisations only aim for significant cost reductions when profits are falling and the outlook for the company is poor. It is significant that the Marks and Spencer organisation started their profit improvement programme when their profit and growth record was excellent and the future showed a continuance of their past good performance.

(b)   The same approach could be used in other companies with good staff and adequate overall control mechanisms. Where the standard of manage-ent is poor it might be asking for trouble to remove detailed control procedures.

Marks and Spencer Ltd were fortunate in being able to reduce staff through the normal wastage and thus avoid redundancy. In other companies, redundancy may be required but the Marks and Spencer approach of communicating their intentions clearly to staff could achieve the desired result.

5   (a)   *Improvement of existing designs*
Cost reduction may be achieved in the following areas:
  (i)   Function: removing unnecessary functions; combining functions
 (ii)   Material: products designed to use another material; design modifica-tion to cut wastage
(iii)   Limits: their relaxation in the design
(iv)   Standardisation and simplification: design modification.

(b)   *Cost of variety*
Cost reduction may be obtained by:
  (i)   The periodic examination of uneconomic variety in designs
 (ii)   The modification of designs of products not selling in large quantities to increase their customer appeal and render such products more economic to produce and sell
(iii)   The grouping of similar components and the classification and coding of drawings and specifications so that at the design stage, duplication of work on similar parts is not carried out
(iv)   Standardisation implemented in all related departments, but in the context of this question working with the design and drawing office staff to achieve cost reduction.

(c)   *Use of the technique of value analysis*
At the design stage, this technique is often referred to as value engineering. The term embraces techniques to identify costs unnecessary according to the value of the product to the user.

192

Cost reductions are achieved at the design stage by assessing product cost, function and esteem value of the product to the customer. When these values are assessed, the specification for the product may be redefined to provide the product to the desired standard at reduced cost.

6   (a)   The initial review should be undertaken by:
  (i)   Identifying cost information required to assess the significance and effectiveness of costs in this area of company operation.
 (ii)   The calculation of the costs ascertained as required in (i).
(iii)   The identification of possible comparable information that may be used to interpret the costs ascertained in (ii). The managing director is using past costs as comparable data and while this information may be useful other independent data should be obtained where possible, e.g., inter-firm comparison data. (The access to comparable information may assist with process (i).) The managing director is also using as comparable data the costs of production. This relationship may not be valid. Distribution costs rarely match production cost movements.
(iv)   The comparison of (ii) with (iii) and an attempt made to interpret the differences disclosed as a basis for possible managerial action.
The major aspects that should receive attention include: packing, ware-housing and despatch.

(b)   Within the above aspects, the items requiring investigation include the follows:
Packing
  (i)   Possible standardisation of packing methods and materials
 (ii)   Assessment of functional packing needs and whether these needs can be met at reduced cost
(iii)   Economies that may be secured with bulk packing requirements.
Warehousing
  (i)   Cost of stock-holding
 (ii)   The balance between finished goods stocks and production output and sales
(iii)   Warehouse location. Additional warehouses may reduce despatch costs.
Despatch
  (i)   Transport costs
 (ii)   The use of own transport compared with outside contractors
(iii)   The type of vehicles used and whether they are satisfactory for the purpose intended.

7   The approach that could be adopted would include the following:

(a)   The calculation of the cost of short manufacturing runs and stockhold-ing costs on inflated costs for parts of non-current models. In relation to these costs an assessment of financial inducements that might be given to companies with old machinery to convert to current models. It is possible that if the problem is as significant as suggested, the costs will be high and a good offer could be given to customers to change their machinery which they would be unlikely to refuse.

(b)   If (a) above does not reduce the problem significantly, a separate department may be formed to manufacture the non-current parts. This would have the effect of reducing the dislocation on the production of the regular lines.

(c)   An attempt to simplify the design of replacement parts and reduce costs.

(d)   A further examination of the product range to identify the less econo-mic products and a reassessment of pricing policy to establish realistic price differentials between products or price inducements to consumers to pur-chase the more profitable lines.

The advantages that may be claimed for this approach are as follows:

(a)   Management policy more closely related to the financial effects of managerial action
(b)   The segregation of the main problem with a concentration of effort possible to solve the problem
(c)   An attempt to remove the basic cause of the problem by a realistic assessment of costs and the inducements that may be offered
(d)   A greater attention to variety reduction and its financial and technical implications.

8   New ideas for profit improvement may be generated and encouraged in the following ways:

(a)   An examination of the attributes of a product with a view to their improvement. Value analysis operates on this basis when the attributes of cost, function and esteem value are considered.
(b)   Standardisation and simplification examination. Ideas may emerge to eliminate, modify or combine operations or procedures.
(c)   Check list assessment. Standard questions regarding a product may be asked to produce ideas, e.g.,
        Fuction: Are all the functions essential? Can they be achieved more easily? Can any be incorporated in another component?

194

Material: Can the specification be revised or another material used? Can dimensions be reduced or increased with a less costly material? Limits: Can they be relaxed to ease manufacture or permit an alternative method?

(d)   The use of employee suggestion schemes.

(e)   The incorporation of profit improvement programmes in the budgetary control system through the use of action plans to achieve a particular objective. In preparing such plans new ideas will be sought and assessed.

(f)   Brainstorming sessions where new ideas are sought from groups by restating problems in different ways as a basis for generating ideas.

(g)   A recognition that management is open to suggestions for improvement and willing to change methods if ideas are proved to be of merit.

9   Unnecessary costs can arise when:

(a)   The quality of management is poor

(b)   The sales can be made at a price that gives a good profit that covers general inefficiency

(c)   The company is operating in a prosperous environment and the effort is primarily directed to meet the demand, giving little time to check inefficiency

(d)   Cost information is inadequate.

Unnecessary costs can also arise in an efficient business for the following reasons:

(a)   Technical information on new materials and processes may not be known

(b)   New ideas not sought with sufficient thoroughness and conventional solutions automatically applied

(c)   A Shortage of time may prevent the best solution to a problem being found

(d)   Temporary arrangements becoming a permanent feature

(e)   Action based on assumptions which are subsequently proved to be invalid

(f)   The reluctance to change accepted practice

(g)   The belief that the limitations that formerly prevented a better method or process are still applicable. This may not be the case.

10   The term 'value analysis' embraces techniques to identify costs unnecessary according to the value of the product to the user, and indicating ways of

eliminating unnecessary costs.

The value analysis procedure is concerned with product cost, function and esteem value to the customers. When these values are assessed, the specification for the product may be redefined to provide the product to the desired standards at reduced cost.

The assessment procedure is carried out by a team representing the various phases of the design and production process with an accountant. In session, their job is to co-ordinate their attitude to the product and produce ideas that will secure the desired result: cost reduction. Ideas are usually encouraged by detailed questioning and recognising that unnecessary costs can be incorporated in any product unless a conscious attempt is made to eliminate them. Value analysis is the conscious attempt.

Value analysis is different from work study in the following features:

(a)   Work study tends to concentrate on the work added by possibly inefficient methods of manufacture. Value analysis is concerned with work added by unnecessary design and specification features.
(b)   Work study is usually carried out by work study officers. Value analysis is carried out by adopting the team approach.
(c)   Work study does not assess the value of the product in the same fundamental way as in value analysis.
(d)   Consultants may be used for work study but value analysis makes use of other outside assistance directly related to the product, e.g., the supplier of components for the product.

11   An examination of the company product range may show that this range is too extensive and many of the products uneconomic. The removal of uneconomic products from the range is variety reduction.

Variety reduction is not confined to the product range − it may cover:

(a)   Improved methods of manufacture to the extent that operations are reduced
(b)   The number of materials used may be reduced and, therefore, the value of stocks
(c)   The unification of specifications and designs to use, where possible, one design for a similar product unit
(d)   The use of coding and classification systems to eliminate duplication, e.g., the production of new drawings which could be provided from existing drawings by an efficient retrieval system.

The analysis necessary for variety reduction proposals may prompt more positive action. For example, a contributory factor to uneconomic variety in the product range is the pricing policy adopted by a business. The price differentials between regular lines and fringe products are often inadequate and this may be due to inaccurate cost information. The variety reduction data may prompt a price incentive to customers to buy regular lines which are more profitable to the business.

12　The approach used in this case could be criticised on the following grounds:

(a)　As a company increases in size one man cannot perform the function described for all expenditure.
(b)　Arising from (a), assuming all the necessary information was available to the cost control manager, delays in administration would be inevitable. The signs are now evident as described in the case.
(c)　The responsibility for cost commitment has been removed from line management. Subject to overall control, it is their responsibility to incur expenditure and be accountable for their actions.
(d)　The suggestion regarding the delegation of power to other cost control officers is of doubtful merit. The power should be delegated to the line management and they should be sufficiently cost conscious to act responsibly. The officials in the case may need educating in this task.

　　The good aspects of the system are:

(a)　The awareness that constant attention must be given to cost control
(b)　The most effective cost control is at source
(c)　The action taken is supported by top management
(d)　Good use has been made of a member of the staff with experience and qualities appropriate to the task allotted to him.

　　The action that could be taken to resolve the problem includes:

(a)　The introduction of a budgetary control system
(b)　The submission of budgets by line managers with a clear understanding that they will be responsible for achieving the objectives of the business in their sections of activity at minimum cost
(c)　The profit improvement procedure incorporated in the assessment phase of submitted budgets for approval
(d)　The control of actual performance against plans approved
(e)　The possible appointment of the cost control manager to the post of budget controller.

17 Standard Costing (1)—Basic Procedure and Primary Variance Analysis

1   To: Managing Director   Date . . . .
        Domestic Electrics Ltd
    From: Consultant
           Proposed Installation of a Standard Costing System
Standard costing is a useful technique to support the managerial control
process and this report answers your queries:

(i)   *Steps involved in the installation of a standard costing system*
(a)   The realistic assessment of overall measures of performance within
      which the standard costing system can be developed and appropriate
      variance analysis planned
(b)   A consideration of the length of time the standards will be in use
(c)   A decision on the most desirable standard of attainment
(d)   The choice of the appropriate level of activity
(e)   The use of available techniques to ensure standard costs are reliable
      measures of performance
(f)   The preparation of standard cost cards
(g)   The documentary support planned for operating the system
(h)   Integration of the standard costing system into the accounting system
      for the business
(i)   Integration of standard costing reporting into the reporting system
      of the business.

(ii) *Benefits expected to accrue from installing a system of standard costing*
(a)   The principle of 'management by exception' can be followed in the
      reporting system
(b)   The fixing of standards will force attention on quantities and rates
      applicable to the elements of cost and improvements in procedure can
      usually be secured
(c)   The standard costs will be valuable for policy formation and profit
      planning. This point is particularly relevant to pricing policies

198

(d)   The standards are a practical measure of efficiency — one of the essential elements of the control process of the business

(e)   Economy in cost accounting procedures may result from the use of a standard costing system.

Further details on the points briefly mentioned in this report will be supplied on request.

Signed. . . . .

2   (a)   A standard cost is a predetermined figure of what the cost should be in a period. The procedure that uses this data as a basis for assisting the management in controlling the business is known as standard costing.

Standard costing operates within the same managerial control cycle as budgetary control and if the techniques of budgetary control and standard costing are compared it may be noted that each technique is based on:

(i)   A predetermined standard of performance — in budgetary control it is called the budget; in standard costing, the standard

(ii)   A comparison of actual performance with the standard of performance

(iii) An analysis of variances by cause to point the way to action that may be taken by managers to improve performance.

The two techniques are interrelated but not interdependent. Standard costing operates in the business context of standardised operations, being concerned with detail, particularly on the production side of the organisation. By comparison, budgetary control is concerned with overall operation of the undertaking and may be applied to any type of business organisation. The overall information that forms the basis of a standard costing system is best provided by budgetary control because greater reliance can be placed on the relative accuracy of this information.

(b)   The forms of standard that are applicable to the business situation are as follows:

(i)   A material model or type to be imitated, e.g., standard pattern, standard product, standard finish or standard material

(ii)   A detailed description of the characteristics of such a model, e.g., a product specification or chemical formula

(iii) The description of a method, e.g., of manufacture, of handling, of installation or of checking

(iv)   A statement of standard condition, e.g., stock level, layout or physical conditions

(v)   A statement of expected achievement or objective, e.g., a budget, production programme or standard cost (all expressed in money or other quantities)

(vi) Statements of standard organisation, e.g., organisation structure charts, job descriptions and departmental establishments.

(c) Clerical work may be reduced when a standard costing system is introduced into a company by taking advantage of repetitive detail. For example, pre-printed job instructions can be prepared with the standard information and if stock is maintained at standard cost, issues or stock values can be ascertained by knowing quantity information because the standard cost is readily available to value this quantity data. If other methods of stock pricing are used, stores ledgers and material requisitions will need to be maintained in value as well as units for each stock movement because prices can change. This procedure is not a complete saving of clerical work since documentation for non-standard activities will need to be provided at additional cost.

Other qualifications on the possible saving of costs should be made:

(i) If the business is not already operating a detailed control procedure, when standard costing is introduced any additional procedure must involve additional clerical cost.

(ii) Where there are a large variety of processes all the usual variances may occur at each stage of the process. The necessary calculations to give management the background information they require to interpret and use the overall variances intelligently can be a time-consuming task. In this situation, all primary control documents need to bear at least the actual and standard data – an increase in clerical work over historical recording.

3   The basis of valuation of each product must be decided and assuming factory cost is adopted, the information required per unit of product would be as follows:

	£
Direct material cost	x
Direct labour cost	x
Factory overhead cost	x
Factory cost	x

For this information to be calculated, reference would be made to the technical specification for the product which provides full information on quantities and times and qualities and grades for each element of cost. Standard cost prices and rates developed from the budget would complete the standard factory cost for each element as follows:

(a)   Direct material cost:

Quantity of each type of material required per unit of product allowing for standard material loss	×	Price that should be paid for each unit of material specified

(b)   Direct labour cost:

Time that should be taken by each type of labour to produce each unit of product analysed by operations and departments	×	The hourly rate of pay that should be paid for each type of labour specified

(c)   Factory overhead cost:

The usage factor for the overhead facilities that should be used in the manufacture of the unit of product	×	The usage rate for each facility obtained from the budget

(The usage factors, for example, may be direct labour hours or machine hours.)

4   The two stages at which the material price variance may be segregated are: (i) at the time of purchase of the material; or (ii) at the time of issue of the material to production.

Description of the procedure – stage (i)
The raw materials stock account will be debited with stock to the value of £1,000 and the cost to production will be the same amount eliminating the input value to the stock account.

As the supplier will be paid £1,020 for the material purchased, the excess £20 will be debited to a material price variance account representing an unfavourable variance.

Description of the procedure – stage (ii)
The raw materials stock account will be debited with stock to the value of £1,020 and the cost to production will be the standard cost of £1,000. As this use of the material removes the material from store and only £1,000 has been credited to the stock account, the remaining £20 must also be credited with a corresponding debit to a material price variance account representing an unfavourable variance.

5   The causes underlying the following variances are as follows:

(a)   *Material price variance*
Change in market price
Emergency purchases where the buyer is unable to use the normal

supplier
Trade discounts not obtained
Special purchases at favourable prices.

(b) *Material usage variance*
Poor quality materials
Change in product or production methods
Careless workmanship
Machinery in need of repair
Savings in materials.

(c) *Labour rate variance*
Using employees with the wrong classification and wage rate for jobs
Paying above or below standard rates during seasonal or emergency operations
New labour not paid established standard rates.

(d) *Labour efficiency variance*
Machine shut-down for adjustment
Inefficiency of inexperienced employee
Extra processing of poor quality material
Delay in receiving material from stock
Sub-standard working conditions.

(e) *Overhead expenditure variance*
Excess or under-spending in the main classifications of expense, usually the natural divisions of costs, e.g., electricity, stationery, repairs, etc.

(f) *Overhead capacity variance*
Lack of sales orders
Shortages of resources such as materials
Labour problems
Machine breakdown
Use of improved methods or equipment
Good supervision
Goodworkmanship.

(g) *Overhead efficiency variance*
As the labour efficiency variance.

6 (a) (Actual price − standard price) x actual quantity =
= material price variance

Material	£	£	grams	£	
P	1.40	1	75	30	(unfavourable)
Q	1.80	2	170	34	(favourable)
				4	(favourable)

(b) (actual quantity − standard quantity for actual production) x
x standard price = material usage variance

Material	grams	grams		£	£	
P	75	80	(40x2)	1	5	(favourable)
Q	170	160	(40x4)	2	20	(unfavourable)
					15	(unfavourable)

(c) Actual material cost − standard material cost for actual production =
= material total cost variance

Material	£		£		£	
P	105	(75x£1.40)	80	(80x£1)	25	(unfavourable)
Q	306	(170x£1.80)	320	(160x£2)	14	(favourable)
	411		400		11	(unfavourable)

(d) (actual rate − standard rate) x actual hours = labour rate variance

Type of labour	£	£	hours	£	
Skilled	1.60	1.50	190	19	(unfavourable)
Unskilled	0.90	0.80	450	45	(unfavourable)
				64	(unfavourable)

(e) (actual hours − standard hours for actual production) x standard rate =
= labour efficiency variance

Type of labour	hours	hours	£	£	
Skilled	190	200	1.50	15	(favourable)
		(40x5)			
Unskilled	450	400	0.80	40	(unfavourable)
		(40x10)			
				25	(unfavourable)

(f) Actual labour cost − standard labour cost for actual production =
                         = labour total cost variance

Type of labour	£	£	£	
Skilled	304	300	4	(unfavourable)
	(190x£1.60)	(200x£1.50)		
Unskilled	405	320	85	(unfavourable)
	(450x£0.90)	(400x£0.80)		
	709	620	89	(unfavourable)

7   (a)   The common factor to the variances is the budgeted cost and
when the actual activity level varies from the budgeted level, this amount
should be 'flexed' to the actual level of activity to produce the budgeted cost
allowance. Both variances should be calculated using the budgeted cost
allowance as shown in answer (b)(ii).

(b)   (i)   Variances on a fixed budget basis:
Actual cost − standard cost for actual production = total overhead
                                          cost variance
£23,000 − £20,000 (1,000 x 5 x (£22,000/5,500)) =
                                        = £3,000   (unfavourable)

Actual cost − budgeted cost = expenditure variance
£23,000 − £2,000   = £1,000   (unfavourable)

(Capacity hours − actual hours) Overhead standard rate per hour =
                          = capacity variance
(5,500 − 5,200) £4   = £1,200   (unfavourable)

(Actual hours − standard hours for actual production) Overhead
              standard rate per hour = efficiency variance
(5,200 − 5,000) £4   = £800   (unfavourable)

(ii)   Variances on a flexible budgeted basis:
Actual cost − standard cost for actual production = total overhead
                                          cost variance
£23,000 − £20,000   = £3,000   (unfavourable)

Actual cost − budgeted cost allowance = expenditure variance
£23,000 − £21,400   = £1,600   (unfavourable)

(Capacity hours − actual hours) Fixed overhead standard rate per hour
= Capacity variance

(5,500 − 5,200) £2   = £600   (unfavourable)

(Actual hours − standard hours for actual production) Overhead standard rate per hour = efficiency variance

(5,200 − 5,000) £4   = £800   (unfavourable)

For every increased in potential hours of 500 there is an increase in budgeted cost of £1,000. Apparently this change is due to variable overhead which gives the variable overhead cost rate of £2 per hour.

The total overhead cost rate is £4 per hour (£22,000/5,500). Therefore, the fixed overhead cost rate is £2 per hour.

	£
Fixed cost: 5,500 hours x £2 per hour =	11,000
Variable cost: 5,200 hours x £2 per hour =	10,400
Budgeted cost allowance	21,400

8   (a)
(i)   For each change in the activity level of 4,000 hours there is a change in the budgeted overhead allowance of £8,000. Apparently, this change is due to variable overhead, therefore, the variable overhead rate per hour is £2.

     Applying the variable overhead rate to each activity level, the fixed overhead is £4,000 (e.g. 7,000 x £2 = £14,000. £18,000 − £14,000 = £4,000).

(ii)   Let x = variable cost, y = activity level required, then

$$\frac{£4,000 + x}{y} = £2.50$$

but x = £2y
by substitution:

$$\frac{£4,000 + £2y}{y} = £2.50$$

$$0.5y = £4,000$$
$$y = 8,000 \text{ hours}$$

(b)   (i)   (Capacity hours − actual hours) Fixed overhead standard rate per hour = capacity variance

(8,000 − 10,000) £0.50   = £1,000   (favourable)

(ii) (Actual cost − budgeted cost allowance) = expenditure variance
£22,000 − 10,000 × £2.00 = £20,000
           8,000 × £0.50 = £ 4,000
                              £24,000   = £2,000 (favourable)

9   The graph required (Figure 17.1):

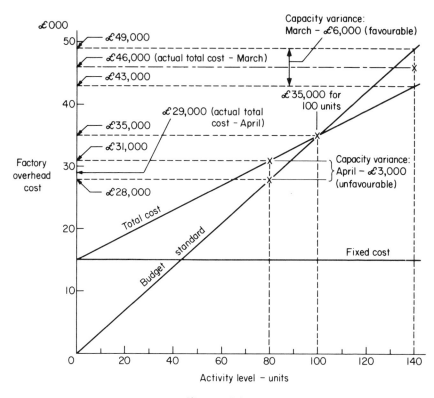

Figure 17.1

The monthly capacity variances on a flexible budget basis may be ascertained from the graph:

    March: £49,000 − £43,000 = £6,000 (favourable)
    April: £31,000 − £28,000 = £3,000 (unfavourable)

Other variances ascertainable from the graph are:

(a) Expenditure variances on a flexible budget basis:

      March: £46,000 – £43,000 = £3,000 (unfavourable)

      April: £29,000 – £31,000 = £2,000 (favourable)

(b) Capacity variances on a fixed budget basis:

      March: £49,000 – £35,000 = £14,000 (favourable)

      April: £28,000 – £35,000 = £7,000 (unfavourable)

(c) Expenditure variances on a fixed budget basis:

      March: £46,000 – £35,000 = £11,000 (unfavourable)

      April: £29,000 – £35,000 = £6,000 (favourable)

(d) Total overhead cost variances:

      March: £46,000 – £49,000 = £3,000 (favourable)

      April: £29,000 – £28,000 = £1,000 (unfavourable)

10

Cost Statement

Week ended ....

	Favourable variance £	Unfavourable variance £	£
Standard cost for actual production			16,650
Add net variance:			
Material price variance		1,808	
Material usage variance		40	
Labour rate variance		168	
Labour efficiency variance	300		
Factory overhead			
Variable:			
Expenditure		25	
Efficiency	250		
Fixed:			
Expenditure		10	
Capacity		200	
Efficiency	100		
	650	2,251	1,601
Actual cost			18,251

Workings

  (i) Standard cost for actual production: 900 x £18.50 = £16,650

  (ii) Material price variance:

     (Actual price – standard price) actual quantity = variance

     £1.20   –   £1   9,040   = £1,808 (unfavourable)

  (iii) Material usage variance:

     (Actual quantity – standard quantity for actual production)

                   Standard price = variance

     9,040 – 9,000 (900 x 10) £1   = £40 (unfavourable)

  (iv) Labour rate variance:

     (actual rate – standard rate) actual hours = variance

     £0.52   £0.50   8,400   = £168 (unfavourable)

  (v) Labour efficiency variance:

     (Actual hours – standard hours for actual production) standard rate

                      = variance

     8,400 – 9,000 (900 x 10) £0.50   = £300 (favourable)

  (vi) Variable expenditure variance:

     (Actual cost – budgeted cost allowance) = variance

     £2,025 – £2,000 (4,000 x £0.50)   = £25 (unfavourable)

  (vii) Variable efficiency variance:

     (Actual hours – standard hours for actual production) variable factory

              overhead standard rate per hour = variance

     4,000 – 4,500 (900 x 5) £0.50   = £250 (favourable)

  (viii) Fixed expenditure variance:

     (Actual cost – budgeted cost) = variance

     £1,010 – £1,000 (1,000 x £1)   = £10 (unfavourable)

  (ix) Fixed capacity variance:

     (Capacity hours – actual hours) fixed factory overhead standard rate

                per hour = variance

     5,000 (1,000 x 5) – 4,000 x £0.20 (£1 ÷ 5)   = £200 (unfavourable)

  (x) Fixed efficiency variance:

     (Actual hours – standard hours for actual production) fixed factory

              overhead standard rate per hour = variance

     (4,000 – 4,500) £0.20   = £100 (favourable)

  (xi) Actual cost:

		£
Labour		4,368
Material		10,848
Overhead:	Variable	2,025
	Fixed	1,010
		18,251

Standard Cost Variance Report
Month ended ....

	Unfav-ourable variance £	Favour-able variance £	£	Product 1, £	Product 2, £	Product 3, £
Standard cost of production			29,300	13,750	8,200	7,350
Direct material price	1,000					
Direct material usage	400					
Direct labour rate	20					
Direct labour efficiency		50		25	50	(25)
Factory overhead:						
Variable:						
Expenditure		5				
Efficiency		20		10	20	(10)
Fixed:						
Expenditure		50				
Capacity	135			(30)	(20)	(85)
Efficiency		10		5	10	(5)
	1,555	135	1,420			
Actual cost			30,720			

Workings

(i) Standard cost of production:

		£
Product 1	2,500 x £5.50 =	13,750
Product 2	2,000 x £4.10 =	8,200
Product 3	1,500 x £4.90 =	7,350
		29,300

(ii) Direct material price variance on the basis of purchases:

(Actual price x actual quantity) − (standard price x actual quantity)
= variance

Material	£	£		£	
A	10,719	10,000			
		(100,000×£0.1)		719	(unfavourable)
B	7,971	7,500			
		(300,000×£0.025)		471	(unfavourable)
C	3,560	3,750			
		(100,000×£0.0375)		190	(favourable)
	22,250	21,250		1,000	(unfavourable)

(iii) Direct material usage variance:

(Actual quantity − standard quantity for actual production) standard
price = variance

Material	grams	grams	£	£	
A	75,000	70,500	0.1	450	(unfavourable)
B	267,560	271,000	0.025	86	(favourable)
C	98,960	98,000	0.0375	36	(unfavourable)
				400	(unfavourable)

Standard quantity for actual production:

Product	Material A	Material B	Material C
	grams	grams	grams
1	37,500	125,000	50,000
	(2,500×15)	(2,500×50)	(2,500×20)
2	−	128,000	48,000
		(2,000×64)	(2,000×24)
3	33,000	18,000	−
	(1,500×22)	(1,500×12)	
	70,500	271,000	98,000

(iv) Direct labour rate variance:

(Actual rate x actual hours) − (standard rate x actual hours) = variance

Product			£		
1		6,200 x £0.50 =	3,100		
2	£7,345	3,900 x £0.50 =	1,950		
3		4,550 x £0.50 =	2,275		
			7,325	£20	(unfavourable)

(v) Direct labour efficiency variance:
(Actual hours x standard rate) – (standard hours x standard rate)
                              = variance

Product	£	£		£	
1	3,100	3,125	(2,500x2½x£0.50)	25	(favourable)
2	1,950	2,000	(2,000x2x£0.50)	50	(favourable)
3	2,275	2,250	(1,500x3x£0.50)	25	(unfavourable)
	7,325	7,375		50	(favourable)

(vi) Variable overhead expenditure variance:
(Actual cost – budgeted cost allowance) = variance

Product		£	
1		1,240	(6,200x£0.20)
2	£2,925	780	(3,900x£0.20)
3		910	(4,550x£0.20)
		2,930	£5 (favourable)

(vii) Variable overhead efficiency variance:
(Actual hours – standard hours for actual production) variable factory
                              overhead rate per hour = variance

Product				£	£	
1	6,200	6,250	(2,500 x 2½)	0.20	10	(favourable)
2	3,900	4,000	(2,000 x 2)	0.20	20	(favourable)
3	4,550	4,500	(1,500 x 3)	0.20	10	(unfavourable)
					20	(favourable)

(viii) Fixed overhead expenditure variance:
Actual cost – budgeted cost = variance

Product		£	
1		650	(2,600 x £0.25)
2	£1,550	410	(2,050 x £0.20)
3		540	(1,800 x £0.30)
		1,600	£50 (favourable)

(ix) Fixed overhead capacity variance:
(Capacity hours – actual hours) fixed factory overhead standard rate
                              per hour = variance

211

Product		£	£	
1	6,500 (2,600 x 2½)	6,200	0.10	30 (unfavourable)
2	4,100 (2,050 x 2)	3,900	0.10	20 (unfavourable)
3	5,400 (1,800 x 3)	4,550	0.10	85 (unfavourable)
				135 (unfavourable)

(x) Fixed overhead efficiency variance:

(Actual hours − standard hours for actual production) fixed factory overhead standard rate per hour = variance

Product			£	£	
1	6,200	6,250	0.10	5	(favourable)
2	3,900	4,000	0.10	10	(favourable)
3	4,550	4,500	0.10	5	(unfavourable)
				10	(favourable)

(xi) Actual cost:

		£	£
Direct material:	A	10,719	
	B	7,971	
	C	3,560	22,250
Direct labour			7,345
Factory overhead:	Fixed	1,550	
	Variable	2,925	4,475
			34,070

Stock increase adjustment:

	Material A grams	Material B grams	Material C grams	
Purchases	100,000	300,000	100,000	
Issues	75,000	267,560	98,960	
	25,000	32,440	1,040	
	x £0.1	x £0.025	x £0.0375	
	= £2,500	= £811	= £39	3,350
			=	
				30,720

12　(a)　The system as described in the case was not meeting the basic concept of cost control intended in the company because the system was essentially historical in application, rather than concentrating wherever possible on preventive action. Where this was not possible, corrective action should have been taken immediately an excess occurred. This was not taking place in the case.

What was taking place was a 'cover up' operation on differences by the reporting of net variances and summarised differences. The averaging process, as described in the case, was also an unsatisfactory cost control measure.

(b)　The standards should represent what the costs should be. The action recommended would be:

(i)　Make the first objective the accurate and fast reporting of detailed information about potential or actual excesses to the people who should take corrective action, leaving the accounting routine to follow

(ii)　Make the later accounting objective to summarise the overall effect for these managers, thus confirming what they already know, but at the same time conveying to top management sufficient detail to show how effective the efforts at departmental level were proving to be

(iii)　Make the estimator the arbiter of what the cost should be and measure everything against that estimate.

(c)　The difficulties expected in applying these recommendations include the following:

(i)　The inadequacies in the knowledge of the estimators to shoulder the increased responsibilities

(ii)　The problem of unifying the preparation and presentation of estimates

(iii)　A general reluctance to change procedures.

(d)　I would attempt to overcome the difficulties expected by ensuring the following:

(i)　Greater management involvement. Top management would need to give effective support to the system to meet difficulty (c)(iii)

(ii)　A greater knowledge on the part of estimators with indirect benefits to the company from the increased work study and training programmes necessary to meet difficulty (c)(i)

(iii)　A simplification in procedure as a result of using the method planning sheet as a basis for all estimates to meet difficulty (c)(ii)

(iv)　In making the detailed estimate for a new product, method study can determine methods; work study can determine layout and appropriate times; and the estimator act as a check on these stages as well as compile the works cost to build up to the selling price (the sales estimate).

When the order is received, revised estimates could be prepared as follows:

The planned estimate – to incorporate revised estimates of cost as material prices or labour and overheads have changed

The current estimate – to incorporate new costs as the job is produced.

These estimates would bring the following benefits:

(a) If the planned estimate exceeds the sales estimate the manager(s) concerned can be immediately informed so that the possibilities of reducing costs can be explored, e.g., the use of different methods

(b) The current estimate can be used as an up-to-date standard to measure actual performance.

18 Standard Costing (2)—Further Variance Analysis

1   A cost variance is the difference between the actual cost for a given period and the standard or budgeted comparable cost for that same period.

The total cost variance for production may be analysed as overleaf (Figure 18.1).

The main divisions are fixed and variable cost variances and the direct material and direct labour cost variances are in the variable category.

Many variances are the net result of a number of calculations which could lead to further analysis. For example, the material variances by type of material and the labour variances by type of labour. The products produced is a natural division for output differences such as efficiency variances.

Any cause identified in the variance analysis that warrants managerial attention should be brought to their attention by separate analysis.

2   Standard cost variance analysis is a mathematical process and the arithmetical calculations are precise, but this procedure may hide a lack of precision in the preparation of the standards for the following reasons:

(a)   Standard costs are predetermined and the future course of events may be very different from those envisaged when the standards were set.

(b)   The basis on which the standards are calculated may vary and generous levels of attainment may hide the inefficiencies that variance analysis is supposed to disclose to management.

(c)   Standards are not necessarily analysed by their controllable and uncontrollable elements.

(d)   There may be difficulties in the evaluation of performance owing to the factors for assessment of the company incorporated in the standard varying over time.

(e)   Poor performance may be outside a band of acceptable performance.

215

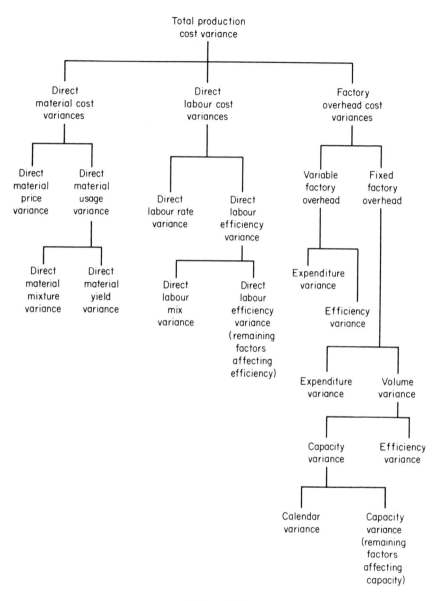

Figure 18.1

Not every variance from a specific standard is unsatisfactory yet a standard cost is generally established to indicate what the cost should be.

Given the basic data, detailed variance analysis can stem from the arithmetical analysis of primary variances and the breakdown of an overall figure into minor elements can produce insignificant figures which are of no value to management.

3   Direct material price variance:
(Actual price − standard price) actual quantity = variance

Material	£	£	Tonnes	£	
X	210	200	200	2,000	(unfavourable)
Y	85	100	50	750	(favourable)
				1,250	

Direct material mixture variance:
(Actual quantities of material inputs in standard proportions − actual quantities of material inputs in actual proportions) standard price per unit of material = variance

Material	Tonnes	Tonnes	£	£	
X	175				
	(70%)	200	200	5,000	(unfavourable)
Y	75				
	(30%)	50	100	2,500	(favourable)
	250	250		2,500	(unfavourable)

Direct material yield variance:
(Actual quantities of material inputs in standard proportions − actual material outputs grossed up to allow for standard wastage in standard proportions) standard price per unit of material = variance

Material	Tonnes	Tonnes	£	£	
X	175	140			
		(70%)	200	7,000	(unfavourable)
Y	75	60			
		(30%)	100	1,500	(unfavourable)
	250	200		8,500	(unfavourable)

$$192 + (4/96) \times 192 = 200 \text{ tonnes}$$

Direct material cost variance:
Actual cost − standard cost for actual production = variance

Material	£	£	
X	42,000	28,000	
	(200 x £210)	(140 x £200)	
Y	4,250	6,000	
	(50 x £85)	(60 x £100)	
	46,250	34,000	£12,250 (unfavourable)

4   *Labour Cost Variances*
                  Week ended ....

	£	
Labour rate variance	16.20	(favourable)
Labour mix variance	34.20	(unfavourable)
Labour efficiency variance	48.00	(favourable)
	30.00	(favourable)

Labour rate variance:
(Actual rate x actual hours) – (standard rate x actual hours) = variance

Type of labour		£		£
Skilled		0.75	x 468 =	351
Semi-skilled }	£450	0.50	x 144 =	72
Unskilled		0.40	x 108 =	43.2
		720		466.2
				16.2 (favourable)

Actual hours for each type of labour:
       Hours per worker = (720/20) = 36

			hours
Skilled	13 x 36 =		468
Semi-skilled	4 x 36 =		144
Unskilled	3 x 36 =		108
			720

Labour mix variance:
(Actual hours of labour employed at standard mix − actual hours of of
labour employed at actual mix) standard labour rate = variance

Type of labour			£	£	
Skilled	360	468	0.75	81	(unfavourable)
Semi-skilled	180	144	0.50	18	(favourable)
Unskilled	180	108	0.40	28.8	(favourable)
	720	720		34.2	(unfavourable)

Labour efficiency variance:
(Standard hours of labour planned to be employed at standard mix −
actual hours of labour employed at standard mix) standard labour rate
= variance

Type of labour			£	£	
Skilled	400				
	(40x10)	360	0.75	30	(favourable)
Semi-skilled	200				
	(40x5)	180	0.50	10	(favourable)
Unskilled	200				
	(40x5)	180	0.40	8	(favourable)
	800	720		48	(favourable)

5   (a)   Standard cost of producing 7,000 units:
Use of ordinary employees: 7,000 x (£1 ÷ 4) = 1,750
Use of temporary employees:
    7,000 x (£0.80 ÷ 4) = 1,400

Variance due to the policy of using
temporaries as against using ordinary staff   350 (favourable)

(b)   Variance due to inefficiency of the temporaries:
(Standard hours for work produced − actual hours) standard rate per
                   hour = variance
    1,750 (7,000 ÷ 4) − 2,000 x £0.80   £200 (unfavourable)

(c)   Variance due to differences in wage rates paid to temporaries:
(Standard rate of pay − actual rate of pay) actual hours = variance
£0.80 − £1.20 x 2,000 =   £800 (unfavourable)

(d)   Amount to be charged in respect of work done by temporaries:
Number of units x standard rate per unit for temporaries
7,000 x £0.20 =   £1,400

6   Method A shows the factory overhead variances calculated on the
basis of:
  (i)   A fixed budget in operation
  (ii) The difference in time taken and the time that should have been
        taken to do the work representing an efficiency factor concerned
        with manufacturing facilities that should be isolated in the variance
        analysis.
        Method B shows the factory overhead efficiency variance calculated
in the same way as Method A but a flexible budget is in operation which has
the effect of altering the expenditure variance to the difference between
actual factory overhead cost and the budgeted cost allowance. The capacity
variance is also altered recognising that this variance occurs with fixed
factory overhead only.
        Method C also assumes a flexible budget but the calculations are made
on the basis that the efficiency factor on variable factory overhead should be
recognised in the expenditure variance.
        Method D similarly assumes a flexible budget and a similar expenditure
variance is calculated as in Method B. The remainder of the factory overhead
variance is analysed on the basis that the difference in time taken and the
time that should have been taken to do the work indicates an efficiency
factor concerned with factory facilities represented by variable factory
overhead only.
        Of the methods described, Method A is not recommended because the
use of the fixed budget can give misleading information to management when
the actual level of activity is different from that used in the original budget.
        Method D is a compromise solution on the difference of opinion
regarding the use of Methods B and C. This solution attempts to isolate
the efficiency variation from the expenditure variation.
        Method B has the advantage over Method C that differences between
actual and budgeted expenditure may be more easily explained. The close
resemblance between the use of labour time and factory facilities cost is
recognised by the calculation of the factory overhead efficiency variance.
Not all authorities would agree with the need for this efficiency calculation
maintaining that the calculation is not worth the effort.

7   Method A shows the sales variances calculated on the basis of value
and Method B on the basis of units. In each case, the sales price variance

is the same but the sales mix variance is different and this varied approach may be illustrated by the following formulae:

Sales mix variance on the basis of value:
(Actual sales quantities x standard prices at budgeted sales value mix)
− (actual sales quantities x standard prices at actual mix) x standard profit %

Sales mix variance on the basis of units:
(Actual quantities of products sold at standard mix − actual quantities of products sold at actual mix) x standard profit per unit of sale

The quantity variances are residual values representing sales volume differences other than sales mix. Given different mix calculations, these variances must also be different as shown in the question.

Unless the units sold are homogeneous, the results of the calculations on a units basis can be misleading because a common measure is not being used. Where the units sold are heterogeneous, the common measure is available in the sales values − the factor used in the sales value approach.

8   Each product has contributed to the increase or decrease in budgeted profit as follows:

A.B. Co. Ltd
Profit Statement − month ended 31st January 19 ....

	Product A	Product B	Product C	Total
	£	£	£	£
Budgeted profit	2,500	600	1,000	4,100
Actual profit	1,500	1,350	550	3,400
Increase/(decrease) in budgeted profit	(1,000)	750	(450)	(700)

Workings

	Product A	Product B	Product C
Budgeted profit	2,500 x £1	1,200 x £0.50	2,000 x £0.50
	= £2,500	= £600	= £1,000
Actual profit	£5,500 −	£4,050 −	£4,950 −
	(2000x£2)	(1,800x£1.50)	(2,200x£2)
	= £1,500	= £1,350	= £550

Sales variance calculations are as follows:

Sales price variance:

(Actual selling price − standard selling price) x actual quantity =

Product	£	£	grams	£	variance
A	2.75	3.00	2,000	500	(unfavourable)
B	2.25	2.00	1,800	450	(favourable)
C	2.25	2.50	2,200	550	(unfavourable)
				600	(unfavourable)

Sales mix variance:

(Actual sales quantities x standard prices at standard mix) − (actual sales quantities x standard prices at actual mix) x standard profit % =

Product	£	£	%	£	variance
A	7,601	6,000	$33\frac{1}{3}$	534	(unfavourable)
	(£7,500 ÷ £14,900 x £15,100)				
B	2,432	3,600	25	292	(favourable)
	(£2,400 ÷ £14,900 x £15,100)				
C	5,067	5,500	20	87	(favourable)
	(£5,000 ÷ £14,900 x £15,100)				
	15,100	15,100		155	(unfavourable)

Workings

Actual sales at standard price:

		£
Product A 2,000 x £3.00 =		6,000
Product B 1,800 x £2.00 =		3,600
Product C 2,200 x £2.50 =		5,500
		15,100

Budgeted sales at standard price:

		£
Product A 2,500 x £3.00 =		7,500
Product B 1,200 x £2.00 =		2,400
Product C 2,000 x £2.50 =		5,000
		14,900

222

Sales quantity variance:
(Budgeted profit − standard profit on actual sales at budgeted mix) = variance

Product	£	£	£	
A	2,500	2,534	34	(favourable)
B	600	608	8	(favourable)
C	1,000	1,013	13	(favourable)
	4,100	4,155	55	(favourable)

Workings

Standard profit % x (actual sales quantities x standard prices at standard mix) = standard profit on actual sales at budgeted mix

Product	%	£	£
A	$33\frac{1}{3}$	7,601	2,534
B	25	2,432	608
C	20	5,067	1,013
			4,155

Proof

	£	
Sales price variance	600	(unfavourable)
Sales mix variance	155	(unfavourable)
Sales quantity variance	55	(favourable)
Total variance for sales	700	(unfavourable)

9   The figures in the question presentations have been calculated as follows:

		Product A	Product B	Total
		£	£	£
(a)	Budgeted sales	100 x £4 = £400	50 x £3 = £150	550
(b)	Standard cost of budgeted sales	100 x £2 = £200	50 x £2 = £100	300
(c)	Actual sales at actual price	50 x £5 = £250	80 x £3 = £240	490
(d)	Standard cost of actual sales	50 x £2 = £100	80 x £2 = £160	260

		Product A £	Product B £	Total £
(e)	Actual sales at standard price	50 x £4 = £200	80 x £3 = £240	440
(f)	Standard profit on actual sales at standard price	50 x £2 = £100	80 x £1 = £80	180
(g)	Standard profit on actual sales	50 x £3 = £150	80 x £1 = £80	230

In Presentation 1 the variances have been calculated as follows:

(Actual selling price − standard selling price) actual quantity = sales price variance

Product	£	£	units	£	
A	5	4	50	50	(favourable)
B	3	3	80	−	
				50	(favourable)

(Actual quantity sold − standard quantity planned to be sold) standard selling price = sales volume variance

Product	units	units	£	£	
A	50	100	4	200	(unfavourable)
B	80	50	3	90	(favourable)
				110	(unfavourable)

In this presentation, the sales volume variance is calculated on the basis of standard selling price and this is not the best form of sales variance information. Management is interested in the profit impact of its sales activities and this information may be given as shown in Presentation 2. In this presentation, the sales price variance is the same but the sales volume variance has been calculated on the basis of standard profit as follows:

(Actual quantity sold − standard quantity planned to be sold) standard profit = sales volume variance

Product	units	units	£	£	
A	50	100	2	100	(unfavourable)
B	80	50	1	30	(favourable)
				70	(unfavourable)

Presentation 2 information may be simplified for statements to management as in Presentation 3 to confine attention to variances arising from actual sales achieved.

10   The relationship between variances is intially not identified by variance analysis using standard terminology. For example, using the case quoted in the question, the use of cheaper material would be disclosed by a favourable material price variance and the lower yield of finished product by an unfavourable yield variance. What is needed is further investigation into underlying causes. This is usually done and the information given to management either by (a) comment on the standard cost variance report, e.g., the favourable material price variance of £x and the unfavourable yield variance of £y is due to the single cause of using cheaper material A for the manufacture of Product M; or (b) the use of a net variance with a title identifying the cause, e.g., production variance due to using cheaper material.

11   *Standard Profit Statement*
                  Four weeks ended ....

			£
Standard profit on actual sales			14,550
Add sales price variance			7,275
	Favour-	*Unfavour-*	21,825
Less net cost variance:	*able*	*able*	
	variances	*variances*	
	£	£	
Material price variance		7,600	
Material usage variance		975	
Labour rate variance		100	
Labour efficiency variance	300		
Overhead			
Fixed:			
Expenditure		100	
Calendar		300	
Efficiency	120		
Semi-variable:			
Expenditure		50	
Calendar		75	
Efficiency	30		
	450	9,200	8,750
Actual profit			13,075

Workings

(i) Standard profit on actual sales: 29,100 x £0.50 = £14,550

(ii) Sales price variance:
(Actual selling price − standard selling price) actual quantity = variance
£2.25 − £2.00 x 29,100 =   £7,275   (favourable)

(iii) Material price variance:
(Actual price − standard price) actual quantity = variance
£0.10 − £0.075 x 304,000 =   £7,600   (unfavourable)

(iv) Material usage variance:
(Actual quantity − standard quantity for actual production) standard
price = variance
304,000 − 291,000 (29,100 x 10) x £0.075 =   £975   (unfavourable)

(v) Labour rate variance:
(Actual rate x actual hours) − (standard rate x actual hours) = variance
£14,350 − £14,250 (57,000 x £0.25) =   £100   (unfavourable)

(vi) Labour efficiency variance:
(Actual hours − standard hours for actual production) standard rate
= variance
57,000 − 58,200 (29,100 x 2) x £0.25 =   £300   (favourable)

(vii) Fixed expenditure variance:
Actual cost − budgeted cost = variance
£6,100 − £6,000 =   £100   (unfavourable)

(viii) Fixed calendar variance:
1 day lost = $\frac{1}{20}$ x 60,000 = 3,000 hours x £0.1 =   £300   (unfavourable)

(ix) Fixed efficiency variance:
(Actual hours − standard hours for actual production) fixed factory
overhead standard rate per hour = variance
57,000 − 58,200 x £0.1 =   £120   (favourable)

(x) Semi-variable expenditure variance:
Actual cost − budgeted cost = variance
£1,550 − £1,500 =   £50   (unfavourable)

(xi) Semi-variable calendar variance:
1 day lost = $\frac{1}{20}$ x 60,000 = 3,000 hours x £0.025 = £75   (unfavourable)

(xii) Semi-variable efficiency variance:
(Actual hours − standard hours for actual production) variable factory
overhead standard rate per hour = variance
57,000 − 58,200 x £0.025 =   £30   (favourable)

(xiii) Actual profit:	£	£
Sales: 29,100 x £2.25		65,475
Less materials: 304,000 x £0.1	30,400	
Labour	14,350	
Overheads:		
Fixed	6,100	
Variable	1,550	52,400
Actual profit		13,075

12   (a)   *Operating Statement – Job H24*

	£	£	£
Standard revenue for the job			3,000
Less standard costs			2,700
Standard profit on the job			300
Less variances			
Materials:			
Price	170		
Waste	50		
Unexplained difference	40	260	
Labour:			
Overtime	300		
Efficiency	100	400	
Direct expense: Expenditure		50	
Overheads:			
Overtime	375		
Efficiency	125	500	1,210
Production loss			910
Add the late penalty on completion			
of the job			150
Actual loss on the job			1,060

Workings

    (i) Standard revenue for the job:

        £2,850 + ($\frac{5}{95}$ x £2,850) =   £3,000

   (ii) Standard costs of the job: £

        Material: standard quantity x standard price

              £32 (£34 − (£4 ÷ 2)) x £25 (£30 − £5)   800

        Labour: 1,600 hours x 50p   800

        Direct expense   100

        Overheads: 125% of £800   1,000

                                         2,700

  (iii) Material price variance:

        (Actual price − standard price) actual quantity = variance

        £30 − £25 x 34 =   £170 (unfavourable)

  (iv) Material waste variance:

        2 x £25 =   £50 (unfavourable)

   (v) Material unexplained difference:

        £1,060 − £800 − £170 − £50 =   £40 (unfavourable)

  (vi) Labour overtime variance:

        25% of £1,200 =   £300 (unfavourable)

 (vii) Labour efficiency variance:

        (Actual hours − standard hours) standard rate = variance

        1,800 ((£1,200 − £300) ÷ 0.5) x 1,600 x £0.50 = £100 (unfavourable)

(viii) Direct expense expenditure variance:

        £150 − £100 =   £50 (unfavourable)

  (ix) Overhead overtime variance:

        125% of £300 =   £375 (unfavourable)

   (x) Overtime efficiency variance:

        125% of £100 =   £125 (unfavourable)

  (xi) Late penalty on completion of the job:

        5% of £3,000 =   £150

Date . . . .

To: Managing Director, Heavy Engineering Co. Ltd

From: Consultant

Comment on the Results of Job H24

I have examined the Category III Job H24 and attach a revised statement of the results.

(A) Advantages of this revised presentation

Based on the limited information available, this presentation is an improvement on the account presented to me for the following reaons:

(a) The statement attempts to indicate what the profit should have been on the job as compared with the actual loss incurred

(b) An attempt is made to identify the reasons why an anticipated profit of £300 was turned into a loss of £1,060.

(B) The weaknesses of the present accounting system

As a result of my examination of the present system, the following weaknesses are evident:

(a) An abnormal cost arising from an abnormal work load had been charged to Job H24. The total amount involved, £170, should not have been charged to this job

(b) On the present procedure, the full labour cost is charged to jobs including overtime premiums. As tender prices are submitted on past experience, presumably the rate of £0.50 per hour includes the averaged allowance for this work. Overtime premiums should be included in overheads unless the job is being carried out in overtime at the specific request of the customer

(c) No attempt has been made to separate fixed and variable expenditure.

Before discontinuing Category III work on the basis of the figures supplied to me, I suggest that further investigation is necessary. Perhaps you would care to discuss this matter with me.

Signed ....

(b) The additional information required before a decision can be made regarding eliminating Category III work includes the following:

(i) Information on costs of all jobs as a basis for future assessment

(ii) Information on the profitability of all jobs as a basis for future assessment

(iii) Information on the technical and marketing factors affecting the grades of jobs

(iv) Information on the future costs and sales of each category of work.

Regarding points (i) and (ii), existing costs should be adjusted to take into account the factors mentioned in the report in part (a).

19 Marginal Costing

1   Marginal costing is a technique of value to management for the following reasons:

(a)   It integrates with other aspects of management accounting, e.g., cost-volume-profit analysis and flexible budgeting.

(b)   Period reports are more easily understood. Management can more readily understand the assignment of costs to products if these are limited to marginal cost because such costs are readily identifiable with the cost unit.

(c)   It emphasises the significance of key factors affecting the performance of the business in the profit-planning and decision-making areas. These key factors may be a lack of sales, shortage of materials, skilled labour, or machine facilities. Contribution to these factors is an important statistic for management.

(d)   There is a close relationship between variable costs and the controllable costs classification. This relationship assists the control function.

(e)   It assists in the provision of relevant costs for decision-making. Without marginal cost data the information for management may be misleading. This is the case, for example, in decisions concerned with:

    (i)   The acceptance of special orders

    (ii)   The possible elimination of a product

    (iii)   The possible outside purchase of components as compared with their internal manufacture

    (iv)   The selling of products in limited markets.

(f)   It assists short-term decision-making particularly those decisions concerned with product short-term pricing.

These factors are of considerable benefit to management but the value of the technique should be assessed with the recognition that:

(a)   It is difficult to analyse costs into their fixed and variable elements

(b)   There is a tendency to concentrate on the short-term situation

(c)   There is a danger in management confusing marginal cost with full cost.

The use of marginal costing has been a controversial subject with accountants and managers for many years but few would dispute its value for profit-planning, control and decision-making.

2   (a)   The disadvantages of adopting marginal costing are as follows:

(i)   The difficulty of analysing costs into their fixed and variable elements. Arbitrary classifications may be used to give this analysis.

(ii)   The tendency to concentrate on the short-term situation. In the long term, fixed costs will vary.

(iii)   Satisfactory long-range decisions can only be made given product full cost data which is not available if product analysis is restricted by marginal costing information only. In the long run fixed costs must be recovered.

(iv)   Attention is focused on the contribution stage and the non-recognition of fixed costs by management may be dangerous.

(v)   In the manufacture of a product, facilities represented by fixed costs are used and the non-assignment of these costs to products is a departure from the accounting principle that when applied attempts to match costs against revenue for profit determination.

(vi)   In a manufacturing plant that is highly automated the amount of variable cost may be small and this situation magnifies the problems of applying the technique.

(b)   If marginal costing is used for stock valuation, research has shown that inaccuracies arising from the difficulty of separating costs into their fixed and variable elements are not significant enough in the average business to distort the result of arbitrary classifications considered necessary. For other purposes, however, the care with which the analysis is carried out assumed a greater significance.

Information for management should be provided in relation to user requirements and if these dictate the supply of marginal cost information, management should be reminded that the information supplied for one purpose should not be used for other requirements, without checking with the accounting department that the detail available is relevant to its intended use. If this rule is observed the danger of confusing marginal cost with full cost will be lessened.

The use of the marginal costing technique should not necessarily mean that full cost data is not available. A fully developed management accounting system will have the basic data available for compilation in the manner required to satisfy the key demands of the management. Where there is the danger that fixed costs will be ignored by management if the marginal costing technique is adopted, it would appear that there are significant weaknesses in the company control system.

Marginal costing has not received much support for external reporting but this does not invalidate its value for internal purposes.

(c)   Part of the answer is in the penultimate paragraph in the previous question. A sound standard costing system can be operated to produce information on the effect on profit of changes in volume or type of output.

The managing director's requirement could be met partly by (i) employing standard absorption costs which show prime cost, variable overhead and fixed overhead; and (ii) presenting reports to management which show both contribution and the conventionally computed profit.

3   (a)   Problems in making the fixed/variable cost classification:
 (i)   Many costs fall into the semi-variable category, i.e., a mixture of variable and fixed costs. It is usually difficult to isolate the fixed and variable elements although statistical methods may be used.
 (ii)   The time period may be crucial: fixed costs which are variable long term may be fixed if a short-term view is taken.
 (iii)   Some costs may be fixed for one range of output and then increase to another level applicable for the next range of output.
 (iv)   The variable factor may not be the unit of output but the incremental effect in the decision-making situation. For example, the work manager's salary is a fixed cost of running a factory but if management is considering closing the factory his salary could be avoided.
 (v)   Certain costs may vary with a change in activity but not in direct proportion to such changes.

(b)   Implications of the difficulties on the provision of marginal costing information for management:
 (i)   There is the need to define the upper and lower limits of the anticipated levels of activity to minimise the distortion in treating an item as, say, a variable cost when it is not a truly variable cost item
 (ii)   The objective for which the information is to be used must be recognised in providing the data so that if marginal costing information is relevant, the variable category may be interpreted accordingly
 (iii)   The classification of costs into their fixed and variable elements may be difficult but the analysis is necessary for such techniques as flexible budgeting and cost-volume-profit analysis in order to aid the planning and control processes of management.

Considerable care should be taken in the classification of costs into their fixed and variable elements and their interpretation.

4   *Absorption costing basis*

Profit Statement

Year ended ....

	£	£
Sales		480,000
Less cost of sales		
Opening stock	37,500	
Add production	325,000	
	362,500	
Less closing stock	62,500	
Standard cost of sales	300,000	
Add variances:		
Variable factor cost	5,000	
Capacity variance	10,000	315,000
Gross profit		165,000
Less selling overhead		
Variable	36,000	
Fixed	30,000	66,000
Net profit		99,000

Workings

  (i) Sales: 120,000 × £4 =   £480,000
 (ii) Opening stock: 15,000 × £2.50 =   £37,500

Variable factory cost per unit	£2.00
Fixed factory cost per unit: (£75,000 ÷ 150,000)	£0.50
	£2.50

(iii) Production: 130,000 × £2.50 =   £325,000
 (iv) Closing stock: 25,000 × £2.50 =   £62,500
  (v) Standard cost of sales: 120,000 × £2.50 = £300,000
 (vi) Capacity variance:
       (150,000 units − 130,000 units) (£75,000 ÷ 150,000) =
                            £10,000   (unfavourable)

(vii) Variable selling overheads: 120,000 x £0.30 = £36,000

Marginal costing basis

Profit Statement
Year ended ....

	£	£
Sales		480,000
Less marginal cost of sales		
Opening stock	30,000	
Add production	260,000	
	290,000	
Less closing stock	50,000	
Standard marginal cost of sales	240,000	
Add variable factory costs variance	5,000	
	245,000	
Add variable selling overhead	36,000	281,000
Contribution		199,000
Less fixed costs		
Factory	75,000	
Selling	30,000	105,000
Net profit		94,000

The stock and production units are multiplied by the variable factory standard cost per unit of £2 to give the figures shown.

The reason for the difference in the profit figures shown is the different basis adopted for stock valuation:

	£	£
Closing stocks	62,500	
	50,000	12,500
Opening stocks	37,500	
	30,000	7,500
Reduction in profit		5,000

5   *Budgeted Profit Statement*

	Year ended			*Results this year*		*Variances*	
	£	£	£	£	£	£	
Sales		356,250		250,000		+106,250	
Less marginal cost of sales							
Prime cost	177,000		118,000		+59,000		
Variable overheads:							
Factory	88,500		59,000		+29,500		
Other	15,000	280,500	10,000	187,000	+5,000	93,500	
		———		———		———	
Contribution		75,750		63,000		+12,750	
Less fixed costs							
factory	30,000		30,000		—		
Other	25,000	55,000	20,000	50,000	+5,000	5,000	
		———		———		———	
Net profit		20,750		13,000		+7,750	
		════				════	
Less stock value adjustment				11,000			
				———			
				2,000			
				════			

Answer to (a)   With the stock
value adjustment
– the answer to
(b)

Workings

(i)   Sales: £250,000 + £125,000 – (5% of £375,000) = £356,250.

(ii) Prime cost: £

	£
Direct materials	100,000
Direct wages	40,000
	———
	140,000
Less stock increase	22,000
	———
	118,000
	════

(iii) Factory variable overhead: £70,000 – (£22,000 ÷ £140,000) x £70,000)
                            (stock valuation adjustment) = £59,000

(iv) Other fixed overhead: £20,000 + £5,000 (additional advertising advert-appropriation) = £25,000.

(v) Remaining items: this year figures + 50% (60% to 90% activity).

6   The reason why management is thinking of closing the depots in the Midlands and/or North:

Budget: Year ended ....

		South £000	Midlands £000	North £000	Total £000
Sales	(A)	1,400	400	200	2,000
Direct materials		336	96	48	480
Direct labour		210	60	30	300
Factory variable overhead		294	84	42	420
Selling and distribution variable overhead		70	32	20	122
Marginal cost	(B)	910	272	140	1,322
Contribution	(A−B = C)	490	128	60	678
Factory fixed overhead		280	80	40	400
Selling and distribution fixed overhead		80	50	30	160
Total fixed overhead	(D)	360	130	70	560
Profit/(loss)	(C − D)	130	(2)	(10)	118

Note: Factory fixed overhead apportioned on the basis of direct labour cost.

Additional information to management:

Possible Courses of Action

		Continue as at present £000	Continue with South and Midlands £000	Continue with South and North £000	Continue with South only £000
Contribution	(A)	678	618	550	490
Factory fixed overhead		400	400	400	400
Selling and distribution fixed overhead		160	130	110	80
Total fixed overhead	(B)	560	530	510	480
Profit	(A − B)	118	88	40	10

Recommendation to management on the basis of the figures above: continue with the depots at present in operation.

236

7   To answer this question it would be useful to know the contribution of Group C business to net profit and fixed costs.

Applying the gross profit percentages to Group C sales the gross profit is as follows:

Product	Gross Profit £	
X	600	(30% x £2,000)
Y	810	(27% x £3,000)
Z	1,250	(25% x £5,000)
	2,660	

No information is given in the question on fixed and variable costs. Assuming salesmen's commission, salesmen's expenses and distribution costs are variable, the remainder being fixed, the contribution of Group C customers may be estimated as follows:

	£	£	
Gross profit		2,660	
Less			
Salesmen's commission	100		(1% x £10,000)
Salesmen's expenses (allotted on the basis of the number of calls)	300		($\frac{3}{20}$ x £2,000)
Distribution expenses (allotted on the basis of sales)	400	800	($\frac{1}{25}$ x £10,000)
Contribution		1,860	

Because the general level of costs is high, if all costs had been allotted to Group C customers, it is understandable that the management should doubt the profitability of this business but the group is making a contribution to profits. On the assumption that the salesmen's time released cannot bring in more profit with A and B customers, if Group C is eliminated the profit will be reduced by £1,860.

Group C customers make the lowest purchases and in that sense they are not as valuable to the business as Group A and B. The main issue is that an investigation is necessary on the variability of the expenditure, future prospects with other customers, and then a decision can be made on the future of keeping Group C customers.

237

8   The additional factors that should be considered in this case before a decision is made are:

(a)   When is it likely that further work will be available?
(b)   Given the answer to (a) will it be possible to negotiate a similar contract to the one proposed?
(c)   What are the future costs anticipated in relation to company manufacture and future contract prices?
(d)   Will the quality of components offered be supplied to the required standard?
(e)   Will the required delivery dates be met and is the supplier considered to be generally reliable? Would one external supplier be a safe proposal for the company?
(f)   Until further work is available would redundancy be expected if the supply of components were subcontracted?

On the basis of the information given in the question, it would be in the interests of the company to continue manufacture of the components at the present time although the supplier's price is £2,000 less than the manufacturing cost. The reason is that since there is no alternative profitable use for the factory facilities at the present time, the fixed factory costs are not relevant to the decision. The marginal cost of £12,000 is the figure to compare with the supplier's price of £15,000 indicating a £3,000 difference in favour of internal manufacture. The points made above could alter this decision.

9   Revised contribution on the basis of more mechanisation:

	£
Sales	34,560
Variable cost	22,464
Contribution	12,096

The extra weekly contribution is £96 (£12,096 − £12,000) which gives an annual return of £4,992 on the capital outlay of £8,000. To evaluate the worth of the project a discounted cash flow calculation is desirable although the payback period of under two years suggests that the investment would be satisfactory.

It has been assumed that the changes proposed involve the business in no incremental costs.

Workings
48,000 units ÷ 160 employees = 300 units per employee
300 units + 60% = 480 units
Weekly output = 480 units x 120 employees = 57,600 units
£30,000 ÷ 48,000 units = £0.625 per unit
£0.625 − 4% = £0.6
57,600 units x £0.6 = £34,560 (sales value)
£30,000 − £12,000 = £18,000
£18,000 ÷ 48,000 units = £0.375 per unit
30% of £0.05 = £0.015
£0.375 + £0.015 = £0.39
57,600 units x £0.39 = £22,464 (variable cost)

		A.B. Ltd contract	C.D. Ltd contract
10 (a)		£	£
Total cost per dozen			
Direct material cost		5.80	2.00
Direct labour cost		2.00	4.00
Overhead:	Variable	4.00	8.00
	Fixed	2.00	4.00
		13.80	18.00
(b) Selling price		15.00	20.00
Profit		1.20	2.00
Profit to sales		8%	10%
(c) The key factor in this case: labour			
Contribution per labour hour		1.60	1.50

On the basis of the figures given, the A.B. Ltd contract should be accepted.
The profit for the quarter for each contract would be as follows:

	A.B. Ltd contract	C.D. Ltd contract
	£	£
Sales	78,000	52,000
Marginal cost	61,360	36,400
Contribution	16,640	15,600
Fixed cost	10,400	10,400
Profit	6,240	5,200

Workings
(i) Variable overhead per dozen = £1,600 ÷ (20 x 40 hours) = £2 per hour
     A.B. Ltd: Direct labour cost: £2
                       Direct labour hours: £2 ÷ £1 = 2
                       2 hours x £2 = £4
     C.D. Ltd: Direct labour cost: £4
                       Direct labour hours: £4 ÷ £1 = 4
                       4 hours x £2 = £8
(ii) Fixed overhead:
     A.B. Ltd: 2 x £1 = £2
     C.D. Ltd: 4 x £1 = £4
(iii) Contribution per labour hour:
     A.B. Ltd: (£15 − £11.8) ÷ 2 = £1.60
     C.D. Ltd: (£20 − £14) ÷ 4 = £1.50
(iv) Costs and selling prices per dozen multiplied by:
     A.B. Ltd: 40 hours x 20 = 800 hours
                       800 ÷ 2 hours = 400 dozens per week
                       13 weeks x 400 dozens = 5,200 dozens
     C.D. Ltd: 800 ÷ 4 hours = 200 dozens per week
                       13 weeks x 200 dozens = 2,600 dozens.

11   The key factor in this problem is available acreage and contribution per acre is the required statistic for deciding on the best use of the 20 acres.

	£
If the 20 acres are used for growing kale	
Value of crop (40 cows x £30)	1,200
Less marginal cost: seed and fertilizers (20 acres x £14)	280
Contribution	920
Contribution per acre	46
If the 20 acres are used for growing barley	
Value of crop (1.5 tonnes x 20 acres x £60)	1,800
Less marginal cost: seed and fertilizers (20 acres x £16)	320
Contribution	1,480
Contribution per acre	74

If the 20 acres are used for grazing cattle	£	£
Value of		
Milk (10 cows x £300)	3,000	
Calves (10 calves x £40)	400	3,400
Less marginal cost		
Kale (10 cows x £30)	300	
Feeding stuffs ((£2,000 ÷ 40) x 10)	500	
Depreciation (10 x £40)	400	1,200
Contribution		2,200
Contribution per acre		110

On the basis of the above figures, the best use of the 20 acres is for grazing cattle and this gives a profit on total operations of £4,400 as follows:

	£	£
Contribution		
Barley: (100 acres x £74)		7,400
Grazing cattle: (100 acres x £110)		11,000
		18,400
Less fixed costs		
Farmworkers' wages	5,000	
Rent, rates, etc.	3,000	
General charges	6,000	14,000
Profit		4,400

12   *Profitability of the Special Contract if Accepted*
Year ended ....

	£	£
Revenue		6,000
Less variable costs per contract vehicle		
Driver's wages	1,456	
Petrol	500	
Tyres	750	
Licence	150	
Insurance	90	
Garage staff overtime	416	

	£	£
Brought forward	3,362	6,000
Stationery and repair material	300	
Depreciation	1,500	5,162
Contribution		838

Workings

(i) Revenue: annual sum (£1,000) + (25,000 x £0.20) = £6,000
(ii) Driver's wages: 40 hours x £0.70 x 52 weeks = £1,456
(iii) Petrol: Note (c) gives an average m.p.g. of 20
 ∴ 25,000 ÷ 20 x £0.40 = £500
(iv) Tyres: 25,000 x £0.005 x 6 = £750
(v) Garage staff overtime: 10% of (£3,120 + £1,040) = £416
 2 x £30 x 52 weeks = £3,120
 1 x £20 x 52 weeks = £1,040
(vi) Stationery and repair materials: £2,700 ÷ 9 vehicles = £300
(vii) Depreciation: (£6,000 − £1,500) ÷ 3 = £1,500.

Costs for Comparison with the Trade Association (25,000 mile basis)
Year ended ....

	With special contract		Without special contract	
	£	£	£	£
Variable costs				
Drivers' wages	14,560		13,104	
Petrol	5,000		4,500	
Tyres	7,500		6,750	
Licence	1,500		1,350	
Insurance	990		900	
Garage staff wages	4,576		4,160	
Stationery and repair material	3,000		2,700	
Depreciation	15,000	52,126	13,500	46,964
Fixed costs				
Partner's remuneration	3,600		3,600	
Garage overhead	900		900	
Administration overhead	1,800	6,300	1,800	6,300
Total cost		58,426		53,264
Average cost per mile		0.234		0.237

Workings

The following costs from the profitability statement are multiplied by 10 and 9 vehicles respectively:

Drivers' wages	Licence
Petrol	Stationery and repair material
Tyres	Depreciation

Insurance
  10 vehicles: £180 + (9 x £90) = £990
  9 vehicles: £180 + (8 x £90) = £900
Garage staff wages
  10 vehicles: £3,120 + £1,040 + £416 = £4,576
  9 vehicles: £3,120 + £1,040 = £1,160

To: John James & Son   Date : . . . .
From: Consultant

Special Contract Decision and Cost Levels

The factors concerned with the proposed contract and your costs have been examined and appropriate comments are as follows:

Cost levels

Reference is made to Appendix A (Costs for Comparison with the Trade Association).

The present cost levels are similar to the figures issued by the Trade Association on a 25,000 mile basis, but as the business operates its vehicles 30,000 miles per year its costs must be less than £0.24 because of the effect of increased activity on the fixed costs.

Special contract decision

Reference is made to Appendix B (Profitability of the Special Contract if Accepted).

If the special contract is accepted, a contribution of £838 will be provided. The explanation of this profitable result is the relative effect of additional costs applicable to the contract as compared with additional revenue to the business. Fixed costs are excluded because they will be incurred whether the contract is accepted or not.

The assumption has been made that the present cost levels will continue and it may be noted that, with the acceptance of the contract the average cost per mile drops to £0.234. On a 30,000 mile per year, per vehicle basis, these costs will be reduced and profitability further increased by excess business revenue from use of the spare capacity as offered by the manufacturing company.

If you wish to discuss the proposed contract further before acceptance, I am available for further consultation.   Signed . . . .

20 Decision-Making Techniques

1   The decisions of management may not be in the interests of the business for the following reasons:

(a)   Inadequate information on which to make a decision given to the decision-maker
(b)   Misunderstanding of the problem
(c)   Not having the time to weigh up alternative opportunities
(d)   Inadequate resources
(e)   Inadequate management experience and training.

Steps that may be taken to reduce the number of decision errors made include the following:

(a)   Clear definition of responsibility for decisions to be made and account-ability for the results of those decisions.
(b)   An improvement in the information system to provide relevant inform-ation as a basis for decision-making.
(c)   The training of subordinates marked for promotion in the decision-making process. Where time permits, it is useful for a manager to give to his subordinate the facts of a problem and ask for his opinion and the action that he would take. If an alternative course is adopted, the explanation of the reasons to the subordinate would help in training the future manager in the way problems should be resolved.
(d)   Concentration of limited managerial time to maximum advantage by giving maximum time and study to the significant problems facing the business.
(e)   Ensuring delegation of decision-making is satisfactory, not only from the point of view of decisions delegated where necessary to managers with the qualifications and experience to make the right decisions, but also with the authority to carry out the action required.

2   What is wanted by the decision-amker is the right answer to the right question. The likelihood that a right answer will be found is reduced if the nature of the problem is not correctly identified at the outset of the decision-making process.

The problem superficially indicated may be different when subjected to detailed investigation. A useful start to defining the problem is to ask the question: why has the need for a decision arisen? The answer to this question may supply clues as to the factors involved in the problem and the key issues requiring attention.

Possible alternative solutions may not be considered if attention is given to problem solution before the nature of the problem is isolated and defined. Many factors must be considered in a major decision but problem definition will simplify problem solution.

3   Alternative solutions may be developed by:

(a)   Considering all related objectives and the interactions of the lines of action possible.
(b)   Determining the time limit effect on the solution to the problem. Given time, additional solutions may be possible.
(c)   Determining the cost and revenue elements of each possible alternative. These factors may be crucial in rating the value of the possibilities open to the decision-maker.
(d)   Considering the uncertainties attached to the alternatives available. Reasonable certainty of a favourable outcome of any alternative considered is necessary.

The qualifications that should be made regarding the use of available alternatives include:

(a)   Significance of the proposals
(b)   Assumptions made regarding each alternative
(c)   Time available before a decision must be made
(d)   Cost of applying each alternative.

Initial reactions to a problem should not restrict the manager's search for other possible solutions, providing the decision-maker is not confused in the process. The aim should be to identify significant possible alternatives, discarding the minor possibilities as soon as possible. The main alternatives can be subjected to detailed investigation in the context of the constraints imposed by the problem.

4   Relevant information is that which bears upon or is useful to the action

it is designed to facilitate or the result it is desired to produce. In the decision-making context this refers to figures designed to assist in solving a specific problem and to arrive at an answer to the problem; appropriate figures may be required for suitable possible alternative solutions. Relevancy in terms of the best estimate that can be given involves the recognition of future costs and revenue for the possible alternatives, and incremental effect used as the criterion for the choice of the figures in the computation.

In the control context, the reported information should be related to the limits of managerial responsibility in all phases of the control process.

5   The statement is true because the costs relevant to a particular decision may be costs emerging from the accounting records as a result of routine processing, such costs modified as necessary, or costs external to the accounting system. Costs external to the accounting system that are relevant in decision-making situations are imputed costs, e.g., interest. Predominently, the traditional accounting records contain historical costs but the future costs are the relevant costs in the decision-making situation. The historical costs may be a valuable guide in the estimation process when recognition is given to future changes affecting such costs.

All costs recorded in the accounting records are not required. The incremental costs are relevant and the basic question to be answered regarding each cost is: would it be incurred if the project was accepted for the company? If the answer is 'yes', such a cost is incremental because if the project is not accepted the cost would be avoided. Expenditure which has taken place in the past and which will not be affected by a particular decision under consideration can be ignored, e.g., sunk costs.

6   (a)   The costs relevant to the make or buy decision are the costs that would be avoided as a result of not making the production units as compared with the cost of equivalent units if purchased.

Such a simple comparison can be justified if other non-quantifiable factors are satisfactory such as supplier reliability regarding quality and delivery dates being met.

If investment is involved in making the units, alternative uses of the funds should also be considered.

(b)   The amounts involved are net cash flows regarding the additional capital expenditure (taking into account taxation factors) discounted at the discounting rate adopted by the company for judging the soundness of capital expenditure proposals. The question refers to costs only but in this case revenue from the new line would also be relevant.

The justification for this approach is to recognise the time value of money.

(c)   The revenue from the products if sold in their present state are the opportunity costs of further processing the products for increased revenue. The product should be further processed if the incremental revenue is greater than the incremental cost of that extra processing. This cost situation can be justified when it is considered that this is the equivalent to the difference between the total revenue of the further processed product, less the additional costs of processing, plus the opportunity cost described.

7   Management accounting is directed to the control aspects of business operation and provides financial information that should be useful to management for that purpose. The information presented from the accounting records is in the form of statistics to the extent that statistics can be defined as numerical data recorded and tabulated and presented in a systematic way. In preparing financial information for management and its interpretation, statistical techniques are often used. These include: (a) averaging; (b) correlating; (c) sampling.

It follows that there is a common area of interest, represented by the disciplines of statistics and management accounting, and management accountants can profit from a knowledge of available statistical techniques and their possible applications.

Much of the information provided by the statistician is in purely numerical terms and while such details may be of value to management as, for example, productivity measurements of output, the economic significance of statistical information as provided by management accounting is vital to the control of a business.

There is an increasing importance in the application of statistical methods to accounting routines and data and statistical probability theory to deal with the uncertainty that is attached to decision problems.

8   The changes in the type of information provided to management, as a basis for the solution of business problems, have arisen with the growth of practical applications of quantitative techniques and the speed with which complex and numerous calculations can be carried out by computers. Another factor contributing to this trend is the training of managers in what they should expect in the way of information to help them in controlling the business. This has meant that more managers are demanding types of information as a basis for decision-making. Prior to this trend there was the tendency for accountants to give management what was

thought to be needed. The inadequate training of accountants in the application of quantitative techniques meant that little use was made of these techniques.

The effect of the trend towards the increasing use of quantitative techniques, and of the types of demands made by managers, means that if the accountant cannot deliver what is required managers will appoint other staff who will give the service demanded. As this type of work is in the senior areas of business activity, such a development would lower the status of accountants. In some companies, this has begun to happen and the accountancy bodies have realised that the remedy is to modify examination syllabuses accordingly. All accountancy bodies have done so but what remains is to practise the skills that are being disseminated to accountants and managers. It is dangerous to pay lip-service to this training or 'window-dress' an accounting syllabus.

9   The definition of operational research given in the question emphasises the scientific approach to problem solving. This approach involves the development of a model of the problem situation with which to predict and compare the outcome of alternative decisions, strategies or controls. The model is used to represent complex problems usually of a type where there is not one correct solution. The aim is to find the best answer to the problem. A broad view is taken by the operational researcher and his approach includes all relevant factors, including accounting data.

Operational research is an approach to a problem which uses all the available tools and techniques to assist in solving the problem. Statistical techniques are particularly valuable in this situation and may come to the aid of the researcher because the volume of information to be studied, for example, may be too much to handle and sampling may be adopted to reduce that volume. The theoretical support and justification for the techniques used in statistics is given by mathematics.

10   A model is a representation of the problem to be solved which enables the investigator to test his theories and produce the best solution to the problem. Types of models include the following:

(a)   Physical models, e.g., the model of an aircraft in a wind tunnel
(b)   Accounting models, e.g., the double entry accounting system is a model
(c)   Planning models, e.g., a company budget
(d)   Mathematical models, e.g., linear programming equations relevant to a transportation problem
(e)   Data processing models, e.g., a computer programme.

Models are useful in the problem solving area because:

(a)   With complex problems, the use of the actual system to test possible solutions would be costly and inconvenient

(b)   If incorrect changes were made in the actual system, chaos might be the result.

The adequacy and reliability of the model largely determines the likelihood of the operational research approach being successful.

11   The TWI scheme was aimed at lower and middle management levels, but factors suggested in the scheme have wider application and the following notes imply this approach:

Notes on the TWI Approach to Problem Solving
Identifying the problem
The decision-making process begins with identifying the problem and an introductory question such as 'why has the need for a decision arisen?' may supply clues as to the factors involved in the problem and the key issues requiring attention.
Determination of the objective
Realistic long-range objectives should be related to attainable short-term objectives. Meeting subsidiary objectives may play a significant part in the achievement of principal objectives.
Getting the facts
As a basis for decision-making, the reporting system must be geared to provide relevant data. This implies that the system facilitates the collection of data, the appropriate data-processing and its interpretation.

Of value to the decision-maker is the quantification in financial terms of the relevant data. Estimated amounts and calculations should be realistic. The estimates used concern the future and the complexity of business inevitably means that precision is not attainable.
Making the decision
There is always a tendency to over-simplify the decision-making process and make decisions before all significant possibilities have been examined, usually because of time and cost considerations.

If the manager is generally successful there can be over-confidence in his decision-making ability. Equally, a manager's confidence can be undermined by a mistake and it should not be forgotten that as a result of such an experience, a manager's decisions can be more reliable.
Taking action
When a decision is made to take action, all aspects of the decision must be

communicated in terms which will be understood to those delegated to carry out the task.

Specific responsibility for the decision and its implementation is crucial.

Follow-up action

The decision-making process is not complete until the results of the action taken are compared with the standards laid down for assessment. The feedback of information from the implementation phase can be useful in refining the quality of the inputs to the decision process.

12   (a)   It appears from the case that managers are not receiving relevant information regarding the problems demanding attention in the business. Managers require this information. Many factors must be considered in a major decision and each step in the decision-making process is complex when placed in the context of the average business. There is the possibility that the information supplied to managers is an over-simplification of the actual situation.

There is nothing unusual regarding a senior executive engaging a personal assistant, such a person investigating specific projects and problems and making appropriate recommendations regarding their solution. What is important is the relative status of such an assistant and if he is a challenge to the chief accountant. If this is so, it is not surprising that the chief accountant would not be agreeable to the proposal. It is important to note that the chief accountant has a tendency to emphasise information in financial terms. It is true that profit impact is vital but in the provision of relevant information as a basis for decision-making, non-quantitative data is important – in fact, this detail may be given greater prominence than relevant costs when making the decision.

(b)   The answer to this question depends on the quality of the chief accountant. The case implies that the management accounting system is poor. This may not be the fault of the management accountant. He may have the necessary experience and may have wanted to develop the existing system, but have been held back by the former management.

The managing director should assess the qualifications and potential of the chief accountant and if he is satisfied, give him the necessary support and encouragement to provide the service to management necessary. If not satisfied regarding the chief accountant's experience but the potential is there, a suitable course of training may be appropriate. If the dissatisfaction goes further than this, a replacement for the chief accountant should be considered.

Whichever course of action is taken regarding the chief accountant, the position of the assistant is a separate issue. Providing desirable relationships are not impaired and functional duties undermined, the appointment could be made.

21 Decision-Making Problems

1   The opinions on the material prices required by the question are as follows:

Material	Price for special order	Price for continuous production of Product 123
(i) A	The price used should be the price foregone as a result of not selling the material at the time the material is used for the special order. This figure is not given in the question. It could be £0.10 per gram because for the last few months the selling price has been steady but the figure may be different because the price can fluctuate widely.	The question refers to the material being a byproduct of irregular production. If continuous production of Product 123 is contemplated, a continuous supply of material A will be necessary. The anticipated supply price of the material should be used.
(ii) B	The price used should be the price foregone as a result of not selling the material at the time the material is used for the special order. It is implied in the question that this price would be £0.30 per gram.	The anticipated price of the material should be used. If the current price is maintained this would be £0.40 per gram.
(iii) C	The price used should be as described for material B. This	Providing the standard is a realistic figure, the standard

(Table continued on facing page)

Material	Price for special order	Price for continuous production of Product 123
(iii) C *(contd.)*	figure is not given in the question. Where the current market purchase price is a reasonable measure of this price (in the question, £0.55 per gram) this figure may be used.	cost of £0.60 per gram should be used.
(iv) D	The replacement price of £0.65 per gram should be used.	The seasonal anticipated prices may be averaged and a weighted average price or standard price used.

Note
Where disposal of the material would involve disposal costs, these should be deducted from the anticipated selling values of the material.

2   (a)   The following preliminary action may be taken:
  (i) Appoint a committee to investigate the position and report back to the main board with recommendations
 (ii) Suggest the development areas to be approached
(iii) Indicate the guiding factors for consideration.

(b)   The further action that should be taken to implement the decision is as follows:
  (i) Investigate the development areas proposed
 (ii) Submit recommendations to the board after consideration of:
        Access to services and labour
        Access to raw materials
        Access to markets
        Facilities in the new area
        Comparative advantages of the proposed move
        Financial assistance from the government
        Financial aspects of the move, including a DCF calculation on
        cash flows (a high figure should be included for contingencies)
(iii) After decision by the board:
        Draw up plans by specialists co-opted to the committee
        Apply for an Industrial Development Certificate

(iv) A careful consideration of employees' problems and company policy before consultation with various representative bodies within the works

(v) Announcement of the move by the managing director

(vi) Maintenance of close liaison between the company and the development corporation

(vii) Carry out the detailed plans.

(c)   Apart from difficulties arising from the above, such as cost changes, delays in the completion of plans, or not anticipating all the problems likely to arise, the main difficulties will concern personnel, such as:

(i) The possibility of unemployment

(ii) Whether experienced staff would move to the new site – training of new employees?

(iii) Employees with children of school age being concerned at the existing shortage of educational facilities in the new area

(iv) The cost of moving and settling in new homes.

(d)   The attempt to overcome the difficulties expected and faced would include the following action:

(i) Full and frank consultation

(ii) Careful detailed planning

(iii) The move carried out in stages, where possible.

3   Initially, the management accountant may assist the direction and depth of the investigation necessary by pointing out the following requirements:

(a) Cost of land and buildings

(b) Whether other suitable sites are available for rental (the rent and the security of tenure)

(c) Construction of buildings and installations including the connexion to the necessary services

(d) Location of inputs: labour and materials availability

(e) The laws relating to the employment of British personnel

(f) The need for and the cost of transferring senior staff to get production started and maintained

(g) Terms and conditions of employment locally recognised

(h) Anticipated costs of operation and profitability

(i) Distribution facilities and access to markets

(j) Taxation factors

(k) Local laws

(l) The stability of the political regime

(m) Currency transfer regulations

(n) Any difficulties in manufacturing, etc., which may be disclosed by discussion with British Consular representatives

(o) The provision of capital (including working capital)

(p) The quality of the product the same by hand or machine methods?

From the financial point of view, the management accountant might provide information to disclose the net effect on total profit as follows:

	£
Profit anticipated from the new factory	—
Less reduction in profits — British factory	—
Net effect on total profit	—

In addition, cost comparisons between hand and machine methods would be provided with cash flows discounted to present values.

4   Before replacement of the machinery is carried out, the following factors should be considered:

(a) The state of the present equipment and the estimated cost of the extensive repairs necessary if the machinery is not replaced.

(b) The type of equipment available to replace the asset(s) and their operational characteristics. For example, will the production output from the new machine be the same or more than the present equipment?

(c) If increased output is expected, will the increased output be saleable at a profit?

(d) The likely technological developments regarding the equipment.

(e) Whether to buy or lease the equipment and if leasing is contemplated, the terms of the lease, including references to possible restrictions of use and maintenance reliability.

(f) Timing considerations regarding the possible introduction of the new asset.

(g) Cash flow comparisons of the old and new machines with regard to inflation, future estimate accuracy and tax considerations.

(h) Capital availability and its cost.

(i) A DCF calculation based on projected cash flows and cost of capital, the aim being to ascertain whether the net present value points in favour of replacement of the machinery.

Statement Showing the Financial Effects of
Various Possibilities open to Management

(a) Continuing with the production and sale of all three products next year:

	Product A £	Product B £	Total £	£
Existing profit				1,250
Less reduction in sales:				
Existing sales	4,200	3,200	7,400	
Revised sales	3,360	2,240	5,600	1,800
				(550)
Add saving in agents' commission (2% of £1,800)				36
Loss				514

(b) Discontinuing one or more products next year:

	Product A £	£	Product B £	£	Product C £	£
The loss (Note (a))		514		514		514
Add						
Lost sales		17,600		3,360		2,240
Incremental costs:						
Maintenance				100		100
Stock				1,200		
		18,114		5,174		2,854
Less						
Avoidable costs:						
Materials	3,000		1,200		500	
Agents' commission	352		67		45	
Railway charges	880	4,232	210	1,477	160	705
Revised loss		13,882		3,697		2,149

	Products A and B £	£	Products B and C £	£	Products C and A £	£
The loss (Note (a))		514		514		514
Add						
Lost sales		20,960		5,600		19,840
Incremental costs:						
Maintenance		100		200		100
Stock		1,200		1,200		
		22,774		7,514		20,454

	Products A and B		Products B and C		Products C and A	
	£	£	£	£	£	£
Brought forward		22,774		7,514		20,454
Less						
Avoidable costs:						
Materials	4,200		1,700		3,500	
Agents' commission	419		112		397	
Railway charges	1,090	5,709	370	2,182	1,040	4,937
Revised loss		17,065		5,332		15,597

Advice to management
It is clear from the above figures that the abandonment of products will worsen the company position and is not to be recommended. On the other hand, the planned performance for next year is poor and it is clear that the company cannot continue on this basis. A further review is needed of the likely profitability of the company in the future. If the future is more hopeful, a loss situation for one year may be sustained; if not, closure of the company is inevitable.

6   *Comparative Statement of Avoidable Cost*
of Making and Buying Containers

	Years 1 to 4 £	Year 5 £	Years 6 to 15 £
Avoidable annual cost of buying containers	20,000	20,000	20,000
Avoidable annual cost of making containers			
Direct material	8,000	8,000	8,000
Direct labour	6,000	6,000	6,000
Departmental overhead:			
Foreman	–	2,500	2,500
Depreciation of machinery	–	–	3,000
Rent	1,500	1,500	1,500
Other expenses	1,500	1,500	1,500
	17,000	19,500	22,500
Annual gain or (loss) from continuing production	3,000	500	(2,500)

Comment

The relevant costs in the decision-making situation are the costs to be avoided if a particular course of action is not taken. On the facts given, it will pay the company to continue production until the machine has to be replaced in five years time. It is assumed the costs will be the same in the future, an unlikely event but a necessary assumption to give an answer to this question.

7   (a)   The problems likely to be met in the situation described in the question are:

(i)   Assessing sales level of each product in each channel of distribution

(ii)   Assessing the selling prices applicable to each product in each channel of distribution

(iii) Assessing the costs appropriate to each product in each channel of distribution.

Some of the information may already be available regarding short-term profitability but in the establishment and continuance of channels of distribution, long-term information will be required. The problems may be dealt with by:

(i)   Using distributor know-how and information from professional sources, trade associations and the Department of Trade and Industry.

(ii)   Identifying specific costs to products and channels of distribution. This should be an easier job in connexion with the fifty products specially manufactured for particular channels.

(iii) Ascertaining product costs by conventional costing methods with particular reference to the identification of marginal costs.

(b)   The relevant management accounting information when deciding whether or not to drop a particular product or a particular channel of distribution is as follows:

(i)   The changes in sales volume and sales revenue as a result of the action contemplated

(ii)   The changes in costs of manufacturing products and distributing products.

Using the above information, the variation in profit would be assessed both in the short and long term. Associated with this financial information, the company would need to consider the normal industrial practice, the characteristics of the products being sold and the nature of the market.

8   To: General Manager   Date . . . .
      From: Accountant
            Rates of Profitability and Proposal Evaluation
As requested, the following information is submitted for consideration:

(a)   Route profitability   *Year* ....

	Route X1 £	Route X2 £	Route X3 £
Revenue from passengers	155,000	96,000	132,000
Variable costs	125,000	75,000	100,000
Contribution before specific fixed costs	30,000	21,000	32,000
Specific fixed costs	8,800	4,800	6,400
Contribution after specific fixed costs	21,200	16,200	25,600

Rates of profitability on the basis of contribution after specific fixed costs:

Per vehicle	£964	£1,350	£1,600
Per mile	£0.042	£0.054	£0.064

(b)   *The proposal to discontinue Route X4*
Providing the vehicles can be used to greater advantage or be disposed of by
the business, this proposal is in the interests of the company because as long
as the route is in operation, total contribution is reduced by £1,200 per year
on the basis of the figures given (£52,000 less £50,000 less £3,200). Any
change in future figures would alter the effect of this proposal.

(c)   *The proposal to reduce the service on Route X4*
Again, on the assumption that unused vehicles on Route X4 can be used
to greater advantage or be disposed of by the business, this proposal would
benefit the company. It would convert an existing contribution reduction
of £1,200 to a contribution increase of £5,400, on the basis of the figures
given, as follows:

	£
Revenue from passengers	32,000
Variable costs	25,000
Contribution before specific fixed costs	7,000
Specific fixed costs	1,600
Contribution after specific fixed costs	5,400

(d) *The proposal to introduce cheap off-peak fares on Route X1*

On the basis of the estimates given this proposal should not be accepted because the profit on this route would be reduced if the proposal was put into effect:

	£	£	£
Present off-peak revenue			80,000
Proposal off-peak revenue			
Revenue at present	80,000		
Less 25% reduction in fares	20,000	60,000	
Add 30% increase in passengers		18,000	78,000
Profit reduced by			2,000

Signed . . . .

9   Incremental revenue and costs for the further processing of each product is as follows:

	Product A		Product B		Product C	
	£	£	£	£	£	£
Incremental sales		20,000		12,000		15,000
Incremental costs						
Direct material	10,000		3,000		7,000	
Direct wages	4,000		2,000		2,000	
Variable overhead						
(see note)	6,000	20,000	3,000	8,000	3,000	12,000
Incremental profit		–		4,000		3,000

Incremental profit for the further processing of any two products or all three products:

Products A and B:	Nil plus £4,000 = £4,000
Products A and C:	Nil plus £3,000 = £3,000
Products B and C:	£4,000 plus £3,000 = £7,000
Products A, B and C:	Nil plus £4,000 plus £3,000 = £7,000.

Recommendation to management: Further process products B and C.

Note

Variable overheads percentage recovery rate:

$$\frac{£45,000}{£30,000} \times 100 = 150\% \text{ on direct wages.}$$

10 The cost of holding the inventory includes the following:

(a) Costs associated with the capital invested in the materials in storage.
(b) Costs associated with storage and clerical routines applicable to such materials, e.g.,
    (i) Store occupancy costs
    (ii) Store labour costs
    (iii) Stock losses
    (iv) Administration and other store overhead costs.

The problems involved in determining these include:

(a) Determining the interest rate to adopt to calculate the interest on capital
(b) Identifying the behaviour of costs to give incremental cost information as a basis for decision
(c) The difficulty of estimating some costs such as deterioration, obsolescence or other stock losses.

The cost of ordering and setting up production facilities includes the following:

(a) Purchases from outside suppliers:
    (i) Supply inquiries
    (ii) Order issue and follow-up
    (iii) Associated clerical routines, e.g., processing of accounts for payment.
(b) Internal manufacture supplies:
    (i) Set-up costs
    (ii) Associated clerical routines, e.g., production control and preparing manufacturing orders.

The principal problems associated with these costs are:

(a) Identifying the behaviour of costs to give incremental cost information as a basis for decision
(b) Assessing the 'out of stock' cost which might arise if a shortage of materials occurs because of incorrect estimates of supplies needed and possible emergency manufacture required.

11 To: Managing Director and   Date . . . .
   Members of the Management Meeting
   From: Management Accountant
   The Selling Price of New Product NP456

In fixing the selling price of new product NP456, the following factors should be taken into account at the forthcoming management meeting:

(a) *General considerations*
(i) Future cost of the product made available for sale
(ii) Expected demand the eleasticity of that demand
(iii) Capacity availability and the expected volume of production
(iv) Customer reactions
(v) Revenue cost-profit relationships
(vi) Competitor(s) reactions.

(b) *Application of the general considerations to product NP456*
(i) *Future costs.* Costs should be analysed into their fixed and variable elements and specific sales promotion costs itemised.
(ii) *Demand.* The anticipated demand should be analysed between home and foreign sales and the special factors affecting the foreign sales identified.
(iii) *Capacity availability and production volume.* The effect of the new product on capacity use at present which is below the usual levels and the likelihood of the recent pattern changing; and special machine use and the limiting effect this machine will have on production volume.
(iv) *Customer reactions.* An assessment is needed of this factor particularly on the likely effects on related products.
(v) *Revenue cost-profit relationships.* As a result of considering points (i) and (iv) above, the profitability of the product should be ascertained given different activity levels. The contribution to fixed costs and profit should also be assessed. The new product requires an initial investment of £50,000 but a DCF calculation on the projected cash flows should also take into account the estimated working capital requirements. Because there is the limiting factor of the special machine, projected contributions to this limiting factor will be additional useful information.
(vi) *Competitor's reactions.* The significant difference between the home and foreign market situation is of particular relevance with the new product.

(c) *Further information*
In preparation for the meeting to discuss the new price for product NP456, if any member of the management wishes to discuss the financial implications of their thoughts on any of the points above, I shall be pleased to assist where possible.

Signed . . . .

12 The problems facing a product manager include the following:

(a) Estimating the potential market for the company products
(b) Planning the share of the market and converting the plan into reality
(c) Planning and controlling selling and distribution costs
(d) Assessing the future of particular products and deciding on the policies and plans for the phasing out of old products and the phasing in of new products
(e) Product pricing
(f) Ensuring a sales revenue level related to costs to give the amount of profit demanded by the board of the company as a return on investment.

The management accountant can assist the product manager with pricing decisions by:

(a) Providing the manager with flexible cost data that can be used to solve different pricing problems — for example, marginal cost data is significant during periods of economic recession but full costs are important because only if full costs are covered by sales revenue can profits be secured.
(b) Through the administration of a budgetary control system provide future costs rather than past costs which are not relevant to pricing decisions.
(c) Providing profitability trends in relation to products as a basis for price adjustments and associated product policies.
(d) Provide non-routine information in connexion with product pricing as the occasion demands, e.g., where special sales promotions are contemplated.

ASSOCIATED TOPICS FOR STUDY

22 Source Documentation and Data Processing

1   The answer to this question depends on whether an integrated system or sub-system is in operation. If an integrated system is in operation its main features are:

(a)   One set of records meeting the requirements for financial and cost accounting opurposes
(b)   Classifications of source data for output requirements for financial and cost reports
(c)   Subsidiary ledgers (financial and costing) controlled through the general ledger
(d)   Each aspect of each transaction is recorded in the books of account thus preserving the double-entry principle.

If a sub-system is in operation its main features are:

(a)   A cost ledger controlling costing requirements rendered self-balancing through the medium of a control account linked to the general ledger. A decision is made on sections of the accounting system to be maintained separately as a sub-system.
(b)   Classification of source data for output requirements primarily limited to costing requirements. There may be overlap, e.g., the provision of stock information for the financial accounts.
(c)   Subsidiary ledgers for costing purposes controlled through the cost ledger.
(d)   As (d) above.
(e)   A need to reconcile the profit per the cost and financial accounts because the costing profit will be calculated on a restricted basis, according to the decision reached on items to be excluded from the cost ledger.

2   (a)   In an integral system of accounting the requirements for financial and cost accounting purposes are obtained from one set of records. The

accounts are maintained in what is usually referred to as a general ledger. It is recognised that a lot of the basic data is common to both requirements which can be met by analysis of this data as necessary.

(b) A coded list of accounts for an integrated system is as follows:

Code	Balance Sheet Accounts
0100	Issued ordinary share capital
0200	General reserve
0300	Profit and loss account
0400	*Current liabilities*
0401	Creditors
0403	Accrued expenses
0405	Taxation
0407	Proposed dividends
0500	*Fixed assets*
0501	Freehold buildings
0502	Plant and machinery
0503	Furniture and fittings
0504	Motor vehicles
0600	*Provision for depreciation*
0601	Plant and machinery
0602	Furniture and fittings
0603	Motor vehicles
0700	*Current assets*
0701	Stock — raw materials
0702	Stock — work-in-progress
0703	Stock — finished goods
0705	Trade debtors
0707	Prepayments
0709	Cash at bank
0710	Cash in hand
	Profit and Loss Accounts
0800	*Controls*
0801	Factory overhead control
0802	Wages control
0803	Administration cost control
0804	Selling and distribution costs control
0900	*Direct expense*
0901	Direct materials
0902	Direct labour
1000	*Factory overhead*

Code	Profit and Loss Accounts
1001	Indirect labour
1002	Indirect material
1003	Salaries
1004	National Insurance
1005	Pension fund
1006	Rent and rates
1007	Light, heat and power
1008	Depreciation
1009	Other expenses
1100	*Administration overhead*
1101	Salaries
1102	National Insurance
1103	Pension fund
1104	Rent and rates
1105	Light, head and power
1106	Car expenses
1107	Insurance
1108	Printing and stationery
1109	Postage and telephones
1110	Bank charges
1111	Legal and professional fees
1112	Depreciation
1113	Other expenses
1200	*Selling and distribution overhead*
1201	Salaries
1202	National Insurance
1203	Pension fund
1204	Rent and rates
1205	Light, head and power
1206	Carriage outwards
1207	Car expenses
1208	Travelling and entertaining
1209	Bad debts
1210	Discounts allowed
1211	Depreciation
1212	Other expenses
1300	*Absorption accounts*
1301	Factory overhead
1302	Administration overhead
1303	Selling and distribution overhead

Code	Profit and Loss Accounts
1400	Sales
1500	Other income – discounts receivable.

3

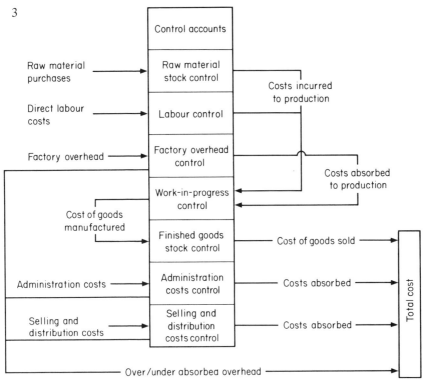

Figure 22.1   Cost data flow in a manufacturing organisation

4

Account	The balance represents	The transactions for the period out of which the balance has arisen
(a) Cost ledger control account	The net total of the outstanding balances in the cost ledger	An opening credit balance A credit entry for raw material and stores items purchased A credit entry for wages paid *(Table continued overleaf)*

Account	The balance represents	The transactions for the period out of which the balance has arisen
		Credit entries for factory, administration and selling and distribution overhead incurred A debit entry for sales A credit entry for profit disclosed by the costing profit and loss account
(b) Stores ledger account	The net total of the outstanding balances in the stores ledger	An opening debit balance A debit entry for purchases of raw materials and stores items A credit entry for issues of raw materials and stores items A credit entry for stock shortages A debit entry for materials returned to stores
(c) Work-in-progress account	The net total of the outstanding balances in the job cost ledger	An opening debit balance A debit entry for direct materials cost to jobs in progress A debit entry for direct labour cost to jobs in progress A debit entry for factory overhead absorbed to jobs in progress A credit entry for the cost of finished jobs transferred to finished stock
(d) Finished goods account	The net total of the outstanding balances in the finished stock	An opening debit balanace A debit entry for goods

(Table continued on facing page)

Account	The balance represents	The transactions for the period out of which the balance has arisen
	ledger	completed and received into finished goods stock A credit entry for the cost of goods sold to customers
(e) Factory overhead account	Under-absorption of factory overhead	A debit entry for factory overhead incurred A credit entry for factory overhead absorbed by goods manufactured
(f) Administration cost account	Over-absorption of administration cost	A debit entry for administration cost incurred A credit entry for administration cost absorbed to period costs

The work-in-progress account in detail is as follows:

Work-in-Progress Control Account

	£		£
Opening balance	6,000	Cost of finished goods	31,000
Direct materials	10,000	Balance carried forward	5,430
Direct wages	8,000		
Factory overhead absorbed	12,430		
	36,430		36,430
Balance brought forward	5,430		

5 (a) *Cost Ledger Accounts for the quarter ended 31st May 19 ....*

Raw Materials Control

	£		£
Opening balance	50,836	Issues to production	16,290
Purchases	22,422	Credits by suppliers	836
		Raw material losses	1,236
		Balance carried forward	54,896
	73,258		73,258
Balance brought forward	54,896		

Work-in-Progress Control

	£		£
Opening balance	12,745	Cost of finished goods	36,834
Direct wages	8,370	Rejected work	1,764
Raw materials	16,290	Balance carried forward	10,593
Factory overhead absorbed	11,786		
	49,191		49,191
Balance brought forward	10,593		

Finished Stock Control

	£		£
Opening balance	25,980	Cost of goods sold	41,389
Cost of finished goods	36,834	Balance carried forward	24,281
Customers returns at cost	2,856		
	65,670		65,670
Balance brought forward	24,281		

Nominal Ledger Control

	£		£
Raw materials credited		Opening balance	89,561
by suppliers	836	Raw material purchases	22,422
Balance carried forward	111,147		
	111,983		111,983
		Balance brought forward	111,147

(b)   For the transactions so far completed, the schedule of remaining balances is as follows:

	Dr	Cr
	£	£
Raw materials control	54,896	
Work-in-progress control	10,593	
Finished goods control	24,281	
Nominal ledger control		111,147
Factory overhead control – see note (i)		8,786
Wages control – see note (ii)		8,370
Profit and loss account – see note (iii)	38,533	
	128,303	128,303

Notes

(i)   The £8,786 balance is calculated as follows:

	£	£
Factory overhead absorbed		11,786
Less		
Raw material losses	1,236	
Work-in-progress rejects		
(assumed to be normal rejects)	1,764	3,000
		8,786

(ii)   The £8,370 balance is the direct wages allocation to work-in-progress
(iii) The £38,533 balance is calculated as follows:

	£
Cost of goods sold	41,389
Less customers returns at cost	2,856
	38,533

6   (a)   *Cost Ledger – quarter ended 31st October 19 ....*

Raw Materials Stock

	£		£
Opening balance	150,000	Work-in-progress	209,000
Purchases	210,000	Balance carried forward	151,000
	360,000		360,000
Balance brought forward	151,000		

Work-in-Progress

	£		£
Opening balance	90,000	Material usage variance (note 4)	3,000
Raw materials	209,000	Finished goods stock (note 5)	715,800
Direct labour	236,800	Balance carried forward	101,600
Factory overhead	268,600		
Labour efficiency variance			
(note 3)	16,000		
	820,400		820,400
Balance brought forward	101,600		

Finished Goods Stock

	£		£
Opening balance	120,000	Cost of goods sold – profit	
Work-in-progress	715,800	and loss account (note 5)	685,800
		Balance carried forward	150,000

	£		£
	835,800		835,800
Balance brought forward	150,000		

Cost Ledger Control

	£		£
Sales	850,000	Opening balance (note 1)	360,000
Balance carried forward	402,600	Purchases	214,000
		Direct wages	230,000
		Production overhead	
		Fixed	74,000
		Variable	185,000
		Administration and selling	
		expenses	80,000
		Profit and loss account	109,600
	1,252,600		1,252,600
		Balance brought forward	402,600

Wages Control

	£		£
Cost ledger control	230,000	Work-in-progress	236,800
Labour rate variance	6,800		
	236,800		236,800

Factory Overhead Control

	£		£
Cost ledger control (fixed overhead)	74,000	Work-in-progress	268,600
Cost ledger control (variable overhead)	185,000	Factory overhead expenditure variance (note 6)	6,400
Factory overhead efficiency variance (note 8)	17,000	Factory overhead capacity variance (note 7)	1,000
	276,000		276,000

Administration and Selling Expenses

	£		£
Cost ledger control	80,000	Profit and loss account	80,000

Sales

	£		£
Profit and loss account	850,000	Cost ledger control	850,000

Material Price Variance

	£		£
Cost ledger control (note 2)	4,000	Profit and loss account	4,000

Material Usage Variance

	£		£
Work-in-progress control	3,000	Profit and loss account	3,000

Labour Rate Variance

	£		£
Profit and loss account	6,800	Wages control	6,800

Labour Efficiency Variance

	£		£
Profit and loss account	16,000	Work-in-progress	16,000

Factory Overhead Expenditure Variance

	£		£
Factory overhead control (variable)	7,400	Factory overhead control (fixed)	1,000
		Profit and loss account	6,400
	7,400		7,400

Factory Overhead Capacity Variance

	£		£
Factory overhead control	1,000	Profit and loss account	1,000

Factory Overhead Efficiency Variance

	£		£
Profit and loss account	17,000	Factory overhead control (fixed)	5,000
		Factory overhead control (variable)	12,000
	17,000		17,000

Profit and Loss Account

	£		£
Cost of goods sold	685,800	Sales	850,000
Administration and selling		Labour rate variance	6,800
expenses	80,000	Labour efficiency variance	16,800
Material price variance	4,000	Factory overhead efficiency	
Material usage variance	3,000	variance	17,000
Factory overhead expenditure			
variance	6,400		
Factory overhead capacity			
variance	1,000		
Profit (cost ledger control)	109,600		
	889,800		889,800

Notes

(1) Opening stock blanaces: £
        Raw materials   150,000
        Work-in-progress   90,000
        Finished goods   120,000
                                                               ─────────
                                                               360,000
                                                               ═════════

(2) Purchases of raw material: £
        At actual cost   214,000
        At standard cost   210,000
                                                               ─────────
        Material price variance   4,000 (unfavourable)
                                                               ═════════

(3) (Production in standard hours − actual hours) x standard labour rate
     (316,000 − 296,000) x £0.80 (£236,800 ÷ 296,000)
        Labour efficiency variance =   £16,000 (favourable)
                                                               ─────────
(4) Issues of raw materials at standard prices: £
        For actual quantities   209,000
        For standard quantities   206,000
                                                               ─────────
        Material usage variance   3,000 (unfavourable)
                                                               ═════════

(5) Balancing figures

(6)   *Fixed*   *Variable*
                                              £   £
        Budgeted cost   75,000   177,600
                                                         (296,000 x £0.60)
        Actual cost   74,000   185,000
                                           ────────   ────────
        Factory overhead expenditure
        variance   1,000   7,400
                                           ════════   ════════

                                        (favourable) (unfavourable)
(7) (Budgeted hours − actual hours) x fixed standard overhead rate
     (300,000 − 296,000) x £0.25 (£75,000 ÷ 300,000)
        Factory overhead capacity variance =   £1,000 (unfavourable)
                                                               ─────────
(8) (Production in standard hours − actual hours) x standard overhead rate
     Fixed: (316,000 − 296,000) x £0.25 =   5,000   (favourable)
     Variable: (316,000 − 296,000) x £0.60 =   12,000   (favourable)
                                                 ────────
        Factory overhead efficiency variance   17,000   (favourable)
                                                 ════════

(b)

Costing Profit and Loss Account
Quarter ended 31st October 19 ....

	Favour-able £	Unfavour-able £	£
Standard profit on actual sales (see note)			84,200
Add variances			
Material price variance		4,000	
Material usage variance		3,000	
Labour rate variance	6,800		
Labour efficiency variance	16,000		
Factory overhead expenditure variance:			
Fixed	1,000		
Variable		7,400	
Factory overhead capacity variance		1,000	
Factory overhead efficiency variance:			
Fixed	5,000		
Variable	12,000		
	40,800	15,400	25,400
Actual profit			109,600

Note	£	£
Sales		850,000
Less		
Cost of goods sold	685,800	
Administration and selling expenses	80,000	765,800
Standard profit on actual sales		84,200

7   (a)   *Integrated Ledger — three months ended 31st October 19 ....*

Fixed Assets

	£	£
Opening balance	200,000	

275

Provision for Depreciation

		£
	Opening balance	40,000
	Factory overhead control	5,000
		45,000

Finished Goods Stock

	£		£
Opening balance	25,000	Revaluation (opening	
Transfer from work-in-progress	67,800	balance – profit and loss)	500
		Cost of goods sold (profit and	
		loss account) (note 1)	65,800
		Balance carried forward	26,500
	92,800		92,800
Balance brought forward	26,500		

Work-in-Progress

	£		£
Opening balance	12,000	Finished goods stock (note 1)	67,800
Revaluation (opening balance		Material usage variance (note 2)	500
– profit and loss)	500	Labour efficiency variance	
Raw materials	29,500	(note 3)	600
Direct wages	21,600	Balance carried forward	11,500
Factory overhead	16,800		
	80,400		80,400
Balance brought forward	11,500		

Raw Materials

	£		£
Opening balance	23,000	Work-in-progress	29,500
Revaluation (opening balance		Material price variance (note 4)	400
– profit and loss)	1,000	Balance carried forward	26,700
Purchases	32,600		
	56,600		56,600
Balance brought forward	26,700		

Debtors

	£		£
Opening balance	33,000	Cash	101,000
Credit sales	98,000	Balance carried forward	30,000
	131,000		131,000
Balance brought forward	30,000		

Cash

	£		£
Opening balance	27,000	Payments to trade creditors	52,300
Receipts from customers	101,000	Payments to other creditors	13,000
		Wages, insurance and tax	28,800
		Balance carried forward	33,900
	128,000		128,000
Balance brought forward	33,900		

Trade Creditors

	£		£
Cash	52,300	Opening balance	26,000
Balance carried forward	12,000	Materials	32,600
		Indirect materials and expenses	5,700
	64,300		64,300
		Balance brought forward	12,000

Other Creditors

	£		£
Cash	13,000	Opening balance	31,000
Balance carried forward	31,000	Administration, selling and	
		distribution expenses	13,000
	44,000		44,000
		Balance brought forward	31,000

Ordinary Share Capital

		£
	Opening balance	200,000

Reserves and Profit and Loss

		£
	Opening balance	23,000
	Revaluation adjustment	
	(note 5)	1,000
	Profit and loss	16,600
		40,600

Factory Overhead Control

	£		£
Provision for depreciation	5,000	Work-in-Progress	16,800
Indirect materials and expenses	5,700	Overhead capacity variance	
Indirect wages	6,300	(note 7)	320
Overhead expenditure variance		Overhead efficiency variance	
(note 6)	600	(note 8)	480
	17,600		17,600

Profit and Loss

	£		£
Cost of goods sold	65,800	Sales	105,000
Material usage variance	500	Administration, selling and	
Material price variance	400	distribution costs variance	125
Labour efficiency variance	600	Factory overhead expenditure	
Labour rate variance	900	variance	600
Factory overhead capacity variance	320		
Factory overhead efficiency variance	480		
Administration, selling and distribution expenses	13,125		
Sales volume variance	5,000		
Sales price variance	2,000		
Reserves and profit and loss	16,600		
	105,725		105,725

Wages Control

	£		£
Cash	28,800	Work-in-progress	21,600
		Labour rate variance (note 9)	900
		Factory overhead	6,300
	28,800		28,800

Material Usage Variance

	£		£
Work-in-progress	500	Profit and loss	500

Labour Efficiency Variance

	£		£
Work-in-progress	600	Profit and loss	600

Materials Price Variance

	£		£
Raw materials stock	400	Profit and loss	400

Sales

	£		£
Profit and loss	105,000	Debtors	98,000
		Sales volume variance (note 10)	5,000
		Sales price variance (note 11)	2,000
	105,000		105,000

Administration, Selling and Distribution Expenses Control

	£		£
Other creditors	13,000	Profit and loss	13,125
Administration, selling and distribution variance (note 1)	125		
	13,125		13,125

Labour Rate Variance

	£		£
Wages control	900	Profit and loss	900

Administration, Selling and Distribution Expenses Variance

	£		£
Profit and loss	125	Administration, selling and distribution expenses control	125

Factory Overhead Expenditure Variance

	£		£
Profit and loss	600	Factory overhead control	600

Factory Overhead Capacity Variance

	£		£
Factory overhead control	320	Profit and loss	320

Factory Overhead Efficiency Variance

	£		£
Factory overhead control	480	Profit and loss	480

Sales Volume Variance

	£		£
Sales	5,000	Profit and loss	5,000

Sales Price Variance

	£		£
Sales	2,000	Profit and loss	2,000

Notes

(1) Balancing figures

(2)

	£	
Materials issued to production	29,500	
Materials input at standard	29,000	
Material usage variance	500	(unfavourable)

(3)

	£	
Wages applicable to production:		
54,000 x £0.40 =	21,600	
Wages at standard: 52,500 x £0.40 =	21,000	
Labour efficiency variance	600	(unfavourable)

(4)

	£	
Purchase of raw materials on credit	32,600	
Purchase of raw materials at standard	32,200	
Material price variance	400	(unfavourable)

(5)

Stocks, 1st August 19	Per Balance Sheet	Per revaluation
	£	£
Raw materials	23,000	24,000
Work-in-progress	12,000	12,500
Finished goods	25,000	24,500
	60,000	61,000

Revaluation adjustment: £1,000

(6)

	£	
Budgeted factory overhead		
(£70,000 ÷ 4) =	17,600	
Actual factory overhead	17,000	
Factory overhead expenditure variance	600	(favourable)

(7)

Budgeted standard hours: 220,000 ÷ 4 =	55,000	hours
Actual hours	54,000	

		£	
Factory overhead capacity variance brought forward		1,000	
1,000 hours x £0.32 (£70,000 ÷ 220,000) =		£320	(unfavourable)
(8)	Actual hours	54,000	
	Standard hours for actual production	52,500	
	Factory overhead efficiency variance	1,500	
	1,500 hours x £0.32 =	£480	(unfavourable)
(9)		£	
	Actual wages cost	22,500	
	Wages applicable to production	21,600	(see note 3)
	Labour rate variance	900	(unfavourable)
(10)		£	
	Budgeted sales (£420,000 ÷ 4) =	105,000	
	Actual sales at standard selling price	100,000	
	Sales volume variance	5,000	(unfavourable)
(11)		£	
	Actual sales at standard selling prices	100,000	
	Actual sales	98,000	
	Sales price variance	2,000	(unfavourable)

(b) (i) *Profit and Loss Account for the quarter ended 31st October 19 ....*

			£
Standard profit on actual sales (see note)			21,075

Less variances	Favour-able £	Unfavour-able £
Sales price variance		2,000
Material price variance		400
Material usage variance		500
Labour rate variance		900
Labour efficiency variance		600
Factory overhead expenditure variance	600	

281

	Favour- able	Unfavour- able	
	£	£	£
Brought forward	600	4,400	21,075
Factory overhead capacity variance		320	
Factory overhead efficiency variance		480	
Administration, selling and distribution expense variance	125		
	725	5,200	4,475
Actual profit			16,600

Note		£
Budgeted sales		105,000
Less sales volume variance		5,000
		100,000
Less	£	
Factory cost of sales	65,800	
Administration, selling and distribution expenses	13,125	78,925
Standard profit on actual sales		21,075

(b)   (ii)   *Balance Sheet as at 31st October 19 ....*

	£	£	£	£
Fixed assets at cost			200,000	
Less depreciation to date			45,000	155,000
Working capital				
Current assets:				
Stocks:				
Raw materials	26,700			
Work-in-progress	11,500			
Finished goods	26,500	64,700		
Debtors		30,000		
Cash		33,900	128,600	
Current liabilities:				
Trade creditors		12,000		
Other creditors		31,000	43,000	85,600
Capital employed				240,600

Represented by	£
Ordinary share capital	200,000
Reserves and profit and loss account	40,600
	240,600

8   To: The Managing Director   Date . . . .
      From: The Accountant
            Integration of the Cost and Financial Accounts

Differences on reconciliation
When reconciliation of the amounts of profit calculated under both systems is made the following differences may cause difficulty:

(a)   Errors in the processing of the data under both systems, e.g., items that should be included in both sets of records but excluded from one system

(b)   Recognising the differences in amounts where items are correctly included in both sets of accounts and correctly at different amounts, e.g., stock valuations

(c)   Recognising differences in the calculated results because items have been correctly excluded from one set of accounts: either included in the cost accounts but not in the financial accounts, e.g., notional rent, or included in the financial accounts but not in the cost accounts, e.g., interest.

Reorganisation procedure
The steps required to reorganise the accounting system to produce an integrated set of records are as follows:

(a)   If sufficient information is not available regarding the existing system, the procedure should be investigated and recorded as necessary to achieve the objective of integration

(b)   Develop the best method to reorganise the system and the stages of possible introduction of the new procedure

(c)   Obtain the approval of management to the reorganisation

(d)   Implement the new procedure.

To implement the integrated procedure, the financial accounts items would be subjected to additional analysis and the subsidiary records and ledgers linked to each other through the medium of control accounts.

Signed . . . .

Reconciliation of the Profit per the Financial Accounts
with the Profit per the Cost Accounts
Year ended 30th June 19 ....

	£	£
Net profit per the financial accounts		60,570
Less item in financial accounts not in the cost accounts:		
Gain on sales of freehold land		3,650
		56,920
Less item in cost accounts not in financial accounts:		
Notional charge for rent		500
		56,420
Less stock valuation difference:		
Closing stock overheads	1,500	
Opening stock overheads	800	700
		55,720

Less items in both sets of books at different amounts:

	Per Financial Accounts £	Per Cost Accounts £	
Works overhead (see note (i))	10,500	10,650	
Selling overhead (see note (ii))	34,220	37,800	
Administration expenses	21,790	22,000	
Depreciation (see note (iii))	12,200	11,425	
Financial income and expenditure (see note (iv))	5,370	3,000	
	84,080	84,875	795
Net profit per the cost accounts			54,925

Notes

(i)	213,000 units x £0.05 =	£10,650
	£22,700 − £12,000 =	£10,500
(ii)	12% of £315,000 =	£37,800
(iii)	½ x £12,200 =	£ 6,100
	Add 213,000 units x £0.025 =	£ 5,325
		£11,425

(iv) £5,470 – £100 = £5,370.

10   The significance of this statement is in the context of the characteristics of a data base system which may be described as:

(a)   A system oriented to informational needs across functional boundaries. The data base is a total package of information.
(b)   Where one type of information is required, a common purpose record is established.
(c)   Storage requirements are dictated by output needs.
(d)   System procedures are established for types of transactions. Transactions have a path to follow in the system to up-date existing data.
(e)   The type of information required governs extraction arrangements, e.g., exception reporting.
(f)   The centralised control of data.

11   An integrated system of accounting is preferred to a sub-system where this is practicable and to that extent Mr Elliott is correct. The significant point here is the practicality of the arrangements required at comparatively short notice.

It is a common feature that when managements decide to have a costing system, they want results quickly. A management accountant may use his influence to limit these requirements to a realistic time-scale but a new man appointed specifically to give management what they want is in a weak position to argue effectively for the limited introduction of a new costing system. The man who should do this is Mr Elliott.

To alter an established system in a fundamental way demands detailed study and the application of sound recommendations. Mr Watkins is correct in this to the extent that any other course can cause considerable trouble and difficult problems for the accountants to resolve in the future.

Mr Elliott's requirements are not only reasonable but necessary. It is dangerous to issue profit figures in management reports without the knowledge that they are accurately reconcilable with the profits per the financial accounts.

In this case, if Mr Elliott could influence the management to reduce their requirements from the system in the near future, the time may be available to introduce the costing system on an integrated basis without reducing the efficiency of the double-entry system. If the management are not prepared to modify their demands it should be clearly understood that, as soon as practicable, methods and procedures will be examined with a view to their improvement and the removal of duplication in clerical work. The introduction of new routines and the improvement of existing routines should be carried out in stages; each stage being consolidated and operating satisfactorily before the next stage is applied. The scale of operations is crucial. An introduction of a new routine on a small scale may include the same type of problems as its introduction on a large scale. The former situation may be managable, the latter a perfect recipe for chaos. If the accounting operations are on a large scale the pilot run of a new routine is invaluable.

12   The first point to emphasise is that because centralised accounting systems were applicable, presumably with advantage, in the companies previously employing the new group accountant, this is not a sufficient reason to alter the arrangements in Paper Products Ltd. The systems adopted should be specific to the company.

The reasons for centralised accounting given by the new group accountant could be described as advantages of such a system in a general way and others might be added to this list such as:

(i)   The use of mdoern data-processing equipment requires the volume of input that centralisation of routines can provide

(ii)   Fewer staff should be required

(iii) Greater flexibility in the use of staff possible.

These general points may need modification in the case of a specific company. For example, in the case of Paper Products Ltd:

(a)   Will a centralised system be cheaper to operate than a decentralised system?

(b)   Will the loss of local accounting control reduce the service to local management? (This seems to be the view of the larger subsidiary companies but it may be significant that only the larger companies take this view. The true reason may be that because they have larger accounting departments they fear losing some of their power.)

(c)   Is it necessary to centralise the accounting system to standardise the accounting routines?

(d)   To what extent is it company policy to eliminate individual company identity?

The disadvantage of centralisation noted in the case may be relevant because:

(a)   The records previously used for day-to-day control may be passed to head office.

(b)   The local link with the practical background to entries on the accounting documents may be lost. An understanding of what the figures on accounting documents represent is important for valid interpretations of information supplied to management.

Additional points may be considered as disadvantages of the centralisation of accounting such as:

(a) The possible employment of additional employees to centralised staff to deal with local requirements previously covered by existing accounting staff.
(b) Higher grades of staff required to cope with the greater demands of a centralised system.
(c) Reduced costing accuracy because of the remoteness of the control.

23 Cost Accounting Methods

1   (a)   In general, the hourly rates of overhead absorption give a more accurate incidence of cost centre costs to cost units. The desire to achieve greater accuracy usually dictates the use of separate cost centre rates where the use of the departmental resources differ in the manufacture of the product. It is also evident in the answer to the remainder of the question that the incidence of the overhead varies between the cost centres.

(b)   *Factory Overhead Distribution Statement*
               Year ended ....

Expense to be allotted below	£
(i) Supervision	7,525
(ii) Indirect workers	6,000
(iii) Holiday pay and company's National Insurance	6,200
(iv) Tooling cost	9,400
(v) Machine maintenance labour cost	4,500
(vi) Power	1,944
(vii) Small tools and supplies	1,171
(viii) Insurance of machinery	185
(ix) Insurance of buildings	150
(x) Rent and rates	2,500
(xi) Depreciation of machinery	9,250
	48,825

Allotment basis		Q	R	S	T
		£	£	£	£
(i)	Actual	2,050	2,200	1,775	1,500
(ii)	No. of indirect workers	2,250	2,250	750	750
(iii)	Total number of workers	1,900	2,400	1,200	700

Machine groups

Allotment basis		Q	Machine groups		
			R	S	T
		£	£	£	£
	Brought forward	6,200	6,850	3,725	2,950
(iv)	Actual	3,500	4,300	1,000	600
(v)	Machine maintenance hrs	1,500	1,000	1,500	500
(vi)	Kilowatt hours	1,080	264	340	260
(vii)	Actual	491	441	66	173
(viii)	Capital cost of machines	75	50	20	40
(ix)	Floor space − sq metres	54	45	24	27
(x)	Ditto	900	750	400	450
(xi)	Capital cost of machines	3,750	2,500	1,000	2,000
		17,550	16,200	8,075	7,000
Machine hour rate		£17,550	£16,200	£8.075	£7,000
		30,000	36,000	19,000	8,000
		= £0.585	= £0.45	= £0.425	= £0.875
		per machine hour	per machine hour	per machine hour	per machine hour

(c) Overhead absorbed by Job A (machine hour rate basis):

	£
Group Q machines: 4 hours x £0.585 =	2.340
Group R machines: 5 hours x £0.450 =	2.250
Group S machines: 1 hour x £0.425 =	0.425
Group T machines: 6 hours x £0.875 =	5.250
	10.265

(d) Overhead absorbed by Job A (direct labour cost percentage basis):
120% of £7 = £8.40

2 (a) *Computation of Results for the Year as a Basis for Comment*

	£	£
Direct material		21,000
Direct wages		18,500
Prime cost		39,500
Factory overheads (149% on direct wages cost)		27,500
Factory cost		67,000

	£	£
Brought forward		67,000
Administration overheads	5,000	
Selling overheads	3,000	
Distribution overheads	1,500	9,500
		(14% on
		factory
		cost)
Total cost (cost of sales)		76,500
Sales		75,000
Net loss		1,500

Observations

(i) The estimating system is inefficient; actual costs have been greater than estimates for work done

(ii) No check has been made on actual costs in relation to estimates

(iii) The actual percentages for absorbed cost are so close to the estimates that selling prices that were too low must have been fixed on under-estimated prime cost.

(b) The advice to management would be:

(i) Introduce a costing system

(ii) Review the estimating methods and institute the checking of estimates to ensure that realistic selling prices are fixed

(iii) Check company profitability on a regular basis.

In connexion with (i) it is noted that there are two departments and the incidence of the overhead varies considerably. Departmental rates should be used and an attempt made to improve the cost absorption methods.

3 The probable reasons for under-absorption are as follows:

(a) The cost incurred may be greater than the cost estimated for the year

(b) The actual activity may be less than the level estimated for the period

(c) During the course of the year, the averaged absorbed cost may be less than the cost incurred in that part of the year because of the seasonal fluctuations in actual cost.

On the assumption that the under-absorption under (c) above is expected to be eliminated by an over-absorption later in the year no action would be taken. Where the differences arise because of cost or activity levels or both being different from estimate, the action taken would depend on the significance of the under-absorption:

(a)   Where the differences are insignificant and, therefore, the cost informa-
      tion given to management is not likely to be misleading, the under-
      absorbed cost would be written off to costing profit and loss account
(b)   Where the differences are significant, i.e., management is likely to be
      misled by understated costs, the rates of overhead absorption would
      be adjusted and costs amended.

The fact that costs are greater than estimated or activity levels less than
anticipated in the period calls for management action where the variations
are unsatisfactory. The techniques of budgetary control and standard costing
are particularly useful in bringin the variances to the attention of management.

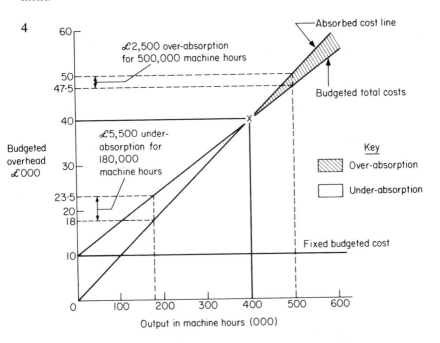

Figure 23.1   Graph showing under- and over-absorption of overheads
               year ....

In the year:
        Budgeted production: 200,000 units
        Budgeted time per unit = 2 machine hours
        Budgeted production time = 200,000 units x 2 hours =
            400,000 machine hours

Total cost for the budgeted production
$$= £10,000 \text{ (fixed cost)} + £30,000 \text{ (variable cost)} = £40,000$$

5   From the range of rates quoted in the case, it is clear that the choice of activity level can significantly affect product costs and this choice is a difficult one to make. It is useful to consider the objectives that may be borne in mind when fixing the activity level to be used in the costing system. These objectives may be: (a) to recover in the period the actual factory overhead incurred; (b) to allow for seasonal and cyclical variations over a reasonable period.

To meet these objectives two activity levels are usually used: (a) practical capacity; and (b) normal capacity.

Practical capacity is the available theoretical capacity reduced by allowance for unavoidable capacity losses such as normal maintenance and holiday interruptions. Normal capacity is the practical capacity adjusted for seasonal and cyclical variations over a sufficient period for these items approximately to cancel out.

In the case, the levels described are on the basis of past performance and future expectations. The recovery of future overhead should be based on future activity levels and three are named in the case (a, d and e). The period covered by the levels is crucial and (d) is too short a time-scale. Levels (a) and (e) are practical and normal capacities respectively. Level (a) is of shorter duration than level (e) and raises the point of the validity of long-term forecasting when it is very difficult to forecast activity levels in the short term.

The factory manager is correct to point out the changes that can occur in activity levels by working overtime and the sub-contracting of the work load. These changes in levels should be incorporated in the plans for the business. Future estimates should, therefore, automatically include adjustments for these items.

Regarding the comments made by the sales manager, practical capacity will recognise sales levels where they do not fluctuate significantly from period to period. Normal capacity gives greater consideration to this factor since this level recognises the long-run ability to manufacture and sell the product. Balancing capacity levels and sales activity is one of the difficult problems for management to resolve and the attempt made is reflected in the use in most companies of normal capacity to recover factory overhead.

Refining Process

	Grams	Cost per gram £	£		Grams	Cost per gram £	£
Material A				Normal loss	900	0.20	180
(see note 1)	2,250	0.70	1,575	Transfer to			
Material B				blending process	3,500	0.90	3,150
(see note 1)	1,500	0.60	900	(see note 3)			
Material C				Abnormal loss	100	0.90	90
(see note 1)	750	0.30	225	(see note 3)			
Labour			120				
Overhead (see note 2)			600				
	4,500		3,420		4,500		3,420

Blending Process

	Grams	Cost per gram £	£		Grams	Cost per gram £	£
Transfer from				Normal loss	560	0.40	224
the refining				Transfer to			
process	3,500	0.90	3,150	finished stock	5,100	1.10	5.610
Material D				(see note 5)			
(see note 4)	1,400	1.00	1,400				
Material E							
(see note 4)	700	1.20	840				
Labour			64				
Analyst's fee			74				
Overhead			240				
Abnormal gain							
(see note 5)	60	1.10	66				
	5,660		5,834		5,660		5,834

Normal Losses in Processes

	Grams	Cost per gram £	£		Grams	Cost per gram £	£
Refining process	900	0.20	180	Abnormal gain			
Blending process	560	0.40	224	on blending	60	0.40	24
				Cash (disposal			
				proceeds):			
				Refining	900	0.20	180
				Blending	500	0.40	200
	1,460		404		1,460		404

Abnormal Losses in Process

	Grams	Cost per gram £	£		Grams	Cost per gram £	£
Refining process	100	0.90	90	Cash (disposal proceeds)	100	0.20	20
				Profit and loss			70
	100		90		100		90

Abnormal Gains from Process

	Grams	Cost per gram £	£		Grams	Cost per gram £	£
Normal loss on blending	60	0.40	24	Blending process	60	1.10	66
Profit and loss			42				
	60		66		60		66

Finished Stock

	Grams	Cost per gram £	£
Blending process	5,100	1.10	5,610

Notes

			Grams
(1)	Material input to the refining process:		
	Material A:	$\frac{3}{6} \times 4{,}500 =$	2,250
	Material B:	$\frac{2}{6} \times 4{,}500 =$	1,500
	Material C:	$\frac{1}{6} \times 4{,}500 =$	750
			4,500

		£
(2)	Overhead apportionment:	
	Refining process: $200 \div 280 \times £840 =$	600
	Blending process: $80 \div 280 \times £840 =$	240
		840

(3) $(£3{,}420 - £180) \div 3{,}600 = £0.90$ per gram

(4) Material input to the blending process:

		Grams
Material D:	$\frac{2}{3}$ × 2,100 =	1,400
Material E:	$\frac{1}{3}$ × 2,100 =	700
		2,100

(5) (£5,768 − £224) ÷ 5,040 = £1.10 per gram

7   To: Managing Director   Date . . . .
     From: Cost Accountant

Scrap Metal Pricing

The suggestion made that scrap metal should be charged to the foundry at market price is preferred to the present practice of charging scrap metal at the average price of metal content.

Comparative Costs under the Different Methods of Pricing Scrap

		Metal cost per tonne Priced on present method £	Priced on suggested method £
% Content Material			
50	A	100	100
20	B	116	116
10	C	12	12
20	Own scrap	57	20
100		285	248
5	Loss in melting	15	13
		300	261

The Position Arising with Varying Scrap Supply

Position	Effect with pricing of scrap on the basis of the average price of metal content	Effect with pricing of scrap on the basis of market price
(a) All scrap cannot be used in future	At present the scrap is credited at £86 (30%	No change in the cost of castings. *(Table continued overleaf)*

Position	Effect with pricing of scrap on the basis of the average price of metal content	Effect with pricing of scrap on the basis of market price
melting processes and must be sold on the market. (In this situation, scrap would be credited to the process at market price.)	of £285). A credit of £30 (30% of £100) will increase the cost of castings.	
(b) (i) The scrap returned to store after pouring is lower than the input of scrap. (In this situation, own scrap used at £285 per tonne and then supplemented as necessary at £100 per tonne.)	Cost of castings reduced because input costs would be reduced by the lower cost of scrap used at £100 per tonne.	No change in the cost of castings.
(b) (ii) The scrap returned to store after pouring is equal to the input of scrap.	No change in the cost of castings.	No change in the cost of castings.

It will be noted that there is no change in the cost of castings in all three situations when scrap metal is priced at market price.

Signed . . . .

Workings

Material A:	50% x £200 = £100
Material B:	20% x £580 = £116
Material C:	10% x £120 = £12
Own scrap:	(20 ÷ 80) x £228 = £57
	20% x £100 = £20
Loss in melting:	(5 ÷ 95) x £285 = £15
	(5 ÷ 95) x £248 = £13

8   *Process Cost Accounts for January 19 ....*

Process A

	Units	£		Units	Unit cost £	£
Opening work-in-progress	1,000	10,000	Transfer to			
Material		9,700	Process B	2,000	11.10	22,200
Labour		3,640	Closing work-in-			
Overhead		5,400	progress	800	11.10	6,540
		28,740				28,740

Unit cost calculation	*Material*	*Labour*	*Overhead*
Equivalent units			
Work-in-progress carried forward	800	400	400
Transfer to Process B	2,000	2,000	2,000
	2,800	2,400	2,400

Unit cost:

Material:	(£5,000 + £9,700) ÷ 2,800 = £5.25	
Labour:	(£2,000 + £3,640) ÷ 2,400 = £2.35	
Overhead:	(£3,000 + £5,400) ÷ 2,400 = £3.50	Total = £11.1

Process B

	Units	£		Units	Unit cost £	£
Opening work-in-progress	3,000	26,800	Transfer to			
Transfer from Process A		22,200	finished goods	5,000	13.0	65,000
Material		2,800	Closing work-in-			
Labour		11,200	progress	2,000	13.0	19,000
Overheads		21,000				
		84,000				84,000

Unit cost calculation	*Material*	*Labour*	*Overhead*
Equivalent units			
Work-in-progress carried forward	2,000	1,000	1,000
Transfer to finished goods	5,000	5,000	5,000
	7,000	6,000	6,000

Unit cost:

Material:	$(£17,000 + £2,800 + £22,200) \div 7,000$	$= £6.00$
Labour:	$(£3,800 + £11,200) \div 6,000$	$= £2.50$
Overhead:	$(£6,000 + £21,000) \div 6,000$	$= £4.50$ Total $=$ £13.00

9   (a)

Figure 23.2   Flow chart for one day

Process

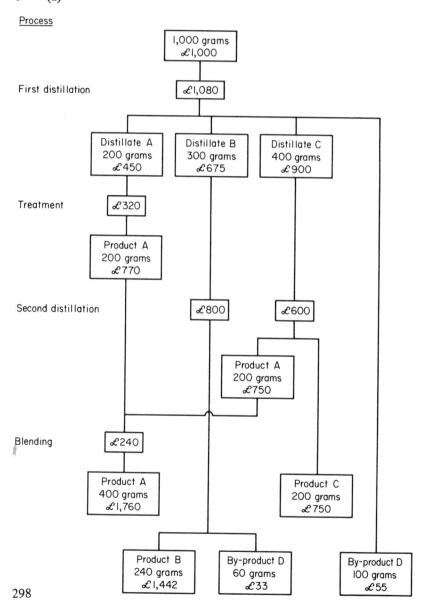

298

Workings
Apportionment of joint cost from the 1st distillation:
£1,000 + £1,080 − £55 = £2,025 (100 grams x £0.55 = £55)
(200 grams ÷ 900 grams) x £2,025 = £450
(300 grams ÷ 900 grams) x £2,025 = £675
(400 grams ÷ 900 grams) x £2,025 = £900
Apportionment of joint cost from the 2nd distillation (Distillate B):
£675 + £800 − £33 = £1,442 (60 grams x £0.55 = £33)

(b) Total cost per gram:
    Product A: (£1,760 ÷ 400 grams) = £4.40 per gram
    Product B: (£1,442 ÷ 240 grams) = £6.00 per gram
    Product C: (£750 ÷ 200 grams) = £3.75 per gram

10   (a)   *Production and Cost Statement − Department C*
Month ended 31st May 19 ....

		Grams	£	
Input				
	Raw materials	160,000	14,400	
	Wages and overhead		10,400	
		160,000	24,800	
Output				
	BP − byproduct to finished stock	40,000	800	(note 1)
	Transfer to Department D	40,000	15,876	(note 2)
	Transfer to Department E	80,000	8,124	
		160,000	24,800	

(b)   *Production and Cost Statement − Department D*
Month ended 31st May 19 ....

			Grams	£
Input				
	Opening work-in-process		7,200	2,592
	Transfer from Deparrtment C	40,000		
	Add 25%	10,000	50,000	15,876
	Wages and overhead			3,968
			57,200	22,436

299

	Grams	£	
Output			
Transfer to finished stock	49,200	19,576	(notes 3
Closing work-in-process	8,000	2,860	and 4)
	57,200	22,436	

Production and Cost Statement – Department E
Month ended 31st May 19 ....

	Grams	£	
Input			
Opening work-in-process	11,000	1,705	
Transfer from Department C	80,000	8,124	
Wages and overhead		8,525	
	91,000	18,354	
Output			
Transfer to finished stock	75,000	15,850	(notes 5
Closing work-in-process	16,000	2,504	and 6)
	91,000	18,354	

(c)

Finished Stock – Product MPA

	Grams	£		Grams	£
Opening stock	2,500	1,000	Cost of sales (note 7)	44,500	17,714
Transfer from Production Department D	49,200	19,576	Closing stock (note 8)	7,200	2,862
	51,700	20,576		51,700	20,576

Finished Stock – Product MPB

	Grams	£		Grams	£
Opening stock	9,000	1,890	Cost of sales (note 9)	77,500	16,366
Transfer from Production Department E	75,000	15,850	Closing stock (note 10)	6,500	1,374
	84,000	17,740		84,000	17,740

Finished Stock – Product BP

	Grams	£		Grams	£
Transfer from Production Department C	40,000	800	Cost of sales	40,000	800

Notes

(1) Value of byproduct: 40,000 grams x (£0.025 – £0.005) = £800

(2) Net sales values:

MPA	£	£
Sales value		30,000
(40,000 grams + (25% x 40,000) x £0.60)		
Less		
Selling and distribution costs	4,000	
(50,000 grams x £0.08)		
Further processing costs	3,968	7,968
		22,032

MPB		
Sales value		24,000
(80,000 grams x £0.30)		
Less		
Selling and distribution costs	4,200	
(80,000 x £0.0525)		
Further processing costs	8,525	12,725
		11,275

Proportion of cost transfer from Department C to Departments D and E: (£24,800 – £800 = £24,000)

Product MPA: (£22,032 ÷ £33,307) x £24,000 = £15,876
Product MPB: (£11,275 ÷ £33,307) x £24,000 = £8,124

(3) Unit cost calculation on a FIFO basis:

	Grams	Material	Equivalent units Wages and over- head
Completed units	7,200		3,600
	42,000	42,000	42,000
Work-in-process	8,000	8,000	4,000
	57,200	50,000	49,600
Period costs		£15,876	£3,968 *Total*
Unit cost		£0.3175	£0.08 £0.3975

(4) Valuations: £

Transfer to finished stock:

	£
Opening balance	2,592
3,600 x £0.08 =	288
42,000 x £0.3975 =	16,696
	19,576

Work-in-process:

	£
8,000 x £0.3175 =	2,540
4,000 x £0.08 =	320
	2,860

Note: The calculation adjusted to agree the total values on page 300.

(5) Unit cost calculation on a FIFO basis:

	Grams	Material	Wages and overhead
		Equivalent units	
Completed units	11,000		5,500
	64,000	64,000	64,000
Work-in-process	16,000	16,000	8,000
	91,000	80,000	77,500
Period costs		£8,124	£8,525 *Total*
Unit cost		£0.1016	£0.11 £0.2116

(6) Valuations: £

Transfer to finished stock:

	£
Opening balance	1,705
5,500 x £0.11 =	605
64,000 x £0.2116 =	13,540
	15,850

Work-in-process:

	£
16,000 x £0.1016 =	1,624
8,000 x £0.11 =	880
	2,504

Note: The calculation adjusted to agree the total values on page 300.

(7)   Valuation of cost of sales, Product MPA:

Grams	£	
2,500	1,000	
7,200	2,880	(£2,592 + £288)
34,800	13,834	(34,800 x £0.3975)
44,500	17,714	

Note: The calculation adjusted to agree the total values on page 300.

(8)   Valuation of closing finished goods stock, Product MPA:
      7,200 x £0.3975 = £2,862

(9)   Valuation of cost of sales, Product MPB:

Grams	£	
9,000	1,890	
11,000	2,310	(£1,705 + £605)
57,500	12,166	(57,500 x £0.2116)
77,500	16,366	

(10) Valuation of closing finished goods stock, Product MPB:
      7,500 x £0.2116 = £1,374.
      Note: The calculation adjusted to agree the values on page 300.

11   Joint products are products that are processed together because they
are not identifiable as separate products until the point of separation. The
costs up to the point of separation are joint costs and cannot be directly
identified with each product produced. If individual product costs are
required, apportionment of cost must take place. The quotation suggests
three methods of apportionment and given the figures in the question, the
product profits would be calculated as follows:

(a)

	Products		
	A	B	Total
	£	£	£
Sales	6,000	2,400	8,400
Cost of sales	3,000	3,600	6,600
Profit/loss	3,000	(1,200)	1,800

Apportionment on
the basis of weight:
$\frac{10}{22}$ x £6,600 = £3,000
$\frac{12}{22}$ x £6,600 = £3,600

(b)

	Products		
	A	B	Total
	£	£	£
Sales	6,000	2,400	8,400
Marginal cost	2,000	2,400	4,400
Contribution	4,000	Nil	4,000
Fixed cost	2,200	–	2,200
Profit	1,800	Nil	1,800

Apportionment on the basis of:
(i) Weight: marginal cost $\frac{10}{22}$ x £4,400 = £2,000
$\frac{12}{22}$ x £4,400 = £2,400
(ii) Contribution: fixed cost

(c)

	Products		
	A	B	Total
	£	£	£
Sales	6,000	2,400	8,400
Cost of sales	4,714	1,886	6,600
Profit	1,286	514	1,800

Apportionment on the basis of the sales value of production:
$\frac{60}{84}$ x £6,600 = £4,714
$\frac{24}{84}$ x £6,600 = £1,886

The apportionment methods are arbitrary and according to the method used widely varying profit figures are calculated for individual products. The total profit remains the same. The only point of apportioning such costs to individual products is to calculate stock values. If apportioned costs are used for decision-making, the results shown above could be very misleading to management. It is not recommended that apportioned joint process costs are used for planning and control.

12 (a)

COST STATEMENT PERIOD ENDED .... (PERIOD 6)	
CRUSHING AND SEPARATING PROCESS	£
RAW MATERIALS	1,200
LABOUR	160
SUNDRY MATERIALS	40
EXPENSES	100
	1,500
SALE OF WASTE	100
TRANSFER TO OIL EXTRACTION PROCESS	70
TRANSFER TO STARCH GRINDING AND DRYING PROCESS	1,330
	1,500
COST PER PRODUCT UNIT (PRODUCTION: 50 UNITS)	28
OIL EXTRACTION PROCESS	£
TRANSFER FROM CRUSHING AND SEPARATING PROCESS	70
LABOUR	120
SUNDRY MATERIALS	40
EXPENSES	170
PACKING COSTS	50
	450
SALE OF WASTE	20
TRANSFER TO FINISHED GOODS (10 PRODUCT UNITS)	430
	450
SELLING PRICE PER UNIT	60
COST PER UNIT	43
PROFIT PER UNIT	17
STARCH GRINDING AND DRYING PROCESS	£
TRANSFER FROM CRUSHING AND SEPARATING PROCESS	1,330
LABOUR	340
SUNDRY MATERIALS	130
EXPENSES	200
PACKING COSTS	100
TRANSFER TO FINISHED GOODS (20 PRODUCT UNITS)	2,100
SELLING PRICE PER UNIT	120
COST PER UNIT	105
PROFIT PER UNIT	15

Figure 23.3

Workings

Packing costs:	£
Labour	80
Sundry materials	40
Expenses	30
	150

Oil extraction process: $\frac{1}{3}$ × £150 = £50
Starch grinding and drying process: $\frac{2}{3}$ × £150 = £100

(b)   The usefulness of the statement produced as in (a) is restricted as a result of the arbitrary apportionments made. It is considered that a statement calculating the contribution to joint costs would be less liable to mislead management. Such a statement is shown in Figure 23.4.

COST STATEMENT

PERIOD ENDED .... (PERIOD 6)

	OIL		STARCH	
SEPARABLE REVENUE AND COSTS	*Per Unit £*	*£*	*Per unit £*	*£*
SALES (A)	60	600	120	2,400
COSTS: LABOUR	12	120	17	340
SUNDRY MATERIALS	4	40	6.5	130
PACKING	4	40	4	80
	20	200	27.5	550
LESS SALE OF WASTE	2	20		–
(B)	18	180	27.5	550
CONTRIBUTION (A – B)	42	420	92.5	1,850

JOINT REVENUE AND COSTS	*Per Unit £*	*£*
CONTRIBUTION:		
OIL		420
STARCH		1,850
(A)		2,270
COST OF GRAIN	24	1,200
LABOUR	3.2	160
SUNDRY MATERIALS	0.8	40
	28	1,400
LESS SALE OF WASTE	2	100
(B)	26	1,300
NET CONTRIBUTION (A – B = C)		970
GENERAL WORKS EXPENSES (D)		500
NET PROFIT (C – D)		470

Figure 23.4

24 Accounting for Changing Price Levels

1   The main principles to be observed in the maintenance of the real capital of the business are:

(a)   The proceeds of the sale of goods or the services by the business should be sufficient to replace the assets consumed in production.

(b)   The balance of the proceeds of the sale of the goods or the services should be sufficient to satisfy the economic claims made against the business not included in costs. These are taxation, interest charges and the necessary payment of dividends to investors.

(c)   The provision of accounts that reflect the real position so that the misleading impression is not given that companies are retaining satisfactory surpluses within the business when, in fact, capital is being eroded.

(d)   The provision of accounting information as a basis for decision-making that will attempt to ensure that when decisions are made, the financial effects of the possible courses of action, in the context of the maintenance of real capital, have been considered.

2   Where an appropriation of profits is made for the excess cost of replacement of assets, costs include only depreciation based on cost, and the profit element in estimates and prices is expected to cover the extra depreciation. The arguments supporting this course of action are as follows:

(a)   Costs are expressed on the basis of costs incurred

(b)   Depreciation is not providing for the replacement of a specific asset

(c)   The increase in replacement cost may be difficult to estimate

(d)   The amount to be provided for replacement is a matter determined by financial policy.

Where the excess cost of replacement of assets is included in the costs of the sale of goods or the provision of services, the arguments put forward for applying this course of action are as follows:

308

(a)   Costs are understated unless the provision for depreciation is sufficient to maintain real capital

(b)   The understatement of costs can seriously mislead management

(c)   The need to cover such additional costs as excess depreciation may not be realised in the fixing of selling prices

(d)   The costs of using equivalent assets are comparable.

Both courses of action have the merit of attempting to ensure that the real capital of the business is not eroded by dividend distributions from over-stated profits.

3   Not all prices change in the same proportions or in the same direction. A general index such as the wholesale or retail price index attempts to indicate general inflation and the overall change in the purchasing power of money. There is no perfect general price index but as an approximate indication of current price levels a general price index may be used. The ASSC in its recommendations considered the following indices in the UK which might be taken as indicators:

(a)   Gross domestic product (GDP) deflator

(b)   Total final expenditure (TFE) deflator

(c)   Consumers' expenditure deflator (CED)

(d)   Retail price index (RPI).

Because changes in the purchasing power of the £ are more often conceived in relation to the purchasing power of money spent by individuals on goods and services for personal use, the ASSC recommend the use of the RPI index. The RPI index is not subject to retrospective revision and is available monthly by about the middle of the following month.

Price level changes of specific assets may be measured by special price indices prepared for them. Advocates of the use of the specific price index, such as company index calculations for each class of asset, make the point that the average change in all prices may not reflect the impact of a price level change on a particular business.

The use of one general index maintains capital in purchasing power units whereas the use of several special indices maintains capital in physical assets. The choice of which index to use to adjust asset original costs to current price levels depends on the objective to be achieved. If price level adjustments only are required, a general index may be used. If the physical assets are to be maintained during a period of changing price levels, specific indices will be used.

4   The arguments for the calculation of the depreciation of fixed assets on their replacement value instead of their original cost are as follows:

(a)   Depreciation would be calculated on a consistent basis. On an original cost basis, the historical cost depreciation would be in terms of varying asset values according to the year of purchase.

(b)   If depreciation was charged against profits on the basis of historic cost in a period of inflation, the charge would be understated and profits overstated.

(c)   By calculating depreciation on replacement values, the book values of assets will be related to current values if assets are included in the accounts on a replacement cost basis.

(d)   Important assessments of profitability such as the return on capital employed ratio are likely to be more meaningful to management.

(e)   In calculating profit in real terms, current revenue should be compared with current costs. Depreciation calculated on replacement cost meets this requirement.

The arguments against the calculation of the depreciation of fixed assets on the above basis are as follows:

(a)   It is difficult to ascertain accurate replacement costs.

(b)   Unless replacement cost values are incorporated into the accounts of the business, the accounts are prepared on an historic basis and depreciation on original costs will be required. Both calculations can be made but this will result in increased effort and clerical cost.

(c)   Costs should be expressed on the basis of costs incurred.

5		*Subsidiary company A*	*Subsidiary company B*
(i)	Current replacement cost:	$\dfrac{150}{40} \times £200,000$ $= \underline{\underline{£750,000}}$	$\dfrac{150}{100} \times £550,000$ $= \underline{\underline{£825,000}}$
(ii)	The accumulated depreciation to date assuming the asset is to be reported at current value:	$\dfrac{27}{40} \times £750,000$ $= \underline{\underline{£506,250}}$	$\dfrac{17}{40} \times £825,000$ $= \underline{\underline{£350,625}}$
(iii)	The depreciation figure for the present year based on current values:	$\dfrac{£750,000}{40}$ $= \underline{\underline{£18,750}}$	$\dfrac{£825,000}{40}$ $= \underline{\underline{£20,625}}$

6   Dear Sir,

Calculating Depreciation on Inflated Cost

There is a difference of opinion regarding the back adjustment for depreciation where replacement costs indicate the charge for earlier years should have been greater than included in the accounts.

The concern in the year when the profits are being ascertained is the amount of depreciation calculated on the value to the business of fixed assets at the time the revenue against which the depreciation can be charged accrues to the company. It would clearly be impracticable to calculate a depreciation charge each time a sale is made by the company and, therefore, the depreciation charge for the year may normally be based on the average value to the business during the year of the fixed assets.

It is not surprising your reader is puzzled by the figures given. Assuming the valuations given are gross replacement costs, their average value to the business is £5,900 (£6,300 + £5,500 ÷ 2). The depreciation for the year is, therefore, 10% of £5,900 = £590. The fact that earlier depreciation will have been calculated on a figure of £5,500 gross replacement cost means that depreciation will have been understated for previous years. The difference between the total depreciation amount charged for previous years and the total depreciation calculated on the revised valuation is the back-log depreciation.

Yours faithfully,

7   The question does not give an indication of the state of these machines now. If the book value is small, the assumption is that the estimated lives of these assets used for depreciation calculations have reduced the book values to nominal values. Replacing the original costs and depreciating on the same lives would reduce the book figures to nominal amounts — probably more than the present book values because of increased values but still low amounts.

If the statement in the question 'book value is small' means that the anticipated life of the asset is still outstanding for a reasonable period and the book value is small merely because of low original cost, the use of replacement costs could be significant. This would increase considerably the depreciation charge based on such replacement costs. From the details given in the question, the depreciation charge has been understated.

Where the life of the asset has been underestimated, the annual charge for product costing should be the depreciation calculated on the basis of the total amount to be written off over the total life of those assets, divided by that useful life now estimated. Preferably, the amount to be written off would be the replacement cost now recognised as four or five times the original purchase price.

8   Monetary items in a closing balance sheet for an accounting period would not be adjusted by the general price index.

Monetary items are those where amounts are fixed by contract or otherwise in terms of numbers of pounds, regardless of changes in general price levels. Examples of monetary items are cash, debtors, creditors and loan capital. Holders of monetary assets lose general purchasing power during a period of inflation to the extent that any income from the assets does not adequately compensate for the loss; the converse applies to those having monetary liabilities.

A company with a material excess on average over the year of monetary liabilities over monetary assets will show, in its supplementary current purchasing power statement, a gain in purchasing power during the year. To calculate this gain, although the monetary items in a closing balance sheet for an accounting period would not be adjusted by the general price index, the opening balances at the beginning of the period would be adjusted by the general price index for that date.

Regarding the profit and loss statement, all items would be adjusted apart from those that occurred at the same price level as that represented by the current general price index.

9   *Balance Sheet as at 31st August 1976*
                       (Current Purchasing Power Basis)

	£	£		£	£
Share capital			Fixed assets		
Ordinary shares			Valuation (note 1)	280,000	
(note iv)		150,000	Less depreciation		
Reserves			(note ii)	92,250	187,750
Profit and loss			Current assets		
account (note v)		18,350	Stock (note iii)	60,600	
10% Debentures		100,000	Debtors	30,000	
Current liabilities			Cash and bank balance	40,000	130,600
Creditors	40,000				
Corporation tax	10,000	50,000			
		318,350			318,350

Notes

(i) Fixed assets valuation:

Date of purchase	Asset original cost £	Conversion factor	CPP value £
1st September 1970	50,000	125	62,500
1st September 1973	150,000	110	165,000
1st Septenber 1975	50,000	105	52,500
	250,000		280,000

(ii) Depreciation calculation:

Asset date of purchase		£
1st September 1970	$\frac{6}{10}$ x £62,500 =	37,500
1st September 1973	$\frac{3}{10}$ x £165,000 =	49,500
1st September 1975	$\frac{1}{10}$ x £52,500 =	5,250
		92,250

(iii) Stock valuation: £60,000 x 101 = £60,600
(iv) Share capital: £100,000 x 150 = £150,000
(v) Profit and loss account — the balancing figure.

10   *Reconciliation of Profit on an Historical Basis with Profit*
on a Current Purchasing Power Basis
Year ended ....

	£	£
Profit before taxation (historical basis)		—
Deduct/add adjustments to convert to current purchasing power basis:		
Stock — additional charge based on restating the cost of stock at the beginning and end of the year in pounds of current purchasing power	—	
Depreciation — additional depreciation based on cost measured in pounds of current purchasing power of fixed assets	—	
Monetary items — net gain or loss in purchasing power resulting from the effects of inflation on the company's net monetary items	—	
carried forward	—	313

	£	£
Brought forward	—	
Sales, purchases and all other costs — as increased by the change in the index between the average date at which they were incurred and the end of the year	—	—
Profit before taxation (current purchasing power basis)		—

11 (a)

Balance Sheets
Note   *(Current Purchasing Power Basis)*

Note	31st December 1975			31st December 1976	
	£	£		£	£
(i)	52,500		Fixed assets	52,500	
(ii)	17,500	35,000	Less accumulated depreciation	19,250	33,250
(iii)	9,947		Stock	18,900	
(iv)	11,053		Debtors	25,000	
(v)	8,842	29,842	Cash	5,000	48,900
		64,842			82,150
(vi)		51,579	Shareholders equity		55,150
(vii)		13,263	Creditors		27,000
		64,842			82,150

Notes

(i)   Fixed assets: £30,000 x (105 ÷ 60) = £52,500
(ii) Accumulated depreciation: £10,000 x (105 ÷ 60) = £17,500
                                  £1,000 x (105 ÷ 60) = £1,750
(iii) Stock: £9,000 x (105 ÷ 95) = £9,947
             £18,000 x (105 ÷ 100) = £18,900 ((95 + 105) ÷ 2)
(iv) Debtors: £10,000 x (105 ÷ 95) = £11,053
(v)   Cash: £8,000 x (105 ÷ 95) = £8,842
(vi) Shareholders equity — the balancing figure
(vii) Creditors: £12,000 x (105 ÷ 95) = £13,263.

(b)   *Profit and Loss Statement for the year ended 31st December 1976*

	£	£	
Sales		42,000	(note i)
Less			
Cost of sales	36,197		(note ii)
Depreciation	1,750	37,947	(note iii)
		4,053	
Less monetary loss		482	(note iv)
Profit		3,571	

Notes

(i)   Sales: £40,000 x (105 ÷ 100) = £42,000

(ii) Cost of sales:

	£		£
	9,000	x 105 ÷ 95	9,947
	25,000	x 105 ÷ 100	26,250
	34,000		36,197

(iii) See note (ii) in part (a)

(iv) *Cash*

	£		£
Opening balance: £8,000 x 105 ÷ 95)	8,842	Suppliers: £18,000 x (105 ÷ 100)	18,900
Debtors: £20,000 x (105 ÷ 100)	21,000	Balance	10,942
	29,842		29,842

Debtors

	£		£
Opening balance: £10,000 x (105 ÷ 95)	11,053	Cash: £20,000 x (105 ÷ 100)	21,000
Sales: £40,000 x (105 ÷ 100)	42,000	Balance	32,053
	53,053		53,053

Creditors

	£		£
Cash: £18,000 x (105 ÷ 100)	18,900	Opening balance: £12,000 x	
Balance	39,513	(105 ÷ 95)	13,263
		Suppies: £43,000 x (105 ÷ 100)	45,150
	58,413		58,413

	Closing balances £	Above balances £	£	
Cash	5,000	10,942	5,942	loss
Debtors	25,000	32,053	7,053	loss
Creditors	27,000	39,513	12,513	gain
			482	loss

(c)

	Shareholders equity £	
Opening balance	51,579	per answer to
Closing balance	55,150	part (a)
Profit per part (b)	3,571	

12   The findings of the 'little Neddy' inquiry have merely reinforced the volume of evidence produced to indicate the shortcomings of conventional accounts. As long ago as 1952 the then Institute of Cost of Works Accountants[1] pointed out that:

(a)   It is possible for the distribution of money profits earned by a business to involve a distribution of real capital, which results in the undermining of the real value of the interests of contributors of business capital

(b)   The measurement in terms of money of the results of the operations of a business do not reflect adequately the results, in terms of real (or stable) values, of these operations.

It is not uncommon to find that people do accept that conventional methods of accounting do not deal adequately with the problem of inflation but relatively few accountants act upon their knowledge of the situation and do something about it.

The General Educational Trust of the Institute of Chartered Accountants in England and Wales produces a survey of published accounts and a copy of their report shows that few companies considered the increased cost of replacement of fixed assets at higher prices. Even these companies differed widely in their choice of method to deal with the problem. This is the difficulty. There is considerable disagreement on the methods that should be employed to deal with the problem.

[1]   *The Accountancy of Charging Price Levels*, ICWA 1952, page 15.

Accountants are reluctant to depart from the base of historical cost into the realms of valuations that are more a matter of opinion than objective verifiable fact. The fact that significant figures in the accounts are a matter of opinion at the present time seems to be ignored or the view is taken that the area of subjectivity should not be increased.

The ASSC has recommended the CPP method as a means of resolving the problem at this stage of progress or lack of it. The historical costs are preserved and the effect of general price level movements are reflected in supplementary statements: these statements prepared on a standard basis by the use of indices capable of verification (the retail price index). The trouble with this approach is the one outlined in the editorial: price movements for specific assets do not necessarily move in line with the general price level.

With a marked reluctance to employ CPP accounting, objections to the use of replacement costs will be considerable, although the Sandilands report is creating the necessary climate for change. The accountant cannot continue to live in a fool's paradise. Some of the changes to be made may not be welcome but they are necessary particularly where accounting information is used by management as a basis for decision-making.

25 Performance Assessment

1   There is a need for adequate standards of comparison in order to isolate the essential areas of business activity demanding managerial attention and possibly further investigation. Such analysis may be useful in indicating the appropriate action that should be taken by management. The problems associated with finding such standards are as follows:

(a)   Ensuring that the standard is comparable with the information to be evaluated. This may be difficult where the standard is external, for example, another company, or internal in the form of data for a comparable period of time which might include the effects of activities not applicable to current performance.

(b)   Ensuring that the standard is a correct measure of performance. It is not unusual for standards to be assessments in the form of single figures of what should be attained in efficient conditions. In fact a range of acceptable performance may be more appropriate.

(c)   Ensuring that the standard is realistic. While many standards are based on rigorous engineering specifications this is obviously not possible with all standards, and loose estimation may creep into the system to such an extent that the standards are of little value.

The standard should represent a reasonable level of attainment. The level of attainment usually adopted is that currently attainable in the conditions reasonably anticipated for efficient operations.

Of the various types of comparable data (budgets, comparable companies or departments, and historical data for comparable periods of time) budgets and standard costs are likely to be better indicators of the required performance of a business. They have their faults like all standards but they are usually prepared as a serious attempt to measure performance in circumstances expected to operate in the business. A clear definition of terms applied and assumptions used in preparing the standards is needed.

318

2   Profitability is usually indicated as the result of expressing profit as a percentage of the sales revenue earned in generating that profit. There are different interpretations of profit and they are measured as follows:

(a)   Gross profit — the difference between the cost of goods sold and their sales value where the revenue is greater than the cost involved.

(b)   Contribution — the difference between sales value and the marginal cost of sales where that marginal cost is less than the revenue involved.

(c)   Net profit — the difference between gross profit and administration, selling and distribution costs. It may also be obtained by deducting fixed costs from contribution.

Increasingly, profitability is being expressed as the ratio of profit to capital employed.

Efficiency is the amount of output per unit of input. It is a productivity measurement and often measured in an engineering sense, e.g., a measured factor of some resource used such as the hours of work produced relative to some standard, as compared with the actual hours taken to produce that work.

Volume may be expressed in terms of sales or production activity. In the case of this question it is the former and may be measured in units or value.

In a general sense the statement is true but it needs to be qualified:

(a)   It is possible to have profitable products (e.g., in terms of contribution) but when fixed costs are deducted a net loss will result. It is true that the expression refers to net profit and it may be inferred that the 'profitability of products' is, therefore, net profit of products but the absorption of costs may be considered as misleading.

(b)   It is possible to have an efficient cost centre but that does not necessarily mean that it is in the profitable interests of the business. What is important is the effectiveness of the cost centres, i.e., how well the objectives of the cost centre have been achieved.

(c)   A company should not aim for volume of sales alone. Net profit achieved can be improved by the increased volume of the more profitable products.

3   An ideal standard is a standard based on performance under the most favourable conditions hence the term 'ideal'. It is an unrealistic standard because perfection is not attainable. If used as a measure of performance, its only justification could be that management would be motivated to high performance on the grounds that a lower standard that is more easily

attainable would not 'stretch' the individual. It is extremely doubtful that this view could be supported when the challenge represented by the ideal is unattainable.

Fundamental to the measurement of performance is the controllability factor and many of the most favourable conditions assumed by the ideal standard are outside the control of a manager. Managers should be judged on the basis of the elements of their job that are under their control.

The currently attainable standard is considerably superior to the ideal standard as a satisfactory measure of performance and the challenge to high performance is usually met by setting the standard on the basis of efficient conditions rather than an unattainable ideal.

4   Information for management regarding the efficiency of the departments and the profitability of products is usually presented as follows:

	Product or Department A £	Product or Department B £	Product or Department C £	Total £
Sales	–	–	–	–
Less cost of sales	–	–	–	–
Profit	–	–	–	–

The departmental information may be limited to costs (cost centres) but if the analysis is by profit centre, marginal cost presentation may be as follows:

	Product A £	Product B £	Product C £	Total £
Sales	–	–	–	–
Less marginal cost of sales	–	–	–	–
Contribution	–	–	–	–
Less fixed costs				–
Profit				–

If standard costing is used, the presentation may be as follows:

	£	£	£
Standard profit on actual sales			–
Add/deduct variances from standard			
Favourable: detailed variances	–		
	–		
	–	–	
Unfavourable: detailed variances	–	–	–
Actual profit			–

Not all variances will be identifiable with specific products or departments but where this is possible the analysis may be given.

Where standard costing is employed, the emphasis is on variances from standard cost as a measure of efficiency. If budgetary control is employed, the variances are indicated as a result of comparing actual and budgeted costs. Budgetary control comparisons may be made without standard costing but where standard costing is in operation, the standards are preferably based on budgetary information and this connexion ensures that the measures of efficiency and profitability are of greater value.

5   *Check List for the Internal Control System*

General aspects of the system
(a)   Does the system of internal control appear to work effectively?
(b)   Are weaknesses in the business being signalled for the attention of management?
(c)   Are the weaknesses requiring action being brought to the attention of appropriate personnel?
(d)   Is action taken promptly regarding problems demanding attention?

Authority and responsibility
(a)   Are centres of responsibility clearly defined?
(b)   Have individual members of management the necessary authority to carry out their assigned responsibilities?
(c)   Are members of staff aware of assigned responsibilities and the extent of authority delegated?

Work allocation
(a)   Is the work fairly distributed and adequately covered by existing staff?
(b)   Is there a rotation of jobs to ensure adequate coverage in terms of sickness and holidays and ensure that internal check is safeguarded?
(c)   Is the work control cycle apportioned between a number of personnel?

Procedures
(a)   Are there effective controls over documentation?
(b)   What is the extent of checking of accuracy incorporated in the system and are the number of errors subsequently revealed reasonable and not of sufficient importance to be a serious problem?
(c)   What discretions are allowed in applying procedures?

(d) What initiates procedures and is there any control on changes made?

(e) What are the independent checking arrangements and the extent of the authority of the personnel given the task, e.g., use of internal auditors?

Relationships

(a) Is the morale in the organisation reasonably good?

(b) Are working relationships between related departments satisfactory?

(c) Are managers in control of their departments?

Specific control systems

(a) Are specific control systems concerned with the acquisition of resources developed to the degree necessary, e.g., capital expenditure control?

(b) Are specific control systems concerned with the use of resources developed to the degree necessary, e.g., material control, labour control and expense control.

6 A system of internal control incorporates the following:

(a) The stipulation of managerial policies and plans to achieve the objectives laid down for the business

(b) A check that methods and measures adopted encourage the adherence to the managerial policies stipulated

(c) An appraisal of accuracy and reliability of the accounting data produced for managerial control

(d) A check on the effectiveness of company procedures

(e) A verification that the assets of the business are safeguarded.

Management responsibilities for such a system are related to company objectives and the successful company emphasises areas of the business where it is vital to be effective; considers where the business must be in one, three, five or more years time; how it is going to get there from the position it is in now; and defines the part to be played by each key executive to overcome problems that could prevent the company achieving its overall objectives. These responsibilities require the design, installation and maintenance of an internal control system, in this context incorporating the features given at the beginning of the answer to this question.

7 Cost audit is the verification of the accuracy and reliability of the cost accounting data and the extent to which the procedures laid down are being followed in practice.

The auditing principles applied in a large company would include the accounting routines concerned with functional sectors of the cost department. This would depend on the form of organisation of the company but cost departments have routines concerned with the elements of cost: wages, material and overheads; and capital expenditure control. The cost audit would include the verification that the costing systems are appropriate in meeting the objectives laid down by the business and in particular, in relation to the business described in the question, that sufficient flexibility is provided in the system to meet the various demands made upon it.

Where job orders for government departments are concerned, the internal audit described above is supplemented by an external audit where the actual costs claimed by the company as a basis for fixing the price will be checked by the government's technical cost officers.

8   The objectives to be borne in mind in transfer pricing are as follows:

(a)   To assist in the measurement of the profitability, efficiency and effectiveness of the company segments in the group
(b)   To motivate management to take action in the overall interests of the group
(c)   To ensure that sections of the group are fairly treated in respect of inter-company transactions
(d)   To facilitate the operations of the group to the extent that a well chosen transfer price system agreed between the affected company managements will not create friction and detrimentally affect personal relationships.

In summary, the primary objective of a system of transfer pricing is to assist in the promotion of the action necessary to achieve the objectives laid down for the company.

9   It is important that proper consideration is given to determining transfer prices for the following reasons:

(a)   Segment management should be motivated to take action in the overall interests of the business rather than the progress of their segment alone
(b)   To ensure that sections of the group are fairly treated in respect of inter-company transactions so that disputes between segment management will be at the minimum and differences that may arise will be of minor significance
(c)   To enable segment management to measure their profitability, efficiency and effectiveness.

The methods of transfer pricing which are available are as follows:

(a)   Cost prices:
      Actual absorption cost
      Standard absorption cost
      Actual marginal cost
      Standard marginal cost
(b)   Cost plus prices:
      Actual absorption cost plus profit
      Standard absorption cost plus profit
      Actual marginal cost plus profit
      Standard marginal cost plus profit
(c)   Market prices:
      Actual market price
      Modified market price
(d)   Linear programming prices.

The advantages and disadvantages of these methods are as follows:

(a)   *Cost prices*
The principal value of the marginal cost price over absorption cost to the receiving unit is in short-term deicision-making but this can be accomplished by analysing the make-up of the full-cost transfer price. Cost is simple to use but may create problems in measuring segment profitability. Because actual costs may include inefficiency costs of the transferring segment, it is an advantage to use standard costs.

(b)   *Cost plus prices*
The advantage is the possibility of the application of a simple standard formula but this may be unfair to the receiving segment to the extent that not only may the transfer price include high costs, but an increased profit margin on these costs.

(c)   *Market prices*
The advantage of the market price is that it is consistent with external pricing policy and profitability assessment but the disadvantage is that a market price may not be available. If the market price is modified, negotiation is involved and the disadvantage is that the result may not be fair to both segments, and disputes might arise.

(d)   *Linear programming prices*
The advantage is the likelihood of optimising the use of company resources, but the disadvantage is the imposition of centralised control on the transfer decision-making process.

10   Factors possibly affecting the transfer price chosen are as follows:

(a)   Cost of materials transferred
(b)   The presently agreed price of £1.30 per gram
(c)   The possibility of a lower price because the material is not in as good a
      condition
(d)   The benefit to Department X by removing the material
(e)   The manufacturing losses of Departments X and Y
(f)   Significant amounts are involved.

Regarding the above points:

(a)   The cost of the materials transferred is not given but it would appear
      that it costs more than £1.30 per gram, seeing a loss is being incurred,
      unless the outside sales are made at a lower figure.
(b)   There should be some allowance for the fact that the material is not in
      as good condition as that normally purchased outside. The Department
      X manager's contention that a price of £1.50 is payable for grade 2
      material is only valid if that normally available of better quality than
      the material from Department X cost £1.50 per gram. If that is the
      case an allowance is being given. If not, no allowance is being given.
(c)   If this material is of no value to Department X it is true that its removal
      would cost the department something which is a charge avoided by the
      transfer to Department Y. Dpeartment Y is not penalised if an equival-
      ent market value is charged for its input and it would appear to be
      reasonable company policy to use its own output profitably.

      Arising from the above points, and assuming an allowance for poorer
quality material has not been given, a transfer price of £1 is suggested
assuming this is the price Department Y would have to pay for equivalent
material. This would have the following effects:

(a)   If the Department Y's belief is correct, the manager would be operating
      on a reasonably autonomous basis and making a profit. His reference
      to profitability might have included an allowance for moving the
      material from Department X in which case, seeing no allowance is
      being given, a loss may result. If this is the case, the operations of this
      department should be reviewed.
(b)   Seeing a loss is already incurred in Department X, the lower transfer
      price of £1 will increase the loss but this is a reasonable presentation
      and should cause the management to question seriously the activities
      in Department X.

      It would be necessary to secure the agreement of the managers of both departments. The Department Y manager would possibly agree but the manager of Department X will need some persuasion. The aim should be to convince all parties that the decision is fair and reasonable and, as profitability in their own departments is an objective, no useful purpose is served by falsifying the position by poor transfer pricing arrangements.

11   To: Managing Director   Date . . . .
      From: Management Accountant
             The Introduction of a Management Audit

I have your memo of the .... intimating that it is your intention to introduce a management audit. There is no generally accepted definition of what a management audit is and the first requirement is to decide the functions you wish the audit to cover in this company.

(a)   *Possible functions covered*

Where management audit is applied the following functions may be included:

  (i)   A check on the effectiveness of the organisation's objectives and policies

 (ii)   A check on the organisation's standards of performance and the extent of their achievement

(iii)   A check on accuracy and relevancy of accounting procedures

(iv)   A check on the effectiveness of the organisation's control systems

 (v)   The recommendation of improvements in the features of the organisation investigated, where the investigation has identified weaknesses that require correction.

(b)   *Deciding on the functions to be covered*

In our company, parts of the possible funtions listed in the previous section are already covered by the internal audit department which checks on the accuracy and relevancy of accounting procedures and has developed a system to minimise the risk of fraud and ensure that the company's resources are preserved. This includes point (iii) with aspects of points (iv) and (v). Our existing management accounting system is concerned with (v) and the check on the achievement of the standards laid down (ii).

From this analysis it would appear that the management audit activities should concentrate on a check on the effectiveness of the organisation's objectives, policies, standards and control systems and provide a supporting role for the procedures already operating in the company.

(c)   *Application of such an audit*

It is suggested that an internal team be appointed to carry out this investigation and at least one member of the management should be seconded to give this work his full-time attention.

                        Signed . . . .

12 (a) The aim would be to obtain a general appreciation of the affairs of the company and try to identify the main problems. The key areas investigated should include:

> Profitability
> Market position
> Productivity
> Product leadership
> Personnel matters
> Balance between short-range and long-range goals.

The type of questions asked should include the following:

 (i)   What are the company's short- and long-range objectives? Why were these chosen?
 (ii) What policies have been developed to achieve the objectives?
 (iii) How is the company organised and has it changed over the years? If so, why?
 (iv) Why have their plans not been geared to give higher performance?
 (v)   What reasons can the company advance for not achieving a better performance?
 (vi) Were there any planned changes to remedy known weaknesses?

(b) The stages to be followed in a detailed investigation, guided by the significant points emerging from the preliminary investigation, would be:

 (i)   Analysis of financial data and control systems
 (ii) Investigation of principal sectors of the business
 (iii) Interpretation of the results of the investigation and discussion of oustanding points and possible recommendations with interested parties.

> After these stages the consultant's report would be completed.

(c) The following action would be taken at the stages named in (b):

Stage (i)
(1) Ratio analysis and the background examined of ratios that demand explanation
(2) Comparison of results with the best available comparable data and an attempt made to put results in perspective and establish trends
(3) Check the effectiveness of control systems and any obvious omissions.
Stage (ii)
The sectors investigated would be the principal divisions of the business: manufacturing, marketing, administration and finance; and would include

the points relevant to these sectors from the preliminary investigation. In particular, an appraisal of the quality and potential of the management should be made.

Stage (iii)

The checking out of impressions and tentative conclusions gained is the principal feature of Stage (iii). It would be very foolish to submit a report which included impractical recommendations which could have been identified as unworkable by simply consulting company personnel.

CONCLUSION

26 The Future of Management Accounting

1   Education in this context is understood to mean the academic study of
the theoretical base of the management accountant's profession, to equip
him to meet the demands which will be made on him during his career. Such
studies are designed to improve the student's capacity to think for himself
in handling new accounting situations and solving new accounting problems.

Training in this context is obtaining adequate practical management
accounting experience to ensure that in a changing business environment the
management accountant can have the practical skills to serve management
adequately. Such training includes the applications of well-tried procedures.

Regarding the balance between these two aspects of study, the emphasis
in the past has been on training to mechanically apply stereotyped methods
to stereotyped situations. This balance is changing in favour of education
because of the pace of change in techniques available to the management
accountant and the views regarding the assumptions on which existing
techniques are based. The appreciation of the implications of these changes
is an important attribute of the future management accountant.

2   After a basic qualification has been obtained, it is necessary to special-
ise since it is impossible to study in depth such a wide range of topics that
are now recognised as the common body of knowledge for accountants.
There is also the situation that the accountant may be employed in many
aspects of the profession and it would appear to be a sensible action to study
in depth the specialism chosen. Professor Solomons suggested a fellowship
qualification awarded in recognition of demonstrated competence in this
specialisation. The fellowship test would be job-oriented not subject-oriented.

Whether the qualified accountant would seek a fellowship qualification
is not directly relevant to this question but it is certain that further study is
required in aspects of the accountant's work that continue to change. The
obvious example of this is when the law is changed and short courses are
usually attended.

Education is recognised as a continuing activity and the accountant cannot escape the need to continue his education to keep up to date. Whether the average accountant makes adequate effort to study his specialisation to the degree necessary, after basic qualification, is open to question. There is evidence that changes are taking place in accounting at such a pace that the accountant who does not respond to these changes will soon find that he will be at a significant disadvantage compared with his more up-to-date colleagues.

A wide range of post-qualification courses are offered by professional bodies, universities, polytechnics, technical colleges and private educational centres. All these facilities will be required and expanded in the future to cope with the demand that will come from accountants wishing to extend their knowledge of their specialism.

3   The management accountant can take the following action to equip himself to take advantage of changes affecting his profession:

(a)   Take advantage of abstracts that convey the essence of the material available on relevant topics of interest. On the basis of this examination, the management accountant can identify published material meriting more detailed study.

(b)   When a good text in management accounting is identified, ensure that time is available to study its contents and understand its message.

(c)   Keep in touch with professional colleagues and follow up promising thoughts prompted by such conversation. Valuable ideas can be generated from discussion with colleagues in disciplines other than accounting.

(d)   Identify deficiencies in knowledge and experience that can be eliminated by attending a course or conference or studying a standard text on the subject.

(e)   Be willing to obtain advice from service organisations organised to give technical information.

(f)   Establish contact with educational institutions that show they can provide relevant up-to-date information on management accounting developments.

4   The management accountant can help the company he serves to profit from changes affecting the organisation by assisting in:

(a)   The integration of objectives and activities at various levels of management through the application of budgetary control

(b) The effectiveness of activities in the organisation by providing a prompt reporting system giving clear signals where anticipated progress is not being made

(c) Isolating problems concerned with the allocation of responsibility and the integration of collective responsibility where co-operative action is needed

(d) The identification of opportunities for improvement in the business by specific reports where a study in depth can signify that managerial action is needed, particularly in the area of strategic decisions

(e) The control of the administration procedure related to action programmes: their agreement and accountability

(f) The search for better methods of performance assessment and the revision of existing methods as necessary

(g) The contribution to the practice of relevant techniques designed to create a favourable climate for profitable changes in the interests of the company, e.g., operational research, organisation and methods study, value analysis, manpower planning, succession and training programmes.

5   This is a question demanding a personal response but the following topics might be considered as promising areas for research:

Ethical considerations in management accouting practice
Concepts of cost — a theoretical and empirical investigation
An evaluation of the effects of accounting policy changes
Management accounting principles — a critical analysis
Empirical research into the financial effects of product diversification
    failures
Financial problems associated with plant maintenance
Communicating management accounting information
Tentative solutions to financial control problems arising from increasing mechanisation and automation
Management control theory applications in accounting techniques
A behavioural approach to the improvement of internal financial
    reporting
Performance measurement problems
Case studies in management accounting for the marketing function
The accountant's role in profit improvement project analysis
Model building problems in long-range planning
Empirical studies in the use of statistical methods in management
    accounting

New directions in social research — their implications in decision-making theory

A classification framework for international financial reporting

Current value accounting models — problems and recommended solutions

Applications of management accounting in areas associated with business failure

Management accounting problems in universities, polytechnics and technical colleges.

6

Topics in the common body of knowledge	Meaning of the common body of knowledge topic	Examples of the coverage in the text	Chapter
Characteristics of information systems	Types of information systems and the attributes of information supplied for management	Types of control systems	8
		Reporting to management	1
The nature and function of accounting	What is meant by the term 'accounting' and its relationship to other disciplines	What is meant by the term 'management accounting'	1
		Management accounting topics	1
		Related disciplines	1
Communication of accounting information	The timing, form and behavioural aspects of the communication of accounting information	The control period	1
		Financial data division	3
		Guidance to management and the communications problem	8
Economics, social, political, legal and organisational interactions with accounting	The effects of the environment on accounting on that influence of accouting on that environment	Organisation structure and the management accountant	1

(Table continued on facing page)

Topics in the common body of knowledge	Meaning of the common body of knowledge topic	Examples of the coverage in the text	Chapter
Mathematical and statistical interactions with accounting	The effects of developments in mathematics and statistics on accounting practice	Operational research techniques Probability theory and the decision-maker	20 20
Valuation concepts and limitations in their implementation	Valuation as an economic measurement process and the problems involved	Work-in-progress and finished goods stock valuation Valuation of assets	16 24
Theoretical framework for economic resource allocation	The justification for the theoretical approach to resource allocation	Project evaluation — net present value	12
The conventional accounting model	The manufacturing, trading, profit statement and balance sheet	Manufacturing statement relationships Trading statement relationships Profit and loss statement relationships Balance sheet relationships	4 4 4 4
Financial statement analysis	How financial statements may be used to assess the performance of a business	Ratio analysis and inter-firm comparison	5
Data accumulation and transformation	The data-processing function as the basis for providing usable accounting information	Characteristics for data division Source documentation and data processing	2 22

(Table continued overleaf)

Topics in the common body of knowledge	Meaning of the common body of knowledge topic	Examples of the coverage in the text	Chapter
Accounting reports	The type of reports issued to users of accounting information	Marketing information	3
		Production cost information	3
		Capital expenditure and research and development cost information	3
		Working capital information	3
		Administration cost information	3
Decision choice, decision implementation and relevant information	Relevant costs for decision-making and the solution of specific decision problems in the financial context	Decision-making techniques	20
		Decision-making problems	21
Accounting tools as comprehensive planning devices	The formal frame-work integrating decisions made as a basis for evaluation	Budgetary control — a management control technique	10
		Budgetary control — budget type aspects	11
Performance evaluation and control	The assessment of performance against satisfactory stand-ards of comparison as a basic for correc-tive action as necessary	The managerial control process	8
		Performance assessment	25